The Island

The Island

A History of Robben Island
1488–1990

edited by Harriet Deacon

Mayibuye History and Literature Series No. 60

Mayibuye Books
University of the Western Cape

David Philip
Cape Town & Johannesburg

The Mayibuye Centre and David Philip Publishers would like to thank the Royal Netherlands Embassy for its sponsorship of this book.

First published 1996 by David Philip Publishers (Pty) Ltd, 208 Werdmuller Centre, Claremont, 7735, and Mayibuye Books, University of the Western Cape, Private Bag X17, Bellville, 7535, South Africa

© 1996 David Philip Publishers

ISBN 0 86486 299 7

The Mayibuye Centre for History and Culture in South Africa is based at the University of the Western Cape. Focussing on all aspects of apartheid, resistance, social life and culture in South Africa, its aim is to help recover the rich heritage of all South Africans and to encourage cultural creativity and expression. The Mayibuye History and Literature Series is part of this project. The series editors are Barry Feinberg and André Odendaal.

The authors would like to thank the staff of the Robben Island Prison and André Odendaal of the Mayibuye Centre.

Printed by Clyson Printers, 11th Avenue, Maitland, Cape Town, South Africa

Contents

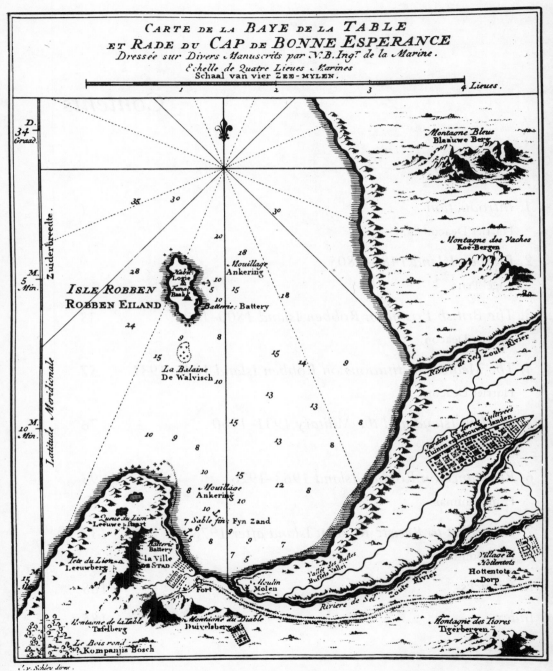

CARTE DE LA BAYE DE LA TABLE
ET RADE DU CAP DE BONNE ESPERANCE
Dressée sur Divers Manuscrits par N.B. Ingr. de la Marine.
Echelle de Quatre Lieues Marines
Schaal van vier ZEE-MYLEN.

1   2   3   4 Lieues.

D.
34
Graad.

Zuiderbreedte.

M.
5
Min.

Latitude Meridionale.

M.
10
Min.

M.
15
Min.

Montagne Bleue
Blaauwe Berg

Montagne des Vaches
Koe-Bergen

35   30

30

20

18

ISLE ROBBEN   Mouillage
ROBBEN EILAND   Ankering

28   Nabit
            Logie
            Kanal
            Baai

15

18

24   Batterie: Battery

9   8

15   15

La Balaine
De Walvisch   10

10   9

8

Riviere de Sel Zoute Rivier

14

13

13

13

12

8

Jardins et Terres Labourées
Tuinen en Bebouwde landen

10   15

Mouillage
Ankering   10

10

7 Sable fin Fyn Zand

Curne du Lion   6
Leeuwe staart   9

Batterie   9
Battery   7

Tete du Lion
Leeuwberg   5

la Ville   7
de STAD

Fort

Moulin
Molen

Vallée des Bustes
Buffels Vallei

Village de
Hottentots
Hottentots
Dorp

Montagne de la Table
Tafelberg

Montagne du Diable
Duivelsberg

Le Bois rond
Kompanjis Bosch

Riviere de Sel   Zoute Rivier

Montagne des Tigres
Tigerbergen

J.v. Schley dimx.

KAART der TAFELBAAI en RÉE van KAAP de GOEDE HOOP,
Geschikt op verscheide HANDSCHRIFTEN, door N.B. Ingenr. des Franssen Zeevaards.

Introduction

Harriet Deacon

Robben Island is a low-lying lozenge of rock and sand, guarding the entrance to Table Bay. Although just a few kilometres long, and a barely swimmable distance from the metropolis of Cape Town, it may well be the most significant historical site in South Africa today. Paradoxically, it symbolises both the repressiveness of the apartheid state and the strength of those who opposed it. Because the Island's future is currently under discussion it is important to consider its past more carefully, for it is a past which has, until recently, been strangely neglected.[1] Interpretations of the history of Robben Island have focused mainly on the harshness of its role as a political prison and the well-known prisoners who were held there, people such as Nelson Mandela, Zephania Mothopeng and Govan Mbeki.

While keeping these important factors in mind, this book seeks to explore the many and varied uses of the Island over the whole period of European involvement in Southern Africa after 1488. Several thousands of people, only a few of whom are now famous, have lived on the Island at various times, voluntarily or involuntarily, since the sixteenth century. Moreover, the experiences of those living on the Island have not always been negative. Some unwilling inhabitants, people who have been subjected to its symbolic strength and practical discomforts, have even been able to use the sentence of banishment there to their common advantage, and thus occasionally to undercut the dominant view of the Island as a place of repression.

In spite of its varied roles, inhabitants and masters, there are continuities in the history of the Island that become evident in a closer reading of its history. The Island and its shores have suffered almost continuous exploitation of their natural resources. Since 1652 the Island has been controlled by the prevailing government of the southern part of Africa; today it is still owned by the state (as Cape Farm no. 432).[2] The authorities have been careful, to varying degrees at different times, to control access to the Island by sailors, fishermen, sportspeople, churchmen, anti-apartheid activists and the general public. The Island

Map of Table Bay from the Abbé Prevost's *Histoire générale des voyages* (1748).

institutions have always been run by white staff, whether Dutch East India Company officials, British military men, doctors and nurses, army and navy officers, or prison guards.

The various functions of Robben Island

For the first two centuries after Bartolomeu Dias first rounded the Cape of Storms in 1488, Robben Island was used as a pantry, to feed the sailors on passing ships, as a postbox for their letters and, occasionally, as a prison for miscreant sailors. During the period of Dutch rule at the Cape, 1652–1806 (with a brief hiatus of British rule between 1795 and 1803), the Island continued to be used as a pantry but it also became increasingly important as a prison, mainly for Cape residents, both black and white, on criminal sentences and for political prisoners from the East Indies. It was during this period that the commercial exploitation of the Island's non-food resources – limestone and shells for lime-burning and stone and slate for building – was begun. Under the British after 1806 the Island was again used as a prison, housing soldiers under sentences of transportation or banishment, Cape residents on criminal sentences who were considered particularly dangerous, and political prisoners from the frontiers of the growing colony. The Island also occasionally housed quarantine cases (for the colonists were very afraid of introducing measles or smallpox into the colony) and a few insane people, mainly those who could not be controlled by their families or kept in the small and rickety country gaols.

In 1846, however, the prison on Robben Island was closed and the prisoners sent to do hard labour in mainland convict stations. In the old prison buildings the colonial government set up a hospital, called the General Infirmary for many years, which was divided into three sections, housing 'chronic sick', 'lunatics' and 'lepers'. These three institutions closed in 1891, 1921 and 1931 respectively. While it acted mainly as a hospital during the nineteenth century, Robben Island also accommodated a small number of political prisoners, mainly from the eastern and northern frontiers of the colony, and, after 1866, convicts on hard-labour sentences who did manual work for the hospital. After the last 'lepers' left the Island in 1931 it stood empty until the outbreak of the Second World War in 1939, when troops were sent there to guard the entrance to Table Bay. Once the war was over in 1945 the garrison was reduced but a Coastal Artillery School operated there from 1946. The South African Marine Corps controlled the Island between 1951 and 1955, when the South African Navy took charge of what became known as *SAS Robbeneiland*. In 1959, however, it was decided that the Island should be taken over by the Prisons Department. From 1961 to 1991 the Island accommodated a maximum security prison, housing those political prisoners considered most threatening to the stability of the apartheid government.

Photograph taken in 1859 of Xhosa prisoners of war housed at Murray's Bay on Robben Island (South African Library).

The physical environment of the Island

The Island is actually the summit of an ancient, now submerged mountain, linked by an undersea saddle to the Blouberg. Its lower strata are of Malmesbury shale forming a rocky and somewhat inhospitable coastline. Above this lies a thick limestone and calcrete deposit covered by windblown sands and shell fragments. The rock formations are similar to those of the mainland except that on Robben Island the stratification is nearly horizontal or gently undulating. The Island is low-lying with the highest point at Minto's Hill (named after a nineteenth-century Surgeon-Superintendent of the General Infirmary) only 24 metres above sea-level. The climate is Mediterranean, as in nearby Cape Town, but the Island experiences stronger wind and colder winters.[3] The Island has a few wells, which were first used by passing sailors in the fifteenth century, but the water is rather brackish. With increasing numbers of people living on the Island in the twentieth century, it became necessary to consider alternative sources of water. Today, water is transported by a cargo ferry boat from the mainland to a reservoir at the Island's harbour.

The Island's inhospitable coastline and the submerged rocks that lie around it have taken many ships by unlucky surprise over the years. In a government

survey of the shipwrecks on the coast of the Island in 1992, it was established
that at least 22 ships are known to have sunk there, 10 of which were British,
3 Dutch and 3 American. Wreckage from 10 of these ships was located and
positively identified. Most of the wrecks occurred on the western or windward
side of the Island, which has a jagged rocky profile. The first reported ship-
wreck near Robben Island was that of the *Yeanger* of Horne, weighing 900
tons, which was wrecked on the northern shore in 1611 while searching for
profits from seal oil. No traces of the *Yeanger* remain today, however. More
recent wrecks include the *Goel no. 1* (1976), which was surveying the offshore
oil potential along the Cape coast, and the *Daeyang Family*, a Korean vessel
carrying iron ore, which sank in 1986.[4]

The types of flora and fauna on Robben Island have been greatly altered by
human settlement. Alien plants (such as rooikrans and eucalyptus varieties)
and animals (such as sheep and cattle, pheasants, rabbits and deer) were
brought in, and the indigenous plants and animals have consequently been
reduced in number or eliminated from the site. But these indigenous forms
were fortunately not unique to the Island, the plants being similar to those
found in the strandveld of the West Coast from Cape Point to the Olifants
River, and the animals mainly penguins and seals. Penguins, which had been
eliminated from the Island shores by the nineteenth century, began to return
in the early 1980s but the seals have not yet re-established a colony.[5]

The built environment of the Island has been carefully researched by Patricia
Riley for the National Monuments Council.[6] She suggests that the earliest
identifiable sites of human occupation are the stone quarry in the south and
the lime quarry towards the centre of the Island, which were probably used in
Van Riebeeck's time. An account of the Island in 1672 by the Danish ship's
surgeon Cortemunde reveals that there were already buildings to accommodate 'many slaves' and 'sometimes 30 to 50 soldiers', gardens behind them, a
'huge lime-burner' and a flag flying from the signal hill (now called Minto's
Hill). Gordon's annotated panorama of 1777 shows an even bigger settlement,
situated at the northern end of the Island (later called Murray's Bay), consisting of the 'Posthouder's huis' (Postholder's house) flanked by long low buildings for the 'bannediten' (convicts) on the left and utility buildings such as a
smithy on the right. The soldiers were accommodated in a line of small houses with vegetable gardens to the north of this, and the slave gardens were situated further away. The caretaker of the signal fire and flag on the hill had a
small house and garden there.

The Postholder's house and convict barracks in the north-east of the Island
were used by the whaler John Murray between 1806 and 1823. In 1806–8 a
new settlement was built at the southern end of the Island to accommodate the
British prison. In 1833 this settlement included a large house for the
Commandant, officers' and soldiers' barracks, overseers' houses (one of which

was roofed with whale bones), a bakery, butchery and smithy, workshops and prison accommodation for over 200 prisoners. During the early 1840s a church, doctor's residence and parsonage were added. All these buildings were used by the General Infirmary, or hospital, after 1846. Prisoners kept on the Island after 1846 were housed in huts and makeshift dwellings at Murray's Bay in the northern part of the Island. A lighthouse was built on Minto's Hill in 1864. During the 1890s there was an upsurge in building activity to accommodate an increasing number of 'lepers' on the Island. Many of these buildings were destroyed or left derelict during the 1930s.

Extensive building activity again took place on the Island in 1939 and 1940: 150,000 tons of building material were transported to the Island in the former year. The present harbour at Murray's Bay was constructed at the same time, unfortunately destroying all evidence of the early Dutch buildings. Gun emplacements, underground magazines, plotting rooms and observation towers, quarters for the garrison and two coastal batteries were built. Many of these buildings are still on the Island today. When the Department of Prisons took over the management of the Island in 1960, further building activity took place: a maximum security and an ordinary criminal prison were built and staff quarters were expanded. In spite of all these changes, however, traces of the more distant history of the Island remain even today.

The symbolism surrounding Robben Island

Regarded as a Hell, Purgatory or rural Eden by various groups at particular times, Robben Island has always been a powerful element within the symbolic geography of the Cape. As Oliver Tambo commented in 1980, 'The tragedy of Africa, in racial and political terms, [has been] concentrated in the southern tip of the continent – in South Africa, Namibia, and, in a special sense, Robben Island.'[7] The symbolic importance of the Island has grown because it is isolated and information about it has long been restricted by the authorities. The representation of Robben Island as the 'hell-hole' of Table Bay, South Africa's Alcatraz, an impregnable place of banishment for those who have opposed the status quo, has long been dominant. But within the South African discourse of liberation, Robben Island has also come to symbolise 'the indestructibility of the spirit of resistance against colonialism, injustice and oppression'.[8] The strong political symbolism of the Island has encouraged the historical emphasis that prevails today on the role of the Island as a prison. Both for the state and for its opponents the Island's symbolic value in this regard has at times outstripped its practical value as a place where the leaders of oppositional forces have been separated from their followers.

'Topologically and symbolically Robben Island has always represented the ultimate margin to which the Pretoria Government banished its opposition.'[9] The idea of the Island as a place of secure banishment, a place for the misfits

of society, those seen as 'Other', was also an important consideration in its use
for quarantine cases, 'lepers' and dangerous 'lunatics' during the nineteenth
century. Examining social classification in modern England, Stallybrass and
White suggest that a symbolic hierarchy ranging from 'high' to 'low' operates
in four interrelated and interdependent domains: psychic forms, the human
body, geographical space and the social order.[10] They use this model to explain
the way in which nineteenth-century environmentalist sanitary theory connected slums to sewerage, sewerage to disease, and disease to moral degrada-
tion. 'The mapping of the city in terms of dirt and cleanliness' was also a division between animal and human, savage and civilised. It is with the 'low' in
all of Stallybrass and White's 'domains' that Robben Island has most frequently been associated – with political opposition, insanity, criminality, dirt,
disease, the poorer classes, the very bottom of Africa. Banishment to the Island
invokes the idea of a symbolic cleansing of the Southern African subcontinent
for the dominant classes.

On the other hand, the discourse of liberation in South Africa has emphasised the ways in which political prisoners have been able to resist the negative implications of their sentences of banishment on Robben Island after
1962. But inhabitants of the Island were also able to do this in the distant past.
While on the Island, a Muslim leader in the eighteenth century transcribed an
important legal text which he was later to use to encourage the development
of an Islamic underclass subculture of resistance in Cape Town. Political and
criminal prisoners in the early nineteenth century plotted a mass escape, lepers in the late nineteenth century organised a programme of resistance to
improve the conditions under which they were detained on the Island, and
political prisoners in the period after 1962 actively learned from each other,
transcending the boundaries of their various political affiliations, and also successfully negotiated for better conditions. The political prisoners in particular
were able to challenge the dominance of the symbolism of the Island as a 'hell-
hole' by also making it into a 'university'.

There are two other strands of symbolic meaning surrounding Robben
Island: its role as Purgatory and as Eden. Professor M. van Wyk Smith has
written of a widespread belief in European culture, dating back to Aristotle's
Meteorologica, that there was another temperate and habitable region, opposite but complementary to the Mediterranean world, beyond the Sahara and
the equator.[12] Coupled to this belief was the idea that there existed a southern
terrestrial paradise, somewhere on a mountain beyond the deserts of Africa –
a location actually depicted on several maps of the early fifteenth century. In
the thirteenth century Dante had invoked this tradition when he placed the terrestrial paradise on the summit of the island of Purgatory in the far south.
Soon after Portuguese explorers returned to Europe with news of the Cape of
Good Hope, European writers began to identify the top of Table Mountain

A party landing on the Island in the late nineteenth century (Cape Archives)

with paradise. Aluigi de Giovanni did so in 1543, and in 1588 Livio Sanuto wrote the following: 'Upon the top of this promontory [Table Mountain] Nature . . . hath formed here a great plain, pleasant in situation, which with the fragrant herbs, variety of flowers, and flourishing verdure of all things, seems a terrestrial paradise.'[13]

There could be no Paradise without Purgatory, no Cape of Good Hope without a Cape of Storms. Nigel Penn has suggested that for the early European visitors to the Cape, Dante's 'Isle of Purgatory' was indeed at the foot of Paradise but separated from it by a dangerous crossing of icy water. Purgatory was Robben Island.[14] For prisoners on transportation sentences, the Island prison was a half-way point between the Cape and the feared Van Diemen's Land or New South Wales convict settlements.

But Robben Island was also sometimes represented as a rural Eden, far from the polluting effects of human settlement. Miasma theories of disease, which dominated medical and popular thinking throughout most of the nineteenth century (even after the first bacteria were discovered in the 1870s), posited that decaying organic matter was the source of foul-smelling emanations, which then produced disease. In the crowded towns, therefore, as one English commentator put it, thousands 'who know no better . . . wallow in the mire and inhale poison at every breath'.[15] Places at some distance from towns were considered more healthy. Islands were particularly recommended as health resorts: 'The insular climate possesses many of the advantages of the sea coast without the land influences [which produce extremes of temperature], and wants [i.e. lacks] many of the more exciting effects of [i.e. overstimulation of the body by] the proximity of table land or mountain.'[16]

A 'change of air' was often prescribed as a cure for chronic disease during the nineteenth century and before. 'Lepers' in particular were thought to benefit from sea-bathing, which improved the condition of their skin; and 'lunatics', from the peace and quiet of a country environment. In the nineteenth century the Robben Island site was thus considered ideal for a hospital because it was both secure (isolating dangerous cases) and healthy (providing a good environment for cure).

Conclusion

Robben Island has played an important part in the history of South Africa at political, practical and symbolic levels. In the reconstruction of the country after apartheid the Island is important as a symbol both of what we have left behind and of the strength we have to go forward. It is a reminder of the horrors of oppression and the heroes of the liberation struggle. But Robben Island is also much more. We need to discover the stories of the Island's forgotten inhabitants: the earliest sailor prisoners, the Khoi leader Autshumato, the Muslim exiles, the Xhosa leaders Nxele and Maqoma, the 'lepers' and 'lunatics' of the General Infirmary, the Second World War soldiers and navy personnel, the less famous political prisoners of the post-1961 era, and the prison and hospital staff who have lived on the Island at various times. These stories are described in the pages which follow, in an attempt to broaden our understanding of the variety of roles the Island has played in the history of South Africa – as pantry, hospital, fishing base, military encampment and prison. Throughout the history of European involvement in Southern Africa, however, Robben Island has served mainly as a repository for those who were considered dangerous to the social order. The history of Robben Island thus provides an off-shore echo of the important events that took place on the mainland. A detailed re-examination of its history is therefore both necessary and timely at a moment when the broader history of South Africa is in the process of popular reconstruction.

Robben Island 1488–1805

Nigel Penn

The first European to round the Cape of Good Hope is generally agreed to have been the Portuguese explorer Bartolomeu Dias in 1488. As the volume of traffic to the East increased over the three centuries thereafter, the commercial shipping companies jockeyed for control of watering and restocking venues along the route. St. Helena, the Cape of Good Hope and Mauritius were among the places used as stopping points for ships of the Dutch, British, Portuguese and other European commercial fleets. After 1652 the Cape was initially merely a refreshment station but rapidly became part of the larger commercial empire of the Dutch East India Company, or Verenigde Oost-Indische Companie (VOC), and the Island played an important part in the Cape's history. By the beginning of the nineteenth century the Island had also become increasingly important in the internal politics of the growing settlement at the Cape.

The period examined in this chapter will be divided into three sections. The first is that which precedes the arrival of Jan van Riebeeck and the establishment of a Dutch refreshment station at the Cape. The second is the period between 1652 and 1700, during which time the refreshment station grew into a colony, and the Island was used less as a pantry and more as a prison. The final phase, 1700 to 1805, is primarily concerned with the Island's history under the VOC in the eighteenth century. For various reasons, however, largely related to the nature of the documentary sources, it is convenient to take the story through to the period of the First British Occupation (1795–1803) and the Batavian Republic (1803–5). The *Bandieten Rollen,* or Convict Rolls, for Robben Island end in 1806 and this, together with the advent of the Second British Occupation, marks the end of one era and the beginning of another.[1]

The period before Dutch settlement, 1488–1652

When Dias reached the Cape in 1488 there was no human settlement on the Island, only thousands of seals and penguins. It is not known for certain whether Dias's men actually visited the Island.[2] But Peter Kolbe, writing in 1727 claimed that in 1498 some Portuguese who happened to be at the Cape (presumably as a support fleet to Vasco da Gama) took refuge on Robben Island, being fearful of the cannibals of the mainland.[3] They sheltered in a large cave (which they called Portugal) and stayed a few days to obtain fresh water from the Island's springs.[4] No doubt they feasted on some penguins and seals, for these creatures were to provide mariners with meals for the next two centuries. In 1503 Antonio de Saldanha and his men 'killed many birds which are called *sutilicarios* [penguins] and sea-wolves and tortoises, of which there was great abundance' on the Island.[5] This slaughter was to accelerate through-out the sixteenth century as more and more ships dared to make the long return voyage to the East and came to rely on replenishing their supplies at the half-way point of the Cape.

In many respects Robben Island was a safer, more reliable refreshment option than the mainland of Table Bay. In the first place the Island was devoid of humans whereas the mainland was inhabited by the Khoikhoi. Though the Khoikhoi were not cannibals, as had been first supposed by the Europeans, they nevertheless retaliated with great vigour when ill used. In 1510 Francisco d'Almeida and more than fifty of his men were killed after they had tried to carry off some cattle belonging to Khoikhoi and kidnap some of their chil-dren.[6] Even when the Khoikhoi were not provoked to hostility they were not always either willing or available to barter their precious flocks and herds for the iron and trinkets of the Europeans. Crews who counted on obtaining fresh mutton or beef at the Cape were often obliged to dine on seal steaks, penguin breasts or penguin eggs on Robben Island. Although these items were not to everyone's taste, the alternative was a six-month diet of salt beef and biscuit.[7]

The Island's natural resources were abundant and free and could be collect-ed with ease, for neither the seals nor penguins were as evasive as the Khoikhoi cattle. An English sailor of 1607 declared that 'In mine opinion there is not an Island in the world more frequented with Fowle and Seales than this Island'.[8] Another Englishman, more practically minded, estimated that in 1604 there were about fifty tons of penguins on the Island.[9] Others remarked that they were there 'in such abundance that you may take them up with your hands, as many as you will' and that 'The eggs of these penguins was there in such abun-dance as we could not almost go for them'.[10] It was possible to drive thou-sands of penguins together in a flock.[11] Some ingenious Englishmen of 1608, finding the penguins to be 'so naturallie simple that you may drive them as you would do a flock of sheep', laid boards from the beach to their boat and herd-ed the 'feathered fish' into it.[12] In a single day one such longboat could remove eleven hundred penguins.[13] It is no wonder that the English called the Island 'Penguin Island'.

The Dutch, though, knew Robben Island as Seal or Sea-dog Island, and it is from the Dutch word for seal – *robbe* – that the present name derives. Indeed, the seals were as impressive as the penguins and found in such numbers as to be 'almost incredible'.[14] Some sailors, such as the crew of the Dutch ship *Oranje* in 1608, were not interested in eating the seals, merely 'clubbing fully a hundred to death' for their own amusement.[15] Others, however, did eat them, preferring young seals to old, the Scandinavians serving them up with prunes and honey.[16] But the principal value of seals was in their oil (train-oil),[17] which was used for a variety of purposes and attracted commercial sealers as early as 1610.[18] One group of Dutchmen thus engaged was shipwrecked on the Island in 1611 but, undeterred, hoped to build a pinnace from the wreckage and sail a cargo of train-oil and seal skins back to Europe.[19] It is not known whether they ever reached their destination but it is likely that they spent at least six months on the Island.

From the beginning of the seventeenth century there were increasing signs that European voyagers to and from the East were finding the Cape to be so crucial a resting place that they wished to improve, regularise and control the facilities of Table Bay. Naturally they started with Robben Island.

It was from about this time that captains began to leave letters or messages, hidden in designated spots on the Island, for other voyagers whom they knew to be at sea. In 1601 the English captain, Sir James Lancaster, generously began the tradition of leaving some sheep on the Island so that they might breed and release future sailors from the necessity of having to barter for meat from the Khoikhoi.[20] Unfortunately the very next fleet, that of Joris van Spilbergen, killed all but one of the sheep for their immediate use.[21] Van Spilbergen also decided to rename the Island 'Isla de Cornelia' in honour of his mother, a change which was not popular enough to persist. More usefully, perhaps, Van Spilbergen left behind some rock dassies from Dassen Island, hoping to establish another source of food.[22] The idea of leaving sheep on the Island was not abandoned, however, for when William Keeling of the *Draggon* dropped anchor in Table Bay in 1607 he received, by a Dutch boat, 'sixe sheepe, the fattest I ever saw, from the Iland: the taile of one of them was eight and twenty inches broad and weighed five and thirty pound weight'. Keeling took other fat sheep from the Island (left by Cornelis Mastlief in 1608) and 'set leane [sheep] in their room'.[23]

The next step towards making commerce with the East Indies safer was to establish a settlement at the Cape of Good Hope. This idea was first raised by Thomas Aldworth, a member of the English East India Company, in 1611. His proposal was to transport about one hundred convicts a year to the Cape and leave them there to fend for themselves. Aldworth had been very impressed by what he had seen of the hinterland of Table Bay, describing it as the best land he had ever encountered in his life, with abundant grass and fresh water, bountiful animal life and courteous and tractable natives.[24] This glowing report encouraged the English East India Company to agree to the idea,[25] but instead of the specified one hundred men they put ashore a mere ten, under the leadership of a certain John Cross, in 1615.²⁶ Unfortunately Aldworth had exaggerated the hospitability of the Khoikhoi, and some of them attacked Cross's men only days after they had landed, severely wounding four of them. Fortuitously for the convicts, the English ship *Hope* was in Table Bay, and Cross begged its skipper, Edward Dodsworth, to provide them with guns and a longboat so that they could base themselves safely on Robben Island. Dodsworth agreed, and so it was that the first group of convicts arrived on Robben Island.²⁷

The English convicts did not stay on Robben Island for very long. In March 1616 Martin Pring of the *Gift* anchored in Table Bay and learnt from one of the Khoikhoi, Coree, that Cross and his men were still on Robben Island. Pring sent a boat there and took off three of the six remaining convicts.

> They reported, that on Saturday last, Captaine Crosse with two others, their boat being split in pieces, made a Gingada [raft] of Timber, and had gotten halfe way betwixt the Island and the ship [Pring's ship] when two whales rose up by them, one of them so near that they strooke him on the backe with a wooden spit; after which they sunke downe and left them. Captain Crosse thus terrified with the whales, and benummed with the water, returned to the Iland; and having shifted a shirt and refreshed himselfe, adventured the second time giving charge to one of the Company to have an eye on him so long as he could see him. This fellow saith, he saw him a great way from the Iland, and on a sudden lost sight of him; which is the last news of him.²⁸

It is possible that Cross made it to the shore. In January 1617 an English fleet at the Cape was told by Coree that Cross and his men (except for two who had been murdered by some evil-minded Khoikhoi) had been taken away by a Portuguese ship.²⁹ Another caller at the Cape, Edward Terry, learnt in June 1616 that two of the men had been taken off by an English fleet and that the three who had been removed by Pring were executed shortly after their return to England for stealing a purse.³⁰

The English did not repeat the experiment of a convict settlement at the Cape,³¹ although Captains Fitzherbert and Shilling did take symbolic possession of Table Bay (and, in fact, all parts of the continent not yet inhabited by a Christian prince) in the name of King James on 3 July 1620.³² Africans and Europeans alike ignored this gesture. The real rulers of the Cape of Good Hope remained the Khoikhoi. It is unlikely, even though there is no written documentation of the period, that any Khoikhoi had lived on the Island before Europeans arrived at the Cape. The Island was too small for prolonged pastoral settlement and the Khoikhoi were not a seafaring people. Indeed, the very usefulness of the Island was at first the absence of a settled Khoikhoi population there. But although the passing sailors could use the Island as a pantry and postbox, they still needed to negotiate with the mainland Khoikhoi for access to cattle.

The Khoikhoi man called Coree, who came from the Table Bay area, was the first person to be groomed by the British as an intermediary between the European visitors and indigenous traders. Coree had been kidnapped by the crew of the *Hector* in May 1613 and taken to England.[33] The intention was to teach him English and return him to the Cape, where, suitably impressed and overawed by his recent experiences, it was hoped he would become a loyal translator and promoter of English interests. Unfortunately Coree did not enjoy his stay in England, despite being the guest of no less a person than Sir Thomas Smythe, Governor of the English East India Company. When he eventually returned to the Cape in June 1614 his resentment at the treatment he had received at British hands made the procurement of livestock from his people more difficult for the Europeans. But the presence of Cross and his convicts on Robben Island and on the Cape Peninsula, fleeting though it was, seems to have convinced Coree that there might be great advantages to be derived from a permanent European settlement at the Cape. Coree thereafter sought to use Europeans to advance his own regional interests, encouraging them to attack his Khoikhoi rivals and building up his own flocks and herds under European protection. His crucial position as intermediary between Khoikhoi and Europeans was not, however, without danger, and in 1626 a Welsh sailor reported that he had been killed by the Dutch for refusing to give them food.[34]

After Coree's death it became even more difficult for Europeans to obtain cattle or sheep, and it was not until 1632 that the English succeeded in grooming another Khoikhoi agent to act for them at the Cape. Harry, Hadah, Herry or Autshumato was the leader of a group of cattleless Khoikhoi who lived in the vicinity of Table Bay and who were known by the Europeans as the Strandlopers or Watermen.[35] They were almost certainly an impoverished offshoot of the Peninsular Khoikhoi but their fortunes began to rise after the English took Autshumato on a voyage to the East Indies in 1631. Here Autshumato learnt English, and by the time he returned he was ready to act as agent of the English in Southern Africa.

In 1632, at his own request, Autshumato asked to be transported to Robben Island with twenty of his followers, and from then until about 1640 he spent long periods in residence there.[36] The advantages of such a position were security from hostile Peninsular Khoikhoi and the copious resources of penguins and seals, both regarded as delectable by the Strandlopers. On the Island Autshumato was useful to the European sailors because he could monitor all of the shipping entering the bay and light signal fires to attract those wishing to forward or receive letters. Peter Mundy, who visited the Island in 1634, described Autshumato as 'Chief of all that dwell ther and governor of the Island'. He was clothed in 'English habit from head to foote' and ruled over sixty followers, who dwelt in seven 'little Cottages'. Captain Pynne, who had first taken Autshumato to the East, had also supplied him with cows, pigs, hens and chickens.[37] There were times when Autshumato and his followers asked to be taken to the mainland and times when they asked to be returned to the Island. It is not known where they were in 1636 when a thrice-keel-hauled mutineer of the Dutch ship *Frederick Henricq* was marooned on Robben Island,[38] but we do know that there were Khoikhoi on the Island in 1639.[39]

By 1638, however, the semi-permanent population of Strandlopers had already begun to have a very destructive effect on the Island's wildlife, for a Dutch sailor reported in that year that when he 'went with the longboat to Robben Island to plant there 109 coconuts, and a large quantity of lemon and pumpkin seeds in some suitable place ... there was nothing there but one penguin, and no wild beasts except a few seals ... all of which must have been exterminated by the blacks who were there for a time'.[40] Although penguins and seals did re-establish themselves in smaller numbers after 1640, the Island had largely lost its attractions for the Strandlopers.

In 1647 the Dutch ship *Haerlem* was wrecked in Table Bay.[41] Those of the crew who camped on the mainland's shore so as to be able to salvage the valuable cargo were able to feed themselves by sending regular foraging parties to Robben Island. These returned with penguins, penguin eggs and cormorants. The successful salvage operation encouraged the Dutch to believe that a permanent settlement at the Cape was feasible. Thus it was that in 1652 Jan van Riebeeck arrived with orders to undertake this task, and the Island (along with Southern Africa as a whole) entered a new phase of history.

The early period of Dutch settlement, 1652–1700

The importance of Robben Island in the history of Dutch settlement at the Cape has not received sufficient attention in the general accounts of this period. Van Riebeeck had instructions to create a refreshment post where passing ships could obtain water, fresh vegetables and meat. In order to supply the last of these requirements the post had to be on the mainland so that cattle and sheep could be obtained from the Khoikhoi. There were many times in the first decade of the settlement, however, when it was impossible not only to supply passing ships with provisions but to feed the Cape garrison itself. At these times the Island acted as a pantry from which emergency supplies of penguins, cormorants and eggs could be obtained. The seals were also used but not so much for their meat – which was given to the Company's slaves – as for their pelts and blubber. It is no exaggeration to say that without Robben Island as a reserve food supply the initial Dutch settlement would have miscarried.[42]

Another function which Robben Island served at this time was that of sheep farm. Like others before him, Van Riebeeck found that sheep deposited on the Island, free of natural and human predators, grew marvellously fat and multiplied at an impressive rate. He attempted, therefore, to have good stocks of fat sheep available on the Island as an insurance against difficult times in the livestock trade with the Khoikhoi. Once livestock had been placed on the Island, however, it became necessary to place shepherds there, partly to prevent foreign sailors from stealing the Company's mutton. In March 1654 four or five men were placed on the Island to erect a shed, suitable for sheltering both men and sheep, to dig a well and to start a vegetable garden. The first Postholder in command of the Island was Corporal Robbeljaert, who was assisted in his duties by Pieter Borgers, the keeper of the sheep.[43] These men oversaw the creation of a little farmyard economy, which in time was to produce the finest cauliflowers in the world.[44]

In the years to come there was to be a fairly high turnover in the Island's Postholders and staff – many were dismissed as careless and lazy by their superiors on the mainland. Lack of supervision and the Island's isolation contributed to the atmosphere of ennui, the absence of urgency that stole over those sent to labour there. Good supplies of sea shells, which could be used in the making of lime, were discovered on the north-western side of the Island. There was thus an incentive to exploit these resources if a sufficiently motivated labour force could be kept to the task. But this was not the reason behind the gradual transformation of the Island into a prison. Political rather than economic considerations prompted Van Riebeeck to begin using the Island as a place of banishment. The first inkling that Robben Island would become a repository for political prisoners is to be found in Van Riebeeck's journal under the entry for 24 November 1652. Significantly the subject of the Commander's meditations was Autshumato, who was then playing the vital role of middleman and translator between the Khoikhoi and the Dutch. Van Riebeeck was apt to blame Autshumato for any breakdown in the livestock trade with the Khoikhoi and believed that supplies would be both cheaper and more plentiful if he were removed:

We are half afraid that the aforesaid Harry – being very much attached to the Saldanhars[45] nowadays whereas formerly they used to be his enemies – instead of acting in our favour, may be brewing mischief ... If he is brewing mischief, it would not be inconceivable for him with his wife and children, together with all the Watermen, to be taken to the Robben Island with sweet words and then left there, so that we might trade more peaceably and satisfactorily with the natives of Saldanha, who appear to be a good type of people. About all of this time will show us more.[46]

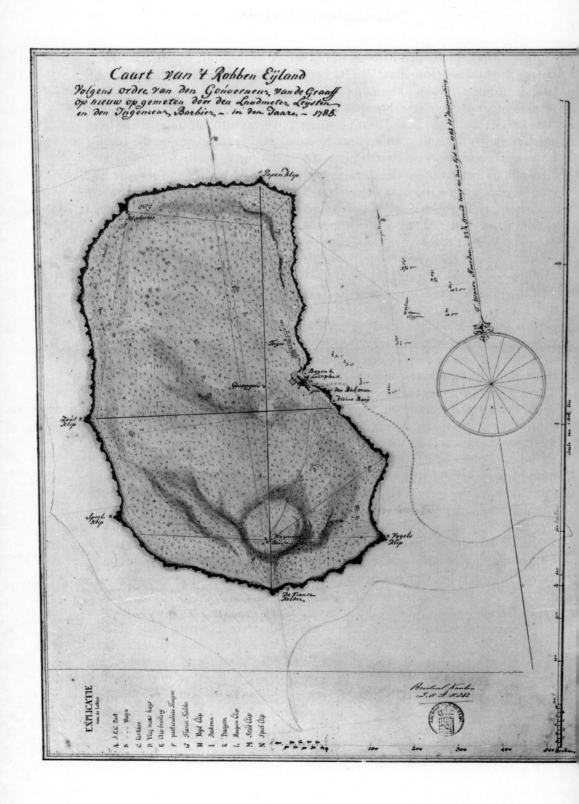

On 10 July 1658 Autshumato, together with two Khoikhoi companions, Jan Cou and Boubo, was indeed placed on Robben Island.[47] The instructions to the Postholder, Rijck Overhagen, were that the Khoikhoi prisoners were to search for their own food but that if they volunteered to help with herding the sheep they were to be given some tobacco. Jan Cou and Boubo had both been released by September 1658 but another Khoikhoi captive was put in their place. Autshumato was taken from the Island on several occasions when his translator's skills were needed, though always in secret, and he was always, emphatically, returned to the Island again. But at the end of November 1659 he and his fellow captive managed to steal the Island's small, leaky rowing boat and make a daring night escape. The authorities thought it impossible that the escapees could have survived the crossing or the breakers of Bloubergstrand. To their chagrin, however, nearly two weeks later they found the boat, safely beached, about one and a half days' journey north of the Castle. About a year later, Autshumato sent a message to the Commander asking for permission to live near the settlement again, and by 1660 he was again acting as an interpreter.[48]

Autshumato and his men were not the first to be banished to the Island by the colonial authorities, for in May 1657 a decision had been made to send some exiles and slaves there to cut and prepare the beautiful soft white stone found on the Island. They included Thomas Mulder, a salaried Company servant; Jasper Duijff, a banished soldier; Lourens Alberts, an exile; Espagniola, a slave; and Eva, a female slave from Madagascar.[49] This diverse group of people worked under the command of the new Postholder, Jan Wouterssen. But the venture was not a success. On 19 July 1657 Wouterssen wrote from the Island to complain that the stone was too crumbly; that Lourens Alberts was weakened by beriberi; that Jasper Duijff had Ceylon disease; and that Eva did nothing but run about the Island chasing sheep and driving them from the lambs. 'She needs somebody to look after her and does not heed and cannot understand signs, gestures or thrashings,' complained Wouterssen. 'No credit can be gained at this work with such people,' he lamented,[50] but he himself had a question mark hanging over his head.

Wouterssen had had a previous spell on Dassen Island collecting train-oil with the assistance of some voluntary, but ineffectual, Khoikhoi labourers.[51] For some reason, however, he fell foul of the authorities in 1657, and so on 15 March was punished for wasting Company provisions and 'blasphemous injuries against the characters of females at the Cape, including the Commander's wife'. He was 'sentenced graciously, in consideration of the pregnancy of his own wife ... to beg pardon on his bare knees, to be bored

Map of Robben Island, 1785, showing the prison (Gevangnis) and garden (Tuijn) (Cape Archives)

through the tongue by the executioner, to forfeit his wages and be banished for three years'.[52] Although the boring of the tongue was not carried out, Wouterssen was banished to the Island, albeit as its supervisor. His wife, a female slave, accompanied him,[53] and her child may well have been born on the Island. After Wouterssen's complaints Van Riebeeck decided to abandon the quarrying and remove the sickly convicts in August 1657, but the rest of the exiles remained on the Island.

In a letter of 28 August 1657 Wouterssen wrote to ask for 'rice instead of barley for our rations, as it goes further when eaten with penguin meat. We also ask for a cock and two or three hens which we wish to keep here, then this place will look like a country village.'[54] Poor Wouterssen's dreams of rural happiness on the Island were not to be realised. Although there were, by this date, 350 sheep on the Island, they were not for the consumption of the inhabitants, and Wouterssen was soon in trouble for neglecting his duties. The following entry was placed in the diary of Van Riebeeck on 20 March 1658:

> With the passage of time it is becoming increasingly evident that Jan Wouterssen, who was deprived last year of his rank of assistant on the grounds of disgraceful conduct, but was graciously allowed to retain the rank of soldier, and in order to enable him to make a living was placed in charge of the Company's sheep on the Robben Island in the hope that he would rehabilitate himself, is behaving as badly as before and is paying no attention to the sheep ... Moreover he is guilty of drunkenness whenever he is able to obtain liquor, either from the rations or by purchase, and completely disregards the repeated instructions concerning various matters issued to him especially the making of beacon fires at the spots indicated, for the purpose of guiding the Company's ships when entering the bay at night.[55]

Wouterssen, his wife and child were therefore removed from the Island and 'transferred' to India in disgrace, and Rijck Overhagen, a cadet, was appointed as the new Postholder. Eva, the female slave, was returned to the mainland. Overhagen's instructions included orders that he should be most diligent in lighting beacon fires for Dutch ships, but that he should extinguish the fires if the incoming ship was foreign. Clearly it was not a priority to ensure the safe arrival of the Company's competitors in Table Bay. Nor were foreigners to be allowed to land on Robben Island.[56] Overhagen had discharged his duties well enough by May 1658 to merit a salary increase.[57] In November work was commenced on a new sheep shed, 100 feet long and 18 feet wide, to provide shelter for the sheep in winter. In order to complete this work nine or ten Company men, as well as three slaves, were sent to work on the Island. When not busy building, they were expected to carry shells to the landing place or exert themselves in killing snakes. Unfortunately the new shed blew down in the winter gales of June 1659, so work had to be renewed. The slaves did not prove to be willing workers, for in August Overhagen wrote that he 'would be glad if your Honour would send me two other slaves, because those who are here would rather be at the Cape, and I can get no work out of them, even if I knock them senseless'.[58]

Despite Overhagen's efforts he seems to have lost favour after Autshumato's escape, but whether this was the reason for his replacement as Postholder in 1660 is uncertain. The new Postholder, Otto Janssen, does not appear to have been as diligent in his duties, and in December 1660 was subject to severe criticisms. In the course of rebuking Janssen, Van Riebeeck fumed prophetically: 'Nothing will come of your request to become a freeman on the Island, as it is inconvenient for the Hon. Company to settle freemen there, so you might as well put that out of your mind.'[59]

Janssen was removed but his successor, Jan Sacharias, was even less suitable. He committed the unpardonable offence of neglecting to light beacon fires for incoming ships though he did not hesitate to signal for help when a female slave on the Island fell ill.[60] His compassionate behaviour was probably influenced by the fact that he had an ex-slave woman as his own wife – Maria of Bengal.[61] His successor, Pieter van Meerhoff, was the third Postholder of the Island to have had a non-European wife – a fact which has led one observer to remark that the authorities may have preferred inter-racial marriages to be out of sight and out of mind.[62] Whether or not this was true, Van Meerhoff's wife was an exceptional woman, whose life became closely bound to the Island.

Her name was Krotoa, or Eva to the Dutch, and she was the niece of Autshumato.[63] Krotoa had replaced Autshumato as the principal translator of the settlement and, having been brought up in Van Riebeeck's household, spoke Dutch much better than her uncle. She had, in addition, been baptised, but her rapid European acculturation had not equipped her with the ability to control her intake (or the effects) of alcohol. It must have been a lonely life on Robben Island with no female companionship, and soon after her arrival there in 1665 Krotoa began displaying the symptoms of a chronic alcoholic. The dispatch of her husband to Madagascar, on a slaving expedition, did not help matters. Van Meerhoff never returned, for he was killed by those he sought to enslave. Krotoa returned to the mainland in September 1668; but her conduct became so unacceptable to the mores of the settlement that she was banished to Robben Island in March 1669. She died or, to quote the journal entry, 'quenched the fire of her sensuality by death' on 29 July 1674.[64]

In the meantime the need for lime, for building work in the settlement, had grown. This necessitated increased exploitation of the shells on Robben Island, and Commander Wagenaar, Van Riebeeck's successor, was industrious in organising the ferrying of volunteer Khoikhoi labourers (their wages paid in brandy and tobacco) to work on the Island. The shell heaps also offered the prospect of combining profit with punishment, and a steady trickle of convicts was now banished to the Island for hard labour. A fine blue stone found suitable for quarrying was now also exploited with convict labour.[65] The first of this new wave of prisoners was Bartholt Keivit, sentenced on 23 August 1664 to five years in chains on Robben Island. More followed, most of them men, although the widow Theilmans, Mayke van der Berg, served a month on the Island in 1677 for theft before being banished to Mauritius.[66] In 1666 Wagenaar could report that there were 350 sheep, 10 cattle, 40 goats, 30 pigs and 25 people, including women and children and 14 convicts. He added that 'the island makes a very good penitentiary where a rogue, after one or two years' work in carrying shells, begins to sing very small'.[67]

In 1672 five Khoikhoi suspected of attacking a shepherd were banished to the Island,[68] but to the amazement of the authorities they succeeded in stealing a boat and escaping in January 1673. In words of grudging admiration the official journal reported that it was 'truly a very bold undertaking, for such savages to trust themselves to such a distance in so small a *jolletje* with only two oars and no rudder; it is proof of the strong desire of freedom which exists in a state of slavery'. The escapees' boat was later found, safely beached, on the mainland.[69]

The later period of Dutch settlement, 1700–1806

By the beginning of the eighteenth century the Island's status as a place of punishment was secure, and this now became its chief function. Prisoners on the Island were referred to as *bandieten* (bandits or, more correctly, convicts) and their numbers included representatives of the great diversity of people who fell victim to the VOC's far-flung empire of commerce and coercion. The first *Bandieten Roll* (or convict roll) for the Island which survives dates from 1728. From this it may be seen that there were then 42 prisoners on the Island, 26 of whom were Europeans and 16 were *Indiaanen*.[70]

The name *Indiaanen* derived from the fact that from 1682 onwards East Indian prisoners were banished to the Island. The first of these was a Prince of Macassar who, in November 1682, was exiled to Robben Island along with his servant.[71] This was the beginning of a trend towards using the Island as a dumping ground for political dissidents and leaders of resistance to the Company's rule in the East Indies during the eighteenth century. Not only high-ranking exiles came from the East but also a more common class of criminal: pirates, robbers, thieves and homicides. There was also a leavening of so-called Mahommedan priests, exiled so that their teachings could be neutralised. Thus did the composition of the Robben Island prison's inhabitants come to be more cosmopolitan than it had been during the early Dutch period, more indeed than it would be after the Dutch had relinquished the Cape to the British.

A great deal of research still has to be done on the Eastern bandits and exiles but some preliminary findings can be recorded.[72] Eastern prisoners first began arriving in significant numbers after 1722. During the period 1722 to 1748 an estimated 312 such men arrived at the Cape. Not all of them were housed on Robben Island – some worked in the harbour area of Cape Town and were lodged in or near the Amsterdam Battery – but the more dangerous or disruptive were. They were called *Indiaanen* primarily to distinguish them from European prisoners, so the term was used loosely and inclusively, gradually including 'Bushmen', 'Bastaards', Chinese, Madagascans, Indians, slaves, Khoikhoi and all others who were not white. Amongst the *Indiaanen* of 1728 were three *Mooren* or Moors (possibly Arabians); one Khoi man; and two East Indian dignitaries: Angenata, head of Jampon, and Ketees Malocco (or Catchiri Daijman Mamoeti), the Prince of Ternaten in the Moluccas.[73] The Prince of Ternaten had initially been banished to Cape Town, but because, once there, he invited Europeans, slaves and slave women to his house for '*dobbel, hoererij als andere onordentelijkheeden* [gambling, whoring and other indecent activities]' he was removed to the Island with a personal slave and an allowance of six rix-dollars a month. He died in captivity in 1747.[74]

It cannot be said from the available evidence whether there were separate living quarters for *Indiaanen* and Europeans on the Island. It is, indeed, very difficult to say anything about the social or living conditions there during the eighteenth century as only scattered incidents are recorded in the archives. Perhaps the best impression of the buildings and accommodation on the Island is to be gained by studying Colonel R. J. Gordon's paintings of the Island of the 1770s.[75] From this it can be learned that there were several buildings erected close to the landing beach at Murray's Bay and that the Postholder, at least, had separate accommodation. We do know that the *bandieten* quarters were known as *die Kraal*,[76] which suggests that there was a continuity between the structure first used to house the Island's sheep and then used to house the Island's prisoners. Indeed, the residence of the Island's nineteenth-century lunatics was also referred to as *die Kraal*,[77] proof that the Island's traditions (if not the actual buildings themselves) died hard. The records also refer to a building known as the *bandiet huisje*;[78] and it is possible that this was used to house the European convicts whilst the *Indiaanen* lived in *die Kraal*. There was also a walled garden and several wells.[79] The size of the Island's staff is unclear but there were always at least one Postholder (invariably a sergeant in the eighteenth century) and two corporals. These Company soldiers had to rely on the collaboration of some of the more privileged convicts, for three men alone could not control all the Island prisoners.[80]

Escape from the Island was only possible by sea, and great efforts were made

A panorama of Robben Island by Colonel R. J. Gordon, 29 July 1777.

to ensure watertight security. In the early years a number of men managed to escape on Company or foreign ships which visited the Island illegally, usually in search of sailors for their undermanned vessels. Small fishing craft from the mainland were frequently obliged to land on the Island in bad weather, and this presented another security leak. Ever since the successful escape of 1673 the Postholder was expected to keep the Island's boat under close guard and its oars and rudder under lock and key. In 1692 there was indeed a recommendation that the *bandieten* should be moved to the mainland and the Island left inhabited solely by three or four Company servants in order to prevent sea-borne escapes.[81] This recommendation was not acted upon, and in 1716 and 1718 groups of prisoners managed to escape, the first in fishing boats belonging to Chinese exiles at the Cape and the second with the connivance of some French and English ships.[82]

A law was passed in February 1718 that in future all fishing boats, even those of foreign ships, should be beached under the eyes of Company guards at nightfall.[83] After these incidents escapes petered off. Seven convicts made an unsuccessful escape attempt in February 1731, which resulted in the death by drowning of three of them.[84] In 1740 four Dutch convicts managed to escape

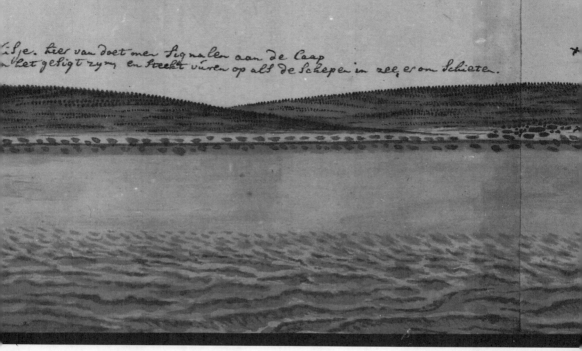

Flag house: people make signals to Cape Town from here when ships come into view and light fires if the ships come into the surrounding sea.

from Dassen Island whilst collecting train-oil, and in 1746 it is recorded that three others escaped from Robben Island.[85] Foreign shipping was kept away by force, for in 1771, when Captain Cook tried to visit the Island, the Dutch guards threatened to open fire on his longboat. Cook remarked that he had heard that some years before this incident a Danish vessel had in fact succeeded in abducting some of the prisoners in order to restock their depleted crew.[86] For the great majority of prisoners, however, escape was impossible. In the summer months howling south-easters turned simple tasks into a trial whilst the heat and glare dazed the senses. In winter the great north-westerly gales rushed curtains of rain across Table Bay, lashing the Island and sometimes preventing the arrival of the ration boat from Cape Town.

Food was, in fact, a constant source of dissatisfaction on the Island. On 9 August 1712 a petition was received from the convicts, who complained that they could not subsist on their monthly rations, which were usually finished as early as the 20th or 24th of the month. At this stage the convicts were not allowed to fish and their monthly ration of forty pounds of rice was obviously inadequate. It was accordingly agreed to increase their rations to the same level as the Company slaves, to allow for some fishing, and to provide a bit of

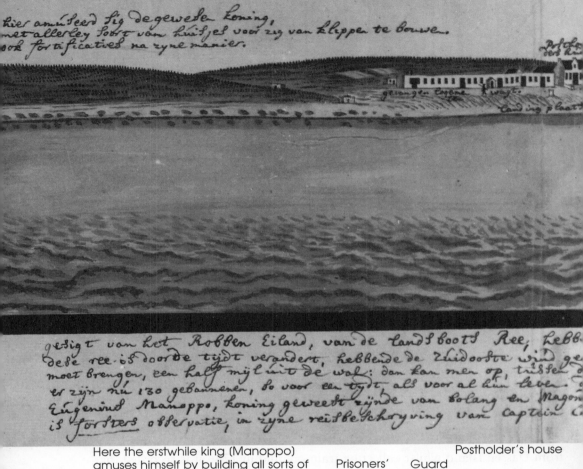

*hier amuseerd sig de geweese koning,
met allerley soort van huisjes voor zig van klippen te bouwe,
ook fortificaties na zyne manier.*

*gesigt van het Robben Eiland, van de Lands boots Ree, hebb.
dese ree is door de tijdt verandert, hebbende de Zuidooste wind ge-
moet brengen, een half mijl uit de wal: dan kan men op, tussel
er zijn nu 130 gebannenen, so voor een tydt als voor al hun leven.
Eugenius Manoppo, koning geweedt zijnde van Bolang en Magon
is forsters observatie, in zyne reisbeschryving van captein C.*

Here the erstwhile king (Manoppo) amuses himself by building all sorts of little houses from stone, and fortifications, after his custom.

Prisoners' living quarters

Guard

Postholder's house

Landing place

View of Robben Island from the landing boat's anchoring place, with the Postholder's house at a distance of 60 *roeden* (an Amsterdam *roede* is about 3,7 metres) to the west, (drawn) on 29 July 1777. (cont. on p. 26)

meat.[87] In July 1721, however, the authorities noted that the meat rations often went bad before they reached the Island, because contrary winds delayed the ration boat. It was thus decided to supply live sheep for the convicts' meat,[88] but the amounts were obviously insufficient and more salt fish than mutton was provided. The consequence was that some of the convicts went into the veld and slaughtered the Island's sheep. For punishment the guilty were sent in chains to the Company's works at Cape Town whilst the rest of the Islanders had their rations of meat, rice and meal suspended. Christoffel Hehlt, the Postholder at that time, was therefore obliged to petition the

woningen en tuinen van 12 gegageerde Solda...
men cultiveert hier veel groente, rekenende m...

kerkhof.

Solje 8 voet hoog, het enige hoge op het eiland: zijnde alles lage struiken

klippen waarop het schip ni...
in maart 1776. gebleven is

Posthouders huis op de distantie van 60 roeden in het westen. Den z...
...t men om de regte ankergrond te hebben voor grote Schepen, het Posth...
...ademen Schone Sandgrond ankeren. dit eiland is vier uren gaans in den om...
...ergaderen Schelpen en klippen tot kalkbranding, en zagen Stenen tot g...
...eken niet en gaan waar zij willen, wordende Schoon zij weinig weinig
...ieus en onwaar.

Churchyard	Dwellings and gardens of 12 salaried soldiers among whom some live here by choice. People grow many vegetables here, in my opinion better ones than those grown in Cape Town.
	Six-foot high bush, the only tall kind on the island: the others are all low shrubs and grass, the terrain mixed, but sandy with stones; full of quails who stay the whole year long, partridges, black snakes, chameleons and lizards.
Stone-cutting place	Rocks on which the ship *Nieuw Rhoon* was damaged in March 1776

authorities for meat on behalf of the convicts on 22 July 1723. He explained that the hungry men were eating the corpses of pigs and sheep that washed up on the Island having fallen off passing ships. They were also eating sheep that had died on the Island and been flung, as carrion, to rot on the beach. Hehlt said that he had more than once been obliged to take away the prisoners' cooking pot and throw it into the sea because the contents smelt too offensively and were doubtless brewing up some foul disease.[89] After this letter rations were improved but convicts would continue to use their spare time foraging, fishing or diving for crayfish in an attempt to supplement their diet.[90]

dewelke hier uit verkiezing wonen.
dezelve bete dan aan de Caap te zijn.
...ras, het terrein gemengt, dog zanderig met klippen. vol kwartels, die het gantsche jaar bly...
Slaven tuinen.

...comie tuin

rheen

July 1777   R: J: Gordon.
...der huis, in het west zuidwest half west, en het flaggeman huis in...
...k. er zijn tegenwoordig 26 man, onder een sergeant, die Posthouder is in...
...lik voor de Caap, wordende s'avonds opgesloten. er zijn 5 indische Staat...
...tgeld krijgen, door den tegenwoordigen Posthouder Bernardi zeer wel onth...

Company garden   Slave gardens

The anchoring place changes over time (with the tide) and if the SE wind blows, one can use the right-hand anchoring ground for large ships if one has the Postholder's house to the W–SW–half W and the flag-house to the SW to S, a half-mile away from the shore; then one finds a lovely sandy anchoring spot at between 12 and 15 *vadems* (an Amsterdam *vadem* is about 1,7 m). This island is about four hours in circumference, and 26 men live on it under a sergeant; the Postholder is in charge, and there are also 12 invalids and now 130 exiles, (confined) either for a (specified) time or for their whole lives.   (cont. on p. 27)

Most of the prisoners had been sentenced to hard labour on the Island, though some of the more exalted Eastern exiles were exempted from this punishment. Work consisted of collecting shells or hacking stone from the quarry. Prisoners could also be set to work chopping firewood, tending the vegetable garden, minding the sheep, or slaughtering seals for the production of train-oil. It would seem as though most of the seals had left the Island by the early eighteenth century and special trips had to be made to the seal colony on

Flat rock

These men gather shells and stones for lime-burning, and quarry stone for use in Cape Town. They are locked up in the evenings. There are five Indian government-prisoners (political prisoners from the East Indies) among whom is a certain Manoppo, erstwhile king of Bolang and Magondo. He does not work and goes where he will, in pursuit of which (privileges) he gets a very small amount of his living allowance; he is very well entertained and is given separate lodgings by the present Postholder, Bernardi. Forster's observation, in his travel account of Captain Cook, is thus injurious and untrue.

Dassen Island. Here prisoners might spend a few nights whilst the work was in progress; they also used the occasion to indulge in some fishing. Work hours on Robben Island were marked by the ringing of a bell, but after the day's labour was done there seems to have been a degree of freedom of movement, at least for those not in chains. Convicts could keep private possessions, for some had trunks and even money to lock up in them. Others buried or hid their prized articles, which ranged from knives to knapsacks. They were also

able to obtain liquor and tobacco. Some of the Eastern exiles were comparatively wealthy. Daing Manganam, for example, the Prince of Macassar, who
had been transported to the Island in 1749, received an allowance of ten rix-
dollars a month towards his upkeep,[91] at a time when the monthly wage of a
Company soldier was a mere two rix-dollars. Such a man must have exerted
a powerful local influence and been at the centre of the Island's rudimentary
exchange economy.

For the less privileged, life was hard and discipline could be extremely harsh.
The sergeants and the corporals seem to have been brutally heavy-handed and
virtually unrestrained in handing out punishment. This is clearly evident from
the records concerning a case of sodomy on the Island, brought to the attention of the Council of Justice in 1735.[92] The last women on the Island had
been removed in 1677, so it is not unlikely that homosexual relationships
existed amongst the convicts. In the eighteenth century such relationships were
viewed as unnatural and abominable, punishable by death. One morning in
August 1735 the slave Panaij van Boegis got up early, planning to catch some
crayfish. Finding that his bait was missing, he was told that it had been taken
by the convict Rijkhaart Jacobsz of Rotterdam, who had already gone ahead
to the beach. Panaij found Jacobsz, but the latter, instead of surrendering the
bait, dropped his pants and proceeded to make most improper suggestions
whilst pointing out the prowess of his private parts. Panaij, according to his
own account, hit Jacobsz in disgust and went to report the matter to Sergeant
Godlieb Willer, the Postholder.[93] Willer beat Jacobsz until, in the presence of
others, he cried out, 'Don't hit me. I did it. Just send me up [before the
court]!'[94] At this stage the convict Hermanus van Munster stepped forward
and told Willer that he knew even worse things about Jacobsz. A fateful tale
began to unfold with its origins back in 1713.

In that year Jacobsz arrived on the Island, sentenced to 25 years. In 1715 he
met the newly arrived Khoikhoi prisoner, Claas Blank, a man with a 50-year
sentence to serve.[95] In 1724 they, together with other convicts, went to Dassen
Island to burn train-oil. There, one night, in the small *bandieten hutje* on the
Island, they were secretly observed 'committing an abhorrent sin' by the slave
Augustijn Matthisz.[96] Nothing was said about this for several years, but in
1732 the same couple were caught in the most compromising of positions in
the *bandieten huijsie* of Robben Island by the convicts Hermanus van Munster
and Jacobus van der Walle. These two went straight to tell Sergeant Scholz,
the Postholder, who said that he could not do anything about such things and
that the evidence of convicts was worthless.[97] Some days later, however, when
Rijkhaart Jacobsz walked past the sergeant, Scholz, on the pretext that
Jacobsz had not raised his hat to him, began to beat Jacobsz with *daggetjes*.[98]
Whereupon Jacobsz, in the presence of others, shouted out, '*Send mij maar op
ek heb hom 'n 't— — [Send me up! I — him in the —].*'

Scholz and his corporal, Wessels, decided to ignore this confession,[99] but their silence did not prevent Jacobsz from committing further indiscretions. Thus it was that finally, in 1735, Sergeant Willer came to know the truth. Jacobsz and Blank confessed to all of the accusations brought against them, though Jacobsz claimed that Panaij was lying and that in 1732 he had been drunk when discovered naked with Blank, and that he had been naked because his pants had accidentally fallen down.[100] It is even possible that Jacobsz had originally been banished to the Island from Batavia in 1713 for the same or similar crimes.[101] There was to be no mercy for him this time or for the unfortunate Claas Blank. On 19 August 1735 the two men had weights tied to their bodies and, somewhere between the Cape and Robben Island, were dropped into the sea to drown.[102]

Jacobsz had confessed to his crimes rather than suffer the beatings of the Island's sergeants. Further testimony to the fear engendered by such beatings is provided by an incident which took place in 1740.[103] A convict by the name of Jan Baptist Caarsteker was caught with stolen property of another prisoner on him. As one of the corporals, Remmer, approached Caarsteker – no doubt to administer punishment – Caarsteker shouted out: 'Here comes the bully to break me on the wheel again. Better a short death than a long one.'[104] So saying, he snatched up a knife and stabbed the nearest convict, killing the unfortunate Michiel Pietersz. 'Now take me to the chains,' said Caarsteker, happy to have guaranteed a speedy execution for himself.[105] The incredulous Fiscal, when prosecuting the case, was told by Caarsteker that similar events were bound to happen given the great cruelty suffered by all on the Island, especially at the hands of Corporal Remmer. Caarsteker was executed, and although Sergeant Willer was ordered to investigate the allegations of cruelty, nothing seems to have resulted from his inquiries.[106]

In 1751 a group of *Indiaanen bandieten* on the Island decided to fight back.[107] They entered into a conspiracy to kill all the Europeans and steal the provision boat on its arrival so that they could sail to the East Indies. The ringleaders of the plot were a certain Radja Boekit, Regent of Padang, and Robbo of Bouton. They succeeded in involving at least 13 other convicts in their plans, mainly of Macassaren or Bouganese origin, and began stealing and hiding specially sharpened seal-slaughtering knives. On 26 June 1751 their intention was to run amok, slaughtering the guards as well as all European convicts. Unfortunately for the conspirators one of their number, September van Ternaten, tried to keep some money that Robbo had entrusted to him by pretending that someone had stolen it. Sergeant Frederick Hofman, in the best tradition of the Postholders of the Island, suspected trickery and tried to beat the truth out of September. He learned more than he had bargained for. Under the pain of his beating September promised the sergeant that if he stopped (for no sooner had he confessed to theft than he began to receive punishment for his crime) he would tell him something of great importance. Sergeant Hofman was interested, and the whole story was slowly wrenched from the conspirators.

Most of those involved tried to implicate Prince Daing Manganam. The Prince denied involvement in the affair, sarcastically observing that he had no reason to be party to such a plot since the Company gave him all he needed plus ten rix-dollars a month. The Prince also pointed out that he could not speak either Bouganese or Malay, the language of the conspirators. Sergeant Hofman was quick to support the Prince, who as the richest man on the Island was doubtless a source of some revenue for the Island's staff. It is significant that several of the conspirators had been slaves on the mainland before having been sent to the Island and were fairly recent arrivals.[108] Four of the nine who were executed for their role in the abortive uprising had been convicted of piracy by the Council of Justice in Batavia in 1748, and it was they no doubt who were to pilot the ship to the East. Robbo had only arrived on the Island in 1750 after having worked in chains at the Cape since 1739. Radja had been banished to the Cape for rebellion in 1749. Six of the condemned men were broken on the cross and three hanged.[109] Security provisions doubtless increased after 1751.

Overt rebellion on the Island was not attempted again, but there were other forms of resistance available to the *Indiaanen* in particular. Robben Island has long held a special significance for the Cape Muslims, who regard it as one of the crucibles for the consolidation of their religion in Southern Africa. According to the *Bandieten Rollen*, the first *Indiaanen* to be specifically described as 'Mahommedan priests' arrived on the Island in 1744. They were Said Aloeurie and Hadje Mattarm, both of whom had been sentenced by the High Court of Batavia to spend the remainder of their lives in chains on Robben Island.[110] The following year, however, Hadje Mattarm died on the Island.[111] In 1761 Said Aloeurie left the Island for Cape Town to become a 'Caffer'[112] – the name given to the Fiscal's assistants – a group of law enforcers, drawn from the ranks of East Indian convicts, whose particular job it was to administer punishment.[113] The Island was frequently used as a recruiting ground for this hated branch of the Cape executive, and several other *Indiaanen* joined the ranks of the Caffers rather than remain on the Island for a life of hard labour.[114] According to the historian Achmat Davids, Said Aloeurie (or Tuan Said as he is known at the Cape) became the first official imam of the Muslim community at the Cape, using his home as a place of worship and using the privileges of his position as 'Caffer' (a name which, ironically, signified 'heathen' to East Indian Muslims) to instruct slaves and prisoners in the teachings of Islam.[115]

The most striking reminder of the close connection which existed between Robben Island and the establishment of Islam at the Cape is that which has been provided by the erection of a *karamat*, or shrine, on the Island in honour of Sheikh Madura. Sheikh Madura (also known as the King, Prince, Pangeran or Raja of Madura) was banished to the Island in the 1740s and died there in 1754. His body was returned to his son and now lies buried in Jakarta. Sheikh Madura had been banished to the Island for leading military resistance to the Dutch in the East Indies, and it is probable that his high rank and reputation as an opponent of Dutch colonialism, rather than his religious zeal, inspired the building of the shrine which now honours him. The shrine was visited by Cape Muslims throughout the nineteenth and twentieth centuries, and today a relatively new edifice still marks the important site.[116]

There are no memorials on the Island for two other men who were there in the 1770s and were also specifically described as 'Mahommedan priests'. One of these men was Jina Apdula from Ternaten (not to be confused with the Prince of Ternaten who had died in 1747) and the other was Noriman from Bantam.[117] Nothing is known about the first of these prisoners but Noriman has left behind a reputation for assisting the oppressed and downtrodden slaves of the Cape. Known by the names Noriman, Sayyed Nuurman, Tuan Nuruman, Imam Norman and Paay Schaapie, Noriman (as he is termed in the archival records) had begun his banishment at the Cape in Cape Town rather than on the Island. In 1786, however, he had assisted a group of runaway slaves by providing them with 'Azeemats', or talismans, for their protection. It was this offence which landed him on Robben Island. Upon his release (date unknown) he continued to propagate the teachings of Islam and served as imam for the steadily growing Muslim community at the Cape.[118]

Tradition has it that the most influential of all the Muslim leaders to have been banished to the Island was Tuan Guru, the first 'Kadi' or 'chief imam' at the Cape. Tuan Guru was a prince from Tidore in the Ternate Islands. He arrived at the Cape in 1780 and was imprisoned on the Island until 1793. During this time he wrote a book on Islamic jurisprudence which, according to Achmat Davids, 'became the main source of reference of the nineteenth-century Cape Muslim community'.[119] There were doubtless many other, less famous Muslim prisoners who spent time on the Island and, in the enforced isolation of their position, established a community of worship with their co-religionists which they transferred to the mainland on their release.

Throughout the eighteenth century the number of prisoners on the Island grew. Between 1730 and 1750 the convict population fluctuated between 40 and 60; a slight majority were European. In 1761 there were 70 prisoners on the Island, 24 of them Europeans and 46 *Indiaanen*. By 1787 the convict population had grown to 124, of whom 98 were *Indiaanen*, and by 1789 of the 134 prisoners 103 were *Indiaanen*. A breakdown of the latter shows that 50 were slaves, 19 Khoikhoi, 3 San, 4 'Bastaards', 26 East Indian and 1 Madagascan. By this date most of the European prisoners were soldiers: the

Fourth Anglo-Dutch War (1780–4) had brought a large influx of troops, from which military offenders were sent to Robben Island. The British managed to press-gang eight of these soldiers on to a Royal Navy vessel in 1781 and seem to have stripped the Island of likely crewmen when they conquered the Cape in 1795.[120]

Just before the British took over the Cape in 1795 there were over 90 prisoners on the Island, some of whom were probably VOC soldiers. The Island prison was reportedly abandoned by the Dutch and the buildings destroyed after the British occupation in 1795. But lists of prisoners on the Island were still recorded from 1786 to 1804, indicating that it continued to function as a prison for that period. During the First British Occupation (1795–1803) the only European prisoners on the Island were one or two British or Dutch soldiers and the number of *Indiaanen* was reduced to between 60 and 80.[121] The Batavians placed 11 Dutch soldiers there as convicts in 1804. But in 1806 all the convicts, both European and *Indiaanen*, were removed to the Amsterdam Battery in preparation for the beginning of a new prison settlement on the Island under British rule.[122]

Conclusion

During the period before 1806, therefore, Robben Island was used primarily as pantry and prison. It was an important stopping and restocking place for sailors undertaking the dangerous journey between Europe and the attractive commercial prospects of the Far East. Once the Dutch East India Company had established itself at the Cape of Good Hope – a process materially aided by the ease of gathering foodstuffs and protecting stock on Robben Island – both political and criminal prisoners were sent to the Island. Its function as a prison became increasingly important during the course of the eighteenth century. The prisoners on the Island worked in the lime and stone quarries, providing materials for the building works being undertaken in the Cape Peninsula as the settlement expanded. By the end of the eighteenth century, Robben Island was already an important practical and symbolic marker in the landscape of the Cape settlement. It was to retain this importance under the British, who first occupied the Cape in 1795.

The British Prison on Robben Island 1800–1896

Harriet Deacon

In 1795 the British annexed the Cape from the Dutch, ushering in a period of eight years known as the First British Occupation. The annexation was approved by the Prince of Orange, who after the invasion of Holland by French troops and the proclamation of the Batavian Republic there, feared the French would capture the strategic post at the Cape. By this time the Dutch East India Company was struggling both with growing opposition from Cape residents and with financial difficulties. The Anglo-Dutch War of 1780, which halted the Company's trade and destroyed many of her ships, had contributed to her bankruptcy by 1794. The British held the Cape until 1803, when under the agreement reached by the Treaty of Amiens in 1802, it was ceded to the Batavian Republic, still under French control. But in 1806 the British retook the Cape, a step which was formally accepted by the Dutch in terms of the London Convention of 1814.[1]

Robben Island was used as a prison almost continuously while the Cape was under British rule although there was a brief hiatus between about 1806 and 1808, and another between 1846 and 1855. The Island prison assisted Britain's military–strategic aims at the Cape and helped to fulfil its quest for symbolic authority over its enemies. Prisoners sentenced under military court-martial, political prisoners and common criminals were all kept on the Island during the nineteenth century.[2] The Island was also used, particularly in the early part of the century, for various private and semi-private commercial enterprises while it formally acted as a prison. In 1846, however, a leper asylum, lunatic asylum and chronic sick hospital were established on the Island, Called the General Infirmary, these hospitals were to dominate the Island for nearly a century, but until the 1890s there were still a few political prisoners and until the 1920s some ordinary convicts also imprisoned on the Island. The importance of the Island as a prison during this time must not be underestimated in spite of the small number of prisoners held there.

The role of Robben Island during the nineteenth century was closely related to the patterns of British involvement at the Cape. It is now generally agreed that British rule had an important influence on the development of the Cape

Three Xhosa chiefs on their release from Robben Island in April 1869: Siyolo, Maqoma and Xhoxho (South African Library)

during the first few decades of the nineteenth century. Even during the short First British Occupation (1795–1803) British officials were concerned to collect as much information on the Cape as possible so that they could govern it more effectively as a colony. Some contemporaries felt that the Cape was mainly of military–strategic importance to Britain, however. Major-General Sir James Carmichael-Smyth commented in 1827 that 'the colony of the Cape of Good Hope is ... generally very much exaggerated as to its value and importance' as its inhabitants were thinly scattered over a large territory, the soil was generally unfit for cultivation, the commercial prospects for British manufactures and imports were poor, and the harbours and roadsteads were not of good quality. The Cape was, all the same, of considerable strategic value in protecting the sea route to the East. [3] Robben Island was of some importance in this regard as it provided a safe harbour for ships in difficulty in Table Bay and guarded the bay.

Carmichael-Smyth was particularly opposed to large investment in military resources to enable the Colony's expansion, especially on its eastern frontier. This frontier was a long-standing problem for both the Dutch and the British.

Conflicts on the eastern and northern frontiers of white settlement in the Colony became intense over the hundred-year period from 1774 to 1879. These conflicts were called the 'frontier wars' by the settlers; from the perspective of indigenous inhabitants, they were 'wars of dispossession'.

A number of black leaders who took part in the frontier conflicts, those who survived the battlefields but failed to escape capture, were punished with exile on Robben Island. The individual stories of these Robben Island prisoners can thus give us an insight into the general pattern of colonial expansion and resistance to it during the nineteenth century. Mostert claims that the conflicts on the frontiers of the Colony and the accompanying 'moral struggle [between the high-minded conscience of the Enlightenment and self-interested commercial expansion] on the Cape frontier provided the main formative experience of South Africa'.[4] While this may be somewhat of an exaggeration, it is indeed true, as Mostert argues, that the frontier came to symbolise the encounter between British 'civilisation' and those they planned to 'civilise'. The leaders of frontier resistance were killed, chased out of their territory or sent to Robben Island. At the same time, as part of the incorporative 'civilising' mission, a network of missions and British institutions was established in their territories in the Eastern Cape, and some of the Xhosa leaders' children were sent to be educated in the British manner at Zonnebloem College in Cape Town. The use of Robben Island as a prison helped to establish British authority over the Colony's black opponents by removing many of their leaders, symbolically drawing a line between the civilisation of Cape Town and the black leaders of resistance from the frontier regions as well as separating these leaders from their subjects.

Against those who stress Britain's military–strategic interests in its empire, a number of historians have suggested that Britain was actively involved in the internal dynamics of its colonies.[5] Bayly argues that Imperial policy in the colonies between 1780 and 1830 was in essence 'a series of attempts to establish overseas despotisms, … characterised by a form of aristocratic military government supporting a viceregal autocracy, by a well-developed imperial style which emphasised hierarchy and racial subordination, and by the patronage of indigenous landed elites'.[6]

When the British took over the Cape they were careful to cultivate the local Dutch gentry, who expanded their farming and retail interests under the more permissive British regime. They retained Dutch law and some of the old administrative infrastructure, but began to reduce the reliance of the Cape legal system on harsh physical punishments such as branding and execution. The British colonial government also assisted the growth of English churches and the anglicisation of administrative structures. English merchants who began to do business at the Cape benefited from the patronage of the Governors and their senior officials. By the 1830s, however, this status quo was threatened both by the growing rights of Khoisan and slaves that came with amelioration and emancipation, and by the pressure of the rising commercial middle classes. With the granting of representative government in 1854, the old aristocratic hierarchy at the Cape finally ceded power to the commercial middle classes in the political arena.

During the early period of British rule, the Robben Island prison acted, much as it had done under the Dutch, as an unattractive place of banishment for political prisoners, for criminals who were considered particularly dangerous, and for some of the insane. The Island also accommodated soldiers and, from 1815, other convicts as a place of intermediate detention until their transportation sentences could be carried into effect. Conditions in the Robben Island prison did improve, though, during the 1820s and 1830s as the colonial government began to place greater emphasis on imprisonment as a punishment in itself rather than as incidental to a range of harsh physical punishments.

These reforms were the result of a broader change in the way punishment was perceived in Europe. During the eighteenth century imprisonment had not been the dominant mode of punishment in Europe and its colonies. Prisons were then mainly used to accommodate suspects and debtors. Convicted criminals were usually punished by public floggings, branding, dismemberment or execution. By the early nineteenth century, however, the philosophies of the Enlightenment had brought a new emphasis on more humane punishments which were intended to reform as well as punish criminals and to deter them and the general public from similar acts. Imprisonment appealed to the Enlightenment reformers as it deprived criminals of their liberty, which every individual supposedly possessed and valued equally. Moreover, it removed the necessity for punishment to be conducted as a public spectacle and was more economical than harsh physical punishments, which could damage the bodies of criminals forever, preventing them from working.

In 1828 a commission of inquiry appointed by the British government to advise on various matters suggested that fines and imprisonment should be imposed for minor offences in the Cape Colony.[7] In practice, however, slaves and free labourers were still often flogged so that they could be returned to work as soon as possible. Both economic considerations – convict labour was also used to reduce the colonial labour shortage – and racism – the belief that black convicts responded less well to the reformative effects of imprisonment than to physical punishment – affected the ways in which the colonial government responded to the prison reform movement.[8] The local state borrowed selectively from Western notions of punishment during the nineteenth century 'as a rational response to the social and economic problems experienced by the colonial government'.[9]

In the 1840s the Cape prison system was reorganised by John Montagu, the

Colonial Secretary at the Cape between 1846 and 1852. He drew on models used in British Tasmania which utilised convict labour for public works.[10] Montagu brought the Cape into line with practices in Europe by continually emphasising the importance of reforming individual criminals, who would then form part of a well-controlled free workforce. He suggested that Robben Island occupy a special place within the new system as a prison where particularly hardened criminals could be sent to work until they showed signs of reform. The creation of graded hardships within the prison system was crucial in encouraging the reform of convicts by means of small punishments and rewards. In 1846, however, the need for extra labour on the Colony's roads and harbours and the need to empty the prisons of the sick poor made Robben Island more attractive as a site for a hospital, and so the prison was closed, opening again only in 1855.

Robben Island under British rule

Although the British had used Robben Island as a prison from 1795, it was only during the Second British Occupation that they built a new prison settlement at the south-eastern end of the Island. In 1805 inspection by a Batavian official had revealed that the old Dutch buildings in the north-east of the Island were in ruins.[11] In 1806, the six white and sixty black prisoners from Robben Island were moved to the Amsterdam Battery on the mainland while new buildings were erected.[12] It was two years before prisoners were again held on the Island, under the command of Postholder J. C. Schultze, who had to build his own house and store, as there was 'no habitation whatsoever' there for him.[13] The new prison settlement was at the south-eastern end of the Island, near the small hill on which a signal post had been sited since the days of Van Riebeeck.

It is important to stress that even while the Island functioned primarily as a prison, it was also used for many other pursuits. The government allowed the Island to be used as a quarantine station for measles and smallpox cases, as a health resort for a few people and as a hunting ground for officials seeking diversion from Cape Town life. In 1802, for example, burgher Matthys Marrien's son was detained there under suspicion of having smallpox.[14] In 1820 a Cape Town resident asked to stay on the Island as part of a health cure.[15] In the 1830s and 1840s, officials from Cape Town came over to the Island to shoot pheasant and quail. In the late 1880s, Captain R. S. S. Baden-Powell (the man who started the Boy Scout movement) applied unsuccessfully to his uncle, Lieutenant-General H. A. Smythe, for permission to raise game birds and animals for sport on Robben Island.[16] But there were also ways in which Robben Island was used for private profit. Fishermen sheltering from bad weather or (illegally) catching rock lobster and fish from the shores exploited the Island's natural resources, as did others who lived on the Island.

Whaling in Table Bay in the early nineteenth century (Cape Archives)

Two Cape businessmen, Thomas Fitzpatrick and John Murray, reaped considerable profits from the Island and its shores in the first thirty years of the nineteenth century, an example which was closely followed with variable success by the prison staff and, somewhat tardily, by the colonial government itself.

Thomas Fitzpatrick petitioned government successfully in 1806, asking for the right to cut stone on Robben Island for his building business in Cape Town.[17] In that year John Murray had also petitioned the newly arrived Lieutenant-Governor, Sir David Baird, for permission to begin a whaling station at Robben Island. He complained that he had lost both his business and his investment in buildings for whaling in 1802, when the Batavian government granted an Amsterdam society the sole rights to whale hunting at the Cape. Murray now wanted to start a new whaling station on the Island, which was far enough away from Cape Town to prevent the smell annoying townsfolk.[18] This was duly granted. In 1806 Murray moved to the Island, using the ruins of the Dutch settlement as a base and converting the old Postholder's house to a residence.[19]

After prisoners arrived back on the Island in late 1808, Murray complained that they might 'contaminate' his slaves, steal his cattle or other property, or escape to the mainland using his boats, and suggested that he might employ and maintain the convicts at his own cost 'as if they were his own slaves', were he allowed to use the whole Island and control access thereto.[20] This grand scheme was rejected by the Governor, but it was in fact somewhat prophetic. Murray's son, who later ran the business, was asked to leave the Island in 1820 after a mass escape of prisoners had been effected by the theft of his whaling boats. He was paid compensation and built a new whaling station near Cape Town.[21] Fitzpatrick was not asked to leave, and continued his stonecutting business on the Island, employing casual labour from Cape Town and even some of the soldiers stationed on the Island.[22] The profitable nature of Fitzpatrick's business later encouraged the authorities to employ convicts in stonecutting.[23]

Whaling too was profitable enough to attract the attention of Postholder Schultze in 1811, who complained to government that he wished to engage in the business to augment his poor salary and provide a pension.[24] This was denied, but the tension between official duties and commercial activity was to be a persistent problem on the Island for much of the century. Fishing in general was an important commercial activity around the Island, and it was a port of call for many Cape Town fishermen. In 1826 the Robben Island commandant, Humphreys, was charged with employing convicts for fishing off the Island, the proceeds of which he sold in Cape Town through an overseer and two convicts.[25] Humphreys, who already had financial problems, was dismissed.[26] Commandant Pedder, his replacement, was also allegedly involved by 1828 in illicit commercial activities on his own account, selling fish and shells from Robben Island in Cape Town.[27] He was dismissed five years later for cruelty and misappropriation of government material for his own use, and replaced by Commandant Wolfe, who was soon to run his own fishery on the Island.[28]

The Robben Island prison and its inmates

Three types of prisoner were kept on Robben Island during the nineteenth century: those sentenced under military court-martial, political prisoners and common criminals.[29] For practical reasons, the monthly returns divided prisoners into 'convicts' who were sentenced to imprisonment (with or without hard labour) on the Island and 'detained prisoners' who awaited transport abroad.[30] Some of the latter were under sentence of banishment (they had to arrange to leave the Colony themselves and fell on government hands if they could not afford passage on a ship or were unfit to work for their passage); others were under sentence of transportation (the government sent them away at its own expense, usually to New South Wales).[31] One such prisoner was Samuel Smith, a private in the Cape Mounted Rifles, who was sentenced to 14 years' transportation to Van Diemen's Land (Tasmania) for drawing his sword on a non-commissioned officer of his regiment in Grahamstown in 1843.[32]

The sentence of transportation was gradually phased out after 1840, after much debate on its utility within the prison-centred penal system.[33]

Military prisoners at Robben Island were few in number, most being sentenced to transportation, although they increased both in absolute terms and as a proportion of total inmates during the 1840s. Most of them were white though a few black soldiers from the 'Hottentot Corps' were also sent to the Island. 'Political' prisoners also formed a minority of the Robben Island inmates; in contrast to the military prisoners, most of them were black. They were treated as ordinary prisoners, but can be roughly distinguished from common criminals either because they were explicitly perceived as enemies of the state or because their actions were directed towards what they perceived as injustices in the status quo.

Common criminals formed the bulk of Robben Island inmates. As in the general prison population at this time, most of them were Khoisan.[34] Those sent to Robben Island formed a small proportion of the criminals sentenced in the Colony, however, as only the most dangerous ones were sent there. From June to September in 1814, only 7 of the 330 criminal convictions in Cape Town carried the sentence of imprisonment with hard labour on Robben Island. Among them were the slave Adam, belonging to Mr Koen, who was charged with escaping and theft, and the 'Hottentot' Spaaie who was charged with an 'unnatural' crime.[35] Other prisoners included Richard Tee, a fairly prominent 1820 settler who was sentenced in 1831 to a year's hard labour on Robben Island for assaulting a 'Hottentot'.[36] The prison also accommodated a small number of female criminals. Pamela, a Cape-born slave charged with theft, was sentenced to Robben Island in 1809.[37] In the late 1820s and early 1830s women comprised a maximum of 10 per cent of the Island's convict population.[38] All of the women prisoners were removed to the House of Correction in Cape Town in 1835.[39]

By 1828 the prison at Robben Island could house 110 inmates in separate cells, although it was underutilised and contained only 38 prisoners in that year.[40] The previous year there had been 60 male and 3 female prisoners, of whom 7 were settlers, 8 were soldiers, 15 were slaves or 'prize negroes', 1 was a 'free black', 5 were 'Kaffres' and 27 were Khoisan.[41] The social profile of the prison inmates, already somewhat different for each of the three groups of prisoners, had changed slightly by the 1840s. In 1844 there were 152 prisoners in the Island prison of whom 38 were British soldiers, 21 were 'Malays and other persons of colour' (including ex-slaves) and 93 were 'Hottentots, Bushmen, Kafirs, Fingoes, etc.'[42] The prisoners performed hard labour during the day, quarrying, sawing and polishing stone. Those who misbehaved were forced to carry crowbars during their rest periods, were shackled in heavy irons, subjected to corporal punishment or put in solitary confinement on a rice-and-water diet. The other prisoners were fed on meat, bread and rice.[43]

Scarcely distinguishable from the prisoners in terms of institutional provision were the sick or insane inmates. These people were sometimes not convicted of any crime but sent to the Island because they were perceived as a threat to the public. In 1815 a number of 'Hottentots', mostly women, with venereal disease were sentenced to the Island, perhaps as part of an attempt to restrict prostitution in Cape Town.[44] In the same year Frederick Ziegler and Thomas Moray were sent to the Island because they were '*gek*' (mad).[45] Although lunatics were removed from the Island to the Old Somerset Hospital in 1823, monthly returns for the Island institution in the late 1820s again show a steady but small number of insane inmates.[46] In June 1827, for example, there were four 'lunatics' on the Island, all 'Hottentots'.[47] These men, named Matroos, Soldaat, Keizer and Vigiland, had been sent to the Island for vagrancy and theft, thereafter becoming insane.[48] Although the formal category of lunatic inmates disappeared from the official returns during the 1830s, some of the convicts, like Platjie Matross in 1844, were considered insane, and could only be pardoned when 'quiet and obedient'.[49] In that year 17 of the 152 inmates were semi-permanently disabled – from old age, skin complaints, hernias and fits.[50]

Early inefficiency and the escape of 1820

When it was re-established in about 1808, the Island prison was poorly staffed with few of the trappings of a prison. This state of affairs changed considerably within a decade. The official in charge, still called a 'Postholder' in 1808, soon became a 'Superintendent of Convicts' and then 'Commandant'. In 1819 Commandant Petrie, who had succeeded Schultze, took charge of a detachment of soldiers who had been sent to guard the prisoners.[51] After many of the prisoners escaped in 1820, security at the prison was tightened up, and during the late 1820s prisoners' living conditions were improved and regulations were drawn up for the prison.

The escape of 1820 involved a number of prisoners, including several important black leaders. Although the number of guards had increased in 1819 the buildings were still insecure and the locks were worn out.[52] A failed escape attempt in March 1820 was followed by a mass escape in August of that year, which the Colonial Secretary ascribed to the 'manifest system of neglect' at the institution.[53] The prisoners who escaped in 1820 were mainly Khoi and Xhosa, led by the detained prisoner Johan Schmidt and the Khoi prisoner Hans Trompetter.[54] They overpowered the guard and took weapons from the store, leaving eight soldiers wounded. They then stole several of Murray's boats and set off for the mainland.[55] Only one of the three boats landed safely at Bloubergstrand, however, and several of the occupants of the capsized boats drowned.[56]

Only two of the survivors of the subsequent shoot-out with the authorities escaped capture – the Khoi prisoners Abraham Leendert and Kieviet. The rest were convicted in Cape Town of 'mutiny and open violence with arms'.[57] The leaders of the escape, Schmidt and Trompetter, were hanged and decapitated, their heads displayed on iron spikes at Robben Island. David Stuurman, another Khoi leader from the Eastern Cape, was treated more leniently because he had saved the life of Murray's overseer during the escape.[58] He was sent to New South Wales in 1823 where he died seven years later.[59] The rest were sentenced to hard labour in irons on Robben Island, and in addition two of the slaves and two of the 'Caffres' (Xhosa) were publicly scourged.[60] These harsh sentences were a legacy of the eighteenth-century tradition of punishment.

Hans Trompetter and David Stuurman were leaders of Khoi opposition to the colonial forces on the Eastern Cape frontier. Trompetter had been banished to Robben Island after his role in the third frontier war (1799–1803).[61] Stuurman, who had also been involved in the third frontier war in the Eastern Cape, was a thorn in the side of the British for some years before his capture in 1819.[62] He had been the central figure in an experiment by which the Batavian government of 1803–6 allowed the Khoi to establish a community on the eastern frontier in order to restore peace and separate them from their former allies against the settlers, the Xhosa.[63] Relations between Stuurman's followers and the British deteriorated by 1809, and after an alleged alliance with the Xhosa under Chungwa (Konga), Stuurman and a few others were arrested and sent to Robben Island for the first time.[64] Stuurman escaped after a year with a few companions, however, and made his way back through the Colony to the Eastern Cape, where he hid among the Xhosa.[65] In 1819, after some involvement on the side of the Xhosa in the fifth frontier war, he was recaptured and rejoined Trompetter on the Island.[66]

Among those who drowned at Bloubergstrand was the Xhosa leader Makhanda. Makhanda, also called 'Nxele' or 'Links' (meaning left-handed in Xhosa and Afrikaans respectively), was a Xhosa warrior–prophet, who had renounced his Christian upbringing to become a strong advocate of Xhosa tradition among the Ndlambe. The Ndlambe (H'lambie) and the Ngqika (Gaika) were sub-groups of the Rharhabe clan of Xhosa, which had been formed by a split within the original Xhosa clan, the Gcaleka. In the frontier war of 1818–19 Makhanda led an unsuccessful attack by combined Gcaleka and Ndlambe forces on Grahamstown, which gave the colonists a much-wanted excuse to drive them across the Keiskamma River. Makhanda surrendered to the British in 1819, wanting to settle for peace as his people were starving, their crops burnt and their stock dying.[67] He was then banished to Robben Island, which soon entered Xhosa mythology as the 'Isle of Makhanda'. At the time the Governor, Lord Charles Somerset, was at pains to indicate that Makhanda was sent to Robben Island to provide 'security of his person'; his banishment involved loss of liberty but no other punishment. He was to be protected from the curious questions of soldiers on the Island, and given a separate room in the garden of the local whaler and fisherman, John Murray.[68] These privileges were not enough to hold him there, however, and he joined the escapees in 1820. After Makhanda's boat capsized during his escape attempt, it is said that for a time he clung to a rock, shouting encouragement to others, before he was lost in the surf.[69]

Also involved in the escape of 1820 was a Xhosa man called Jacob or Jackot by the settlers and the British military, later named Hlambamanzi by the Zulu, who accompanied Makhanda as a prisoner to the Island in 1819. Early in his life he had come into conflict with Dutch settlers on the eastern frontier and had then been captured by British forces on the frontier. For a time he worked as an interpreter for them before escaping across the Fish River. On his return into the Colony, he was recaptured and sent to the Island. After the 1820 escape attempt he was given a further sentence of 14 years' hard labour in irons but was released in 1822 to accompany the survey ship HMS *Leven* as an interpreter.[70] He left the ship at Algoa Bay to travel with Lieutenant James Farewell to St Lucia, and there escaped again. He later became an ambassador for the Zulu leader Shaka and his successor, Dingane.[71]

The natural security of the Island continued to ensure its use as a place of confinement for the most threatening of those who challenged the authority of the government and the settler class. In 1821 eight slaves from Stellenbosch were together convicted of theft, murder and escaping from their masters: their punishment included branding, flogging and imprisonment on Robben Island.[72] In 1825 there was a slave and Khoisan uprising in the Koue Bokkeveld – the Bokkeveld Rebellion – which caused the deaths of six white farmers. At his trial, the slave leader Galant said he had learned that the government was to free the slaves but his master was adamant that they should not be freed. He then determined to free himself.[73] After the rebellion, a number of Afrikaner farmers from Worcester, the district to which the accused had been sentenced to hard labour, wrote to the government that they feared their slaves or Khoi servants might converse with the convicts and 'form a new plot'. They asked that the criminals be sent to Robben Island instead.[74]

A tightening of control

After the escape of 1820 the whaler John Murray was asked to leave in the interests of security, and fishing boats were no longer allowed to beach on the Island.[75] With the tightening of control over access to the Island, opportunities for escape decreased.[76] White prisoners and those awaiting transportation were now segregated from the other prisoners to improve control within the prison.[77] But in 1828 the Commandant complained that the 'present construction of the Prison does not admit of any classification' (i.e. separation) of prisoners.[78] It was only at this stage that substantial changes were brought about, both with regard to living conditions for inmates and with regard to the administration of the prison. Discipline was tightened and codified in regulations drawn up for the regiment, civilian staff and inmates, first in 1828 and again in 1841 and 1844.[79] The conduct of Commandant Humphreys also came under scrutiny when some prisoners complained about him to the Colonial Secretary.[80] Although Humphreys was replaced by the more conscientious Pedder late in 1826, subsequent improvements in living conditions and discipline at the prison did not stem solely from the initial solicitude of the new Commandant.[81]

The colonial government began to intervene more actively in the administrative structure of the Cape during the 1820s. Faced with an outdated and culturally distinct legal system based on eighteenth-century Dutch practice, it had appointed a commission in 1823 to advise on reform. The government was anxious to modernise the colonial prisons because as imprisonment became the most usual form of punishment, conditions within them increasingly came under the spotlight. The commission proposed that an independent higher court be established, that the Fiscal be replaced by an Attorney-General and that a Superintendent of Police be appointed.[82] The last appointment was intended to improve supervision of convict labour and thus to regularise the colony's prison system. This focus on hard manual labour for convicts, often outside prison walls, was to become a characteristic of the South African prison system.[83] In many reformist European prisons, in contrast, the employment of prisoners in 'useless' labour on treadmills and other devices within prisons was favoured. But because of a shortage of 'free' labour, convict labour, employed on road works to aid commercial and territorial expansion, was an attractive resource in the Cape after the 1840s.

One of the objects of better regulation of prisons was the deterrence of crime. This was to be achieved by maintaining systematically harsh conditions, especially by providing hard manual labour for all convicts. 'The proper object of all punishments being to deter from crime by the suffering actually endured by the criminal and by the exhibition of it to others, it becomes absolutely necessary that the condition of convicts in this Colony should not ... be ... improved and rendered easier by the sentence of the Law.'[84]

To regularise the experience of punishment, convicts were no longer to be employed as overseers or servants of the prison staff.[85] The Robben Island overseer, who now lost his convict servant, requested a salary commensurate with that of constables in Cape Town, a comparatively princely sum of £45 per annum.[86] For the prisoners, the new emphasis on hard manual labour did not mean equally harsh conditions for all, however. Although it was deemed important to make the prison experience harsher than the conditions experienced outside the prison, prisoners with different social statuses had different perceptions of hardship. It was suggested that for 'a convicted Slave or Hottentot who is worked less and perhaps fed and clothed better [in prison] than with his master the sentence of the Law is ... not a punishment'.[87] This justified harsher treatment for black prisoners than their white counterparts even as the prison system was undergoing a process of 'humanitarian reform' after the 1820s. By the end of the century, indeed, the prison system was to channel black prisoners into hard manual labour and white prisoners into semi-skilled workshop activities.

During the Dutch period prisoners had been put to work in quarrying stone and slate and collecting shells on Robben Island and on public works on the mainland. But by the 1820s convict labour was more effectively organised. The emphasis on hard labour for the Robben Island convicts increased as stonecutting and lime-burning were resumed by the prison authorities.[88] A jetty, built with convict labour of Robben Island stone, was completed in 1827, considerably easing the landing of stores and passengers.[89] Two years later a visitor commented,

> Before the pier was built the landing was very disagreeable, and often very difficult on account of the surf and the quantity of sea-weed which covered the beach, and which sometimes became very offensive when in a state of decomposition during the hot weather. Through both of these impediments persons were either obliged to wade, or be carried on the shoulders of a convict, an experiment which was not infrequently attended by a ducking. The new pier is 600 ft long by 20 wide, and 21 feet high from its base, at the extremity, near which there are some good stone steps for the convenience of landing.[90]

There was some tension within the new labour-intensive system, however, as some of the Robben Island prisoners had not been sentenced to hard labour and were, Pedder complained, 'desperate characters', difficult to control. The Colonial Secretary replied that

> convicts confined at Robben Island under sentences or order of transportation or banishment may be kept to hard labor [*sic*] if their health permits, and the time during which such convicts are confined on the Island shall be taken and reckoned in discharge or part discharge of their times of transportation or banishment ... It does not appear that persons confined there NOT under such sentence, can be legally ordered or kept at hard labor unless specially sentenced thereto.[91]

In spite of the dominant emphasis on deterrence as the purpose of punishment at this time, there was increasing interest in the reform of the criminal by gentler means. An organised system of convict rehabilitation through hard labour on public works was introduced for the first time under John Montagu in the 1840s. Already in the late 1820s the Robben Island prisoners had begun to receive 'reformatory' religious instruction from a fellow convict, Van Graan.[92] The government paid for Bibles and prayerbooks to be issued to the prisoners, although they did not allow Pedder to buy any additional books.[93] Rewarding good behaviour was an essential part of the reformist approach. On account of his teaching duties Van Graan was allowed the privilege of occasional visits to Cape Town and received an allowance.[94] After petitioning the Governor in 1825, the prisoners received payment for extra work to allow them to purchase soap for washing their linen and some tobacco, which was not issued to them as part of their rations.[95] Living conditions also improved as part of the prison reforms. In 1827 Commandant Pedder suggested that a boiler be purchased so that soup could be made for the prisoners. Hitherto they had been required to cook their own rations; this had been problematic as there were no cooking facilities provided and most of them had had to go without food at lunch-time.[96]

Further improvements in conditions for prisoners were not to come from Pedder, however. In 1833, after earlier complaints about his use of convict labour for private fishing, he was dismissed on account of cruelty.[97] Lieutenant Wall of the British regiment on the Island (the 98th) accused Pedder of making the pregnant slave Louisa, a prisoner, carry heavy stones, thus causing her to miscarry.[98] On Pedder's dismissal, Richard Wolfe of the 93rd Regiment was appointed as the new Commandant.[99] Wolfe was an ambitious civil servant. Later he became Resident Magistrate of Wynberg, and employed the artist Thomas Bowler as tutor to his children.[100] Wolfe effected reforms at the Robben Island prison, although he was at the same time absorbed in private profit-making through his fishery business on the Island.

In the year of Wolfe's appointment as Commandant, an inspection of the Robben Island staff barracks concluded that it was 'a substantial building, affording sufficient accommodation for a subaltern's party'. It also noted that there was room in the barracks 'for a few convalescents and invalids, who are sometimes sent there from Headquarters for the improvement of their health. There is no hospital, the sick being forwarded for treatment to Cape Town.'[101] Robben Island thus continued to accommodate those who got sick on the mainland and required a 'change of air' or better security arrangements. A continuing emphasis on prison regulations, now explicitly designed to 'provide for the security, the well being and the moral reformation of the Prisoners', encouraged further improvements in living conditions for the prisoners under Wolfe.[102] Sick prisoners, who had previously been treated by the prison staff or sent to the Somerset Hospital in Cape Town, now had the advantage of occasional treatment from a doctor, Bickersteth, who was appointed Surgeon at the Somerset Hospital and medical attendant to the convicts at Robben Island in 1834.[103] After a complaint from the transportation convicts later in that year, hats were issued to those prisoners 'who may have been accustomed to wear Hats previously to their confinement'.[104]

Wolfe's term of office as Commandant on Robben Island (1833–46) coincided with greater government investment in the lime works as a commercial venture, longer working hours for the prisoners and the purchase of the first large boat to be run from the Island for the use of the prison.[105] Convicts were now used as overseers and boatmen.[106] To counteract the potentially disruptive effects of these greater opportunities for contact with the mainland, the prison regulations of 1844 tightened up control of the prisoners. They included directions that 'No tobacco or snuff is ever to be ... used by any Prisoner' and 'No Prisoner is allowed to receive or send away a letter, or letters ... except by the permission of the Commandant'. The regulations also stipulated that the prison officers should not 'pass over the slightest irregularity they may observe among the Convicts, however trifling it may be', as the Commandant was 'determined to establish a system of the most rigidly severe discipline' at the prison. Rewards or 'indulgences' would, however, be issued to prisoners who showed a willingness to reform their ways.[107] This combination of rewards and strict discipline, coupled with the focus on rehabilitation and training, was characteristic of the humanitarian reforms that John Montagu had promised to bring to the colonial prison system after 1843.

By the 1840s the Robben Island prison occupied a unique place within the colonial prison system as it had been reorganised under Governor Napier and John Montagu. The relative isolation of the Island and the general fear of imprisonment there, especially among the 'lower orders', still made the prison particularly important as a place 'where the very worst of criminals' could be sent.[108] The Robben Island prison could thus provide a more severe punishment for serious offenders without necessitating any additional physical sanctions.[109]

Prisoners may have feared the stigma of the Island prison, but middle-class families sometimes favoured its isolation above the public nature of labour in the Town. 'Jafta', sentenced to five years' imprisonment on the Island, complained in 1845 that although he submitted to his sentence 'without a murmur', his transfer to Robben Island was to take place not for his own misdemeanour, which was simple theft, but so that he could be employed in the fish house, to copper the Commandant's casks (a reference to Wolfe's fishery business). Jafta asked to remain at Tigervalley Convict Station instead.[110] But for some prominent Cape Town families, the stigma of working in chains in full view of Cape Town society weighed more heavily than the terrors of Robben Island. The family and friends of Jan van Eijk, who had been convicted of

Robben Island drawn by G. M. Smith *c.* 1860, a 'lunatic' patient on the Island
(South African Library)

forgery and sentenced to four years' hard labour in Cape Town, pleaded with government to send him to Robben Island in 1840 'that he may not be ordered to work in chains to the disgrace of his Respectable Relations and friends'.[111] A tailor's son, called Hendricks, was sent to the Island in 1842 for similar reasons.[112]

In spite of the adapted role of the Island prison under the new convict system, other uses for the Island became more attractive as more of its inmates were needed for work on the roads and transportation sentences became less common. In 1845 John Montagu decided to establish a hospital on the Island for all those potentially dangerous and incurable medical cases which were filling up district gaols and town hospitals. The prison was thereupon closed in 1846. It would be another ten years before a political prisoner was to return to the Island and twenty years before criminal prisoners were again housed there, now as labourers for the medical institutions.

Political prisoners on Robben Island after 1846

During the War of Mlanjeni (1850–53) – also known as the Eighth Frontier War – the British captured a Ndlambe Xhosa chief called Siyolo, named after a prophet who claimed to be the reincarnation of Makhanda. Siyolo was sent to Robben Island in May 1855, accompanied by his wife, and was initially imprisoned in a house at the village, a separate section of the female leper asylum. There were, according to the Superintendent, several men on Robben Island at the time who spoke Xhosa; Mrs Fairbank, the baker's wife, had learned some Xhosa in Natal.[113] The Fairbanks were employed to look after the prisoner and his wife.[114] By June, the Robben Island officials had stopped locking Siyolo up at night, and the prisoners received weekly supplies of flour, tobacco and sheep fat in addition to their daily ration of candles, bread, meat, potatoes, tea and sugar. This ration was a full hospital diet with two extra pounds of flour. The prisoners were also allowed to herd a small flock of goats.[115]

In August 1855, Siyolo's wife requested permission to visit Cape Town. She and Maqoma's wife were certainly allowed to do this by 1862.[116] From there they were able to smuggle messages home.[117] By 1862 Siyolo, too, was straining against the Island's restrictions. He sent a petition to the Colonial Secretary saying he no longer wished to remain on the Island but wanted to live in Cape Town. He was often blamed by Island officials for misconduct, which included beating an attendant with a knobkierie.[118] After his release in 1869, Siyolo returned to the Eastern Cape. In 1878 he again joined forces with the Ngqika in the last frontier war, during which he was shot and killed.

Several other Xhosa chiefs came as prisoners to Robben Island in 1858 after the Cattle Killing of 1856–7, part of a millenarian Xhosa offensive against the encroaching British which nearly destroyed the Xhosa themselves. Among those imprisoned on Robben Island was Maqoma. Born in 1798, Maqoma (or Macomo) was a son of Ngqika. His biographer charges that Maqoma has been 'characterized as a drunken troublemaker and cattle thief who masterminded an unprovoked irruption into the Colony in 1834 and eventually led his subjects into the irrational Cattle Killing catastrophe of 1856–7'.[119] In fact, he was one of the most important nineteenth-century Xhosa leaders, considered even by his British opponents a formidable tactician, a masterful politician and a brilliant orator. He placated European raiders with cattle tribute in the 1820s and 1830s, only retaliating against the British in 1834 after he had been forced off his land three times.[120] He could not have been a confirmed alcoholic, asserts his biographer, as he sustained successful guerrilla insurgency tactics during the War of Mlanjeni. He drank mainly at meetings with colonial officials, who deliberately plied him with alcohol to try and befuddle his judgement. He supported the Cattle Killing only once it had become such

Maqoma, photographed by Gustav Fritsch in the early 1860s
(South African Library)

Maqoma and his wife Katyi, c. 1860 (South African Library)

a powerful movement that failure to do so would have threatened his chiefly power and prestige.[121]

Maqoma and his wife Katyi were banished to Robben Island after he was convicted in 1857 of having been party to the murder of another chief, who had refused to destroy his cattle in the Cattle Killing. For the first month of his stay he was put in solitary confinement by Superintendent Minto, who 'was afraid of him by the report [he had] had'.[122] Maqoma raged that he was 'much discontented' about being imprisoned on Robben Island and demanded a trial or freedom in 1858, but to no avail. His wife, then ill on the Island, apparently refused medicine, saying, 'No, my heart is sore, I want to die.'[123]

By 1859 there were eight Xhosa leaders on the Island: Maqoma, his brother Xhoxho, Mhala (the son of Ndlambe), Fadana, Kenti, Dilima (the son of Phato, leader of a Khoi–Xhosa clan) and his two younger brothers.[124] The prisoners had little contact with their relatives: Mhala was fortunate to have a son at Zonnebloem College in Cape Town, who in 1861 asked whether he could visit his father on Robben Island.[125] Mhala's and Xhoxho's wives, however, refused to come from the Transkei. The prisoners wrote lonely letters home requesting news. Although they received adequate food they received no alcohol. They were, however, able to hunt hares and Cape pheasants on the Island.[126] Their accommodation consisted of huts covered with tarpaulins at Murray's Bay, where they slept first on mattresses on the sand, and then on stretchers.[127] Other Xhosa captives, who had been temporarily imprisoned in Cape Town, joined the prisoners at Murray's Bay in 1862.[128] The prisoners were now given three weather-boarded houses instead of huts, and a few cows which soon died.[129]

Several of the Xhosa chiefs were released in 1863, leaving six male prisoners of war and two of their wives on the Island.[130] On 19 April 1869, the last three prisoners, Maqoma, Siyolo and Xhoxho, left the Island by boat. Reverend Baker, the resident Anglican chaplain on the Island, wrote in his diary that they thanked him on their departure, accepted some small gifts and said they hoped the Bishop would send them a good missionary.[131] They were all allowed to return home, but Maqoma was unfortunately soon re-convicted. While he had been on the Island, Maqoma's land in the Ciskei, near Fort Beaufort, was taken by the British. After trying to reoccupy his land, he was re-imprisoned on Robben Island in 1871, this time without his wife. He died in the pauper wards, 'from natural causes', a weak and lonely old man, in September 1873.[132] Praise poems described him as 'a black snake who crosses rivers' and ascribed his death 'on the white people's island' to a gunshot wound inflicted by his white prison guards. There is no contemporary documentary evidence to substantiate the claim that he was murdered, however.[133] In 1978 a traditional seer claimed to have found Maqoma's grave on the Island; his bones were reburied in his old territory in the Ciskei.

After Maqoma had died in 1873, the Island was without political prisoners for barely a year. The Hlubi chief, Langalibalele, was to arrive in 1874, in rather inauspicious circumstances. Langalibalele, or Mthethwa (1818–89), became the chief of the Hlubi in 1873, one of the most powerful independent black groups remaining in Natal. The Hlubi had been relocated by Theophilus Shepstone to the upper stretches of the Bushman's River near the Drakensberg in order to form a buffer between the San in the Drakensberg and the colonists. Langalibalele's growing following, and his influence as a visionary, rain-maker and independent leader, began to threaten the colonists and

Langalibalele, chief of the Hlubi, in captivity (Cape Archives)

Shepstone's 'native policy'. But the spark for what was called the 'Langa-libalele Rebellion' was the refusal by the Hlubi to register weapons which they were bringing back from the diamond fields in Griqualand West. In 1873 Shepstone finally sent troops after Langalibalele, but he escaped to Lesotho. The Hlubi were disbanded, and their land and their stock confiscated.[134]

Langalibalele was finally arrested in Lesotho, and tried early in 1874. His trial is still regarded today as a major travesty of justice, as his lawyer was not given the assurance that British law would prevail. The lawyer withdrew in protest, and Langalibalele was not represented. He was convicted of treason, murder and rebellion, with trivial support for these accusations. J. W. Colenso, the Bishop of Natal, protested in vain against the trial, even going to England to plead the chief's cause with the Secretary of State for the Colonies. Langalibalele was banished to Robben Island for life under a special Act of the Cape parliament, called the Natal Criminals Act.[135] Colenso continued to fight for redress, however. After a visit to the Island, Colenso requested that the prisoner be relieved of convict dress and given a change of diet. Super-intendent Biccard replied that the chief and his son had already been given civilian-style canvas clothing, and that they would in future receive more bread and meat, and a ration of beer daily. They were not allowed bottles with

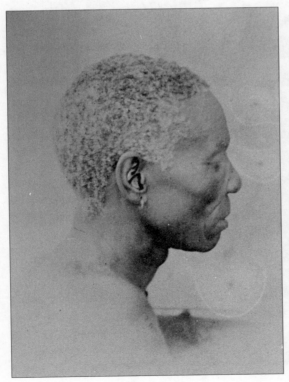

their beer or wine because their room opened into the convict barracks, and it was feared that they might trade the items with the convicts.[136]

Later in 1875 the Secretary of State in London, Lord Carnarvon, finally succeeded in forcing the Cape parliament to reconsider Langalibalele's sentence. Carnarvon felt that lifelong banishment on Robben Island was too severe in relation to the crime com-mitted and he complained also that the trial had been irregu-lar. Parliament grudgingly repealed the Natal Criminals Act and Langalibalele was

Stokwe, photographed by Gustav Fritsch in the early 1860s (South African Library)

released from Robben Island in August 1875. Still considered a threat to settler security, he was imprisoned instead on the farm Uitvlugt, near present-day
Pinelands in Cape Town, where the Zulu king Cetshwayo was later to be held
in 1879.[137] While at Uitvlugt, Langalibalele asked the authorities to fulfil their
promise of sending one of his wives down from Natal. He asked his favourite
wife, Vokwe (or Voko), to 'go to him, and cook for him and stay with him'
but she refused, saying that she did not want to go alone, as she was afraid
that 'the Authorities have killed him long ago' and she did not want to be singled out because 'all the Chief wives want to go'.[138] In 1877 Langalibalele was
taken back to Natal where he died in 1889.

The last phase of colonial consolidation in the area west of the Fish River
and south of the Orange drew to Robben Island a new group of political prisoners. By early 1880 there were about 26 prisoners in all, on whom the government spent about £100 per month in maintenance and security.[139] It was
more expensive to keep prisoners on Robben Island than on the mainland, but
this was compensated for by the greater symbolic value of exiling the leaders
of indigenous opposition forces to the Island and the practical value of the
cheap security that the Island situation offered.

In 1877 on the eastern frontier of the Colony, tension developed between the
Gcaleka and the Mfengu, in the area east of the Kei. The Mfengu, called
Fingoes by the colonists, were a group of refugees, rather than a coherent clan,
who had fought on the side of the British, and had been relocated north of the
Gcaleka, in land the Gcaleka had previously occupied. When in 1877 the
British stepped in to 'protect' the Mfengu and their interests in the frontier
region, the last, and ninth, frontier war broke out. In 1878 the Ngqika and
Ndlambe Xhosa joined on the side of the Gcaleka against the British. The
Xhosa were finally crushed in that year.

After the war, eleven Gcaleka Xhosa and the sons of Maqoma, Mhala and
Sandile of the Ngqika and Ndlambe clans were imprisoned on Robben Island.
Although a general amnesty had been given to the 'rebels' after the war, their
leaders were tried, but because of public sympathy for the brutal British inter-
vention in the war, their sentences were commuted to life or less. On Robben
Island, the Xhosa were kept separate from other political prisoners, in a wood
and iron hut near Murray's Bay. Some of the Xhosa prisoners may have been
transferred as early as 1880[140] to the Breakwater Prison, where Edmund
Sandile and his brothers were assigned to gangs working on the docks.
Edmund was still at the Breakwater Prison in 1884. One of the prisoners on
Robben Island was Stokwe Tyhali, a chief from Thembuland, who had been
charged with high treason. Although several, like Tyhali, had been given life
sentences, they were all released from the Island in 1883. In 1888 those
remaining in the Breakwater Prison received an amnesty.

Korana chiefs from the northern frontier of the Cape were also sentenced to

Robben Island in 1870 and 1879. Piet Rooy, Jan Kivido, David Diedericks and Carel Ruyter were captured in the Korana war of 1869–70. Kivido was classified as a chronic sick patient soon after his arrival, and died on the Island in the 1880s. The other three were classed with the ordinary convicts by the time the second group of Koranas arrived in 1879.[141] They were finally released from Robben Island in 1884.

The second Korana War, which lasted from 1877 to 1878, was centred along the middle reaches of the Orange River. Many of the Korana leaders were captured and sentenced to Robben Island. Thomas Pofadder, Jan Malgas and five other Koranas were sent from Robben Island to the Breakwater Prison in late 1880.[142] The Koranas, except the three who had been on the Island since 1870, were kept in a room adjacent to the convict station. A conditional release was offered to the Korana chiefs in 1883. They were not to be recognised by the colonial government and were not allowed to establish themselves near or within colonial borders or to gather any following.[143] These restrictions were a way of controlling the chiefs without the colonial government bearing the stigma of imprisoning them.

Conclusion

The prison on Robben Island during the nineteenth century was thus an important card in the British hand. Britain's possession of the Island symbolised its control over the Cape as a guarantee of its sea route to the East. The Island also provided a secure place of detention for the undesirables in colonial society. The prison on the Island merely accommodated these undesirables – in itself it did little to contain and control or even reform the prisoners before the 1840s because it was not well regulated or adequately staffed. The prison inmates included criminals, court-martialled soldiers, and the insane or infectious sick (such as smallpox cases). At the same time, throughout the nineteenth century the Island inmates also included black leaders who had played an important part in the struggle against colonial expansion on the eastern and northern frontiers of the Colony. A number of these men died on the Island, while others were released only when the British had established formal control over their lands or were in a position to demand obedience from them and their peoples.

The establishment of the General Infirmary on the Island in 1846 formally closed the prison for ten years. The new hospital drew on the long association which the Island had had with the exile of undesirables, as its patients were considered incurable or dangerous. But it also drew on an almost equally long-standing association of the Island site with the restoration of the sick to a state of health.

The Medical Institutions on Robben Island 1846–1931

Harriet Deacon

Although for many years it had been solely a prison or a pantry, for nearly a century – between 1846 and 1931 – Robben Island accommodated a hospital for 'lunatics', 'lepers' and the chronically ill poor. The patients in the General Infirmary, as it was called for many years, were those perceived as the most dangerous and incurable of the sick. Even so, an increasing number of middle-class white patients were also admitted during and after the 1860s, heightening tension between the curative and custodial, or punitive, aspects of the Island institutions. By the 1890s this tension was partially resolved by the removal of the supposedly less dangerous and more curable patients from the Island (chronic sick patients and white non-criminal lunatics respectively) to curative institutions on the mainland. By 1913, only lepers and black lunatics remained on Robben Island. Within less than a decade the lunatics were all sent to mainland institutions, as the Robben Island asylum was becoming disproportionately expensive in relation to the low social status of its patients. The decreasing incidence of leprosy in the Western Cape also contributed to the closure of the Robben Island leper asylum in 1931.

The establishment of the General Infirmary

The General Infirmary was the brainchild of John Montagu, who came to the Cape in 1843 from Tasmania as Secretary to the Government (later Colonial Secretary). Montagu suggested in 1844 that

> As the salubrity of Robben Island has long been acknowledged, and there is abundance of stone, lime and labour on the spot to erect the necessary buildings, I would strongly recommend ... the expediency of removing the leper and pauper establishments of Hemel-en-Aarde [near Caledon] and Port Elizabeth, to Robben Island, also the pauper establishment of Cape Town, and the lunatics at present confined in the Somerset Hospital at Cape Town [which] are ... wretchedly conducted, at very heavy annual expense to the public.[1]

Altogether 17 chronic sick from the Port Elizabeth Pauper Asylum, 51 lunatics from the Somerset Hospital, 101 paupers from the Cape Town Pauper Asylum, and 56 lepers from mission-run settlements at Hemel-en-Aarde and Baken's River were to be sent to the Island.[2] When the plan was put into effect in 1845–6, however, only those paupers considered incurably sick were dispatched, in addition to the lunatics and lepers.

The beginnings of the General Infirmary on Robben Island were inauspicious. At the Moravian-run settlement near Caledon, Hemel-en-Aarde, 'the Magistrate had to use strong language to get [the lepers'] cooperation' to leave for Robben Island in 1845; they consented only on condition that their pastor, Rev. Lehmann, was to follow soon.[3] At the Somerset Hospital in Cape Town, a few chronic sick patients flatly refused to leave the mainland for what seemed an endless exile on Robben Island.[4] In 1845 the Island was still thinly populated with convicts on transportation sentences; with the encouraging promise of pardon, they were transforming their prison into a hospital.[5] A few lepers from Hemel-en-Aarde were the first to arrive at the end of 1845 and were joined by lepers from Port Elizabeth in January 1846. The chronic sick, many of them ex-slaves bent with age and rheumatism, filled the hastily converted prison buildings on the Island. Lunatics from overflowing gaol infirmaries and the Somerset Hospital came too, shouting, deluded and morose, on the arduous boat trip from the harbour at Table Bay and then disembarked through the breakers on to the Island beach.

The General Infirmary was the product of a more general process of increasing state intervention in the lives of the Colony's subjects during the 1840s, but not of any greater commitment towards curing the sick poor. Montagu expanded the executive role of the Colonial Secretary, plundering welfare funds for 'prize negroes', legal wards and distressed British settlers, and trying to tax local commerce in order to reduce the Cape government's deficit.[6] His plans to use convict labour on road and harbour works made it important to empty district gaols of the sick poor and insane. The General Infirmary received these 'incurable' cases, providing cheap centralised custodial care outside Cape Town for those considered beyond reform.

The colonial government had never been eager to provide welfare at the Cape, leaving much of the responsibility to churches and communities. But the Imperial government did encourage action on slave emancipation, aboriginal rights and the emigration of British subjects to the colonies.[7] After emancipation in the 1830s the Cape government wanted to place ex-slaves in the position of workers within a new social hierarchy and to control the growing urban underclasses. It also felt some responsibility to provide for the growing number of British immigrants who had left the benefits of the Poor Laws behind for a new country where they often found themselves in temporary destitution without friends or family. The Infirmary catered for these two groups, but it was also designed to control and limit state welfare provision by providing relief only for those of the poor who could not work through sickness or old age and were prepared to receive indoor relief on the Island, far from their friends and families.

Living on the Island

The convict settlement on the south-east of the Island, constructed piecemeal between 1807 and about 1843, was dominated by a large rambling house occupied by the Commandant, Major Wolfe. Next to it were gardens and shacks for curing fish, and behind it a parsonage, church and the resident surgeon's dwelling, which had been built to generous specifications in the early 1840s. The prison, guard houses, lime houses and stables, next to the church and parsonage, formed a row facing the sea. The lepers were housed in the old stables and their pastor, Mr Lehmann, moved into the adjacent parsonage. Lunatics occupied the old prison, next to the church. Male chronic sick were housed in the guard house, the overseer's house, a converted lime kiln (the Flagstaff ward) and another two cottages. When Commandant Wolfe left to become Resident Magistrate of Wynberg in 1847, female chronic sick were housed in his residence, which became the 'Female Hospital'.

By May 1847 there were 72 chronic sick, 68 lunatics and 54 lepers on the Island.[8] During the course of the next half-century, first the lunatics and then the lepers were to surpass the chronic sick in number and importance. The three patient groups had strikingly different social profiles. The chronic sick consisted largely of male patients from Cape Town, of whom about two-fifths were white until the 1860s. There was a small but steady proportion of middle-class patients (who were all white), representing about one-fifth of the chronic sick.[9] Although the lepers initially showed a fairly even gender balance, the intake gradually favoured men.[10] Almost all of them were black, all of them were destitute, and most of them were in the advanced stages of the disease. By 1855, lepers from the Western Cape predominated (four-fifths of the total), and these were mainly from the Cape District. A quarter of the lepers came from Cape Town. The lunatics, by contrast, comprised a growing number of middle-class patients (a tenth of the total in 1855),[11] and although initial admissions were mainly black,[12] by 1855 about a third of the lunatics were white. The gender balance among lunatics was fairly even, perhaps slightly favouring men. About half came from Cape Town.[13]

After the first intake from mission stations like Hemel-en-Aarde, most of the Robben Island patients came through the Old Somerset Hospital. The hospital admitted most of its chronic sick patients from in and around Cape Town, while leper and lunatic cases were more often sent from the country. Doctors

Christmas party for female lepers in the early twentieth century (Cape Archives)

at the Old Somerset Hospital were allowed to admit emergency cases as in-patients without certificates, and others were referred to the authorities for permission.[14] Many chronic sick patients applied by memorial for admission to the hospital. George Tinehan, for example, wrote to Montagu at the Colonial Office in 1851, saying that he had been laid up with an ulcerated leg for six months and was unable to pay for medical care, and asking for admission to the Old Somerset Hospital as a pauper.[15]

Destitute ex-slaves were admitted automatically to pauper institutions by order of the Governor after 1838.[16] Admission of other pauper cases to the Old Hospital was governed by municipal regulations drafted in 1840. The regulations stipulated that those sick paupers who were unable to pay a deposit or fees of two or three shillings a day[17] could be admitted to the hospital free if they provided a certificate from the local wardmaster certifying that they were destitute and 'fit objects of charity'.[18] Dr Bickersteth commented in 1845 that wardmasters' certificates were often unreliable as many were provided for country patients or sailors whom the wardmasters could not know personally.[19] Unfit objects of charity included a pauper, William de Vries, who was refused in-patient treatment in 1853 because he had no dependants and was deemed responsible for his own illness. For him, the attraction of the hospital was its provision of food and lodging rather than the treatment, which he could get free as an out-patient.[20] As in European and American hospitals,[21] the Cape hospitals were often more important in providing board and lodging to their clientele than in promoting cures. In 1865 Dr Landsberg, who attended the poor on behalf of several charitable societies, sent only the poorest patients to the Old Somerset Hospital; these needed food more than medicine to effect a cure.[22]

Few of the patients had any alternative source of care. In 1862 it was noted that 'the helplessly destitute leper alone resorts to the asylum on Robben Island'.[23] Dr Ebden commented that 'in the upper parts of the town [Cape Town] there are many cases of ... lepers living with their friends'.[24] The asylum keeper suggested too that if the male lunatics had 'any one to come for them ... they would be sent away'.[25] There was much demand for the limited Island places,[26] which meant that dangerous or violent cases usually enjoyed precedence.[27] Even in the 1880s, the asylums at Robben Island and Grahamstown were so full that cases had to be kept in gaols for many months where they were 'aggravated by becoming the butt and amusement of the prisoners'.[28]

Many of the chronic sick were black, the poorest of the colonial population, and the rest were European immigrants who had few community support structures in the Colony. Widow Hennessy, for example, who emigrated to the Colony in 1851, was 'reduced to actual want of the common necessaries of life, caused by sickness and unable to use her right hand during the last six months' in 1863 and thus applied for admission to the Old Somerset Hospital.[29] Once on the Island most of the patients (and many of the staff) had no alternative but to stay, where they were fed and housed for free. Not all were allowed to stay, however. A couple named Davies protested in vain for readmission in 1857 when, after returning from leave in Cape Town, they were excluded from their chronic sick hospital quarters because of alleged immorality.[30]

The Island staff was small and, because of the importance of maintaining links with the mainland, about half were boatmen in 1846.[31] The upper echelon of the staff consisted of the Surgeon-Superintendent, the chaplain, and the clerk and storekeeper. The subordinate staff, or 'servants', were paid much less than the staff 'aristocracy' and initially also less than domestic servants in Cape Town.[32] Most of them were recent British immigrants who had found it difficult to support their families in Cape Town or were attracted to Robben Island because of personal connections, such as a relative in the hospital.[33] Many of the male attendants had been previously employed by the colonial government as soldiers or policemen.[34] Their wives often worked as nurses and matrons at the Infirmary.

Life on the Island was not easy. All three patient groups were expected to help with the nursing; the lunatics and chronic sick were expected to work at other chores, carrying water and landing stores, mending and washing clothes. One lunatic was even employed on the Island boat, until he escaped.[35] The water was brackish, sanitation poor and all food had to be brought from the mainland. Low diet was perceived to be a beneficial 'depletory' measure for the insane and the sick. The patients' diet – bread and tea in the morning and evening, and a meat and vegetable soup at midday – was so scanty until changes were made in 1863 that many of them collected crayfish and other foods on the beach, or killed the institution's sheep at night.[36] Only the lepers were allowed the full diet.

The lepers complained of the food, the glare, their separation from friends and family, and the inadequate medical attention they received.[37] Treatments administered during the 1850s were cursory and 'heroic'.[38] Birtwhistle's 'house medicine', a 'tartar emetic and salts', was a purgative, administered daily to refractory patients and three times a week to the rest, in half-pint doses.[39] Without effective chemical cures and with a large number of avowedly chronic cases, medical treatment was never extensive. In the 1870s a doctor commented: 'In no sense of the word [was] there a hospital for lepers [on Robben Island], but simply a number of wards set apart for those paupers who are suffering from the disease, to prevent them contaminating the others.'[40]

The isolation of the Infirmary gave staff members, especially the Surgeon-Superintendent, great control over the lives of patients. One patient wrote to a local paper in 1862:

> Many are suffering very bad from a bowel complaint caused by bad
> food and water, and three were buried yesterday in one grave, two white
> men and a leper. Many of us felt strange enough when we saw this way
> of burying the dead; but we dare not say anything about it to the
> authorities here, because if we make complaints it only makes matters
> worse ... [The clerk, Murray] is the only one who seems to pity [the
> patients] ... All hands are kept busy from morning till night making the
> new jetty ... A lunatic of the name of Varney, who used to be a sort of
> manager, and is a good mason, refuses to work any more, and says he
> has worked long enough for nothing ... I hope you will continue to
> advocate our cause till we are removed from this place.[41]

The unsuitable doctor and the unsuitable site

Although the General Infirmary was not destined to reduce medical expen-
diture significantly after 1846 by centralising hospital facilities,[42] its first six
years were seen at the time as a period of relative success. But a series of scandals in the 1850s highlighted deficiencies in the management of the institution
and brought into question its original rationale. The Island site now became
problematic and attempts were made to recast the lunatic asylum in particular as a humane and curative institution that could be clearly distinguished
from the custodial and punitive prison.

In 1852 the first scandal broke when the Robben Island clerk and storekeeper, David Thompson, wrote to the Lieutenant-Governor, Darling,

> imploring your interference on behalf of the General Infirmary, Robben
> Island, which has long suffered under the incompetence and tyranny of
> its Surgeon-Superintendent, Mr. John Birtwhistle. It may be that for sev-
> eral years past, the government and the public have heard nothing but
> approving and flattering accounts of the establishment; but all these
> accounts have been fallacious and deluding.[43]

The Superintendent, Dr Birtwhistle, was criticised for being too familiar with
the 'servants' and some patients, for intentional cruelty towards some patients
and favouritism towards others. He was shown by the subsequent government
inquiries to have been cruel and dishonest, although in some respects his mode
of treatment was simply old-fashioned. He was finally dismissed in 1855.

The role of the clerk in bringing the scandals to light, the involvement of
Darling and the delay in Birtwhistle's dismissal were not circumstantial.
Birtwhistle wrote to the Parliamentary Commissioners investigating the case
in 1854, 'You can be expected to know but little of what goes on at Robben

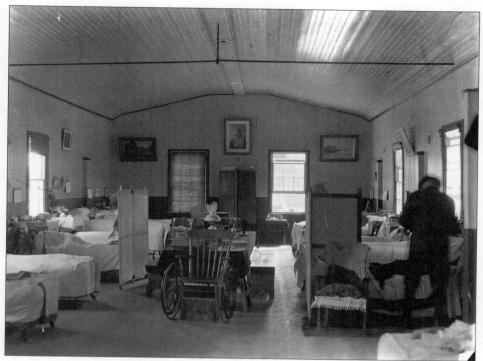

A leper ward in the early twentieth century (Cape Archives)

Island, in that miniature world, where human passions and feelings, pent up within limits on which society on the mainland can afford no parallel, operate upon all within their influence.'[44] The clerk was resentful of the doctor's increasing power within the General Infirmary after changes to the regulations in 1847, which removed some of Thompson's responsibilities for patient and staff management and made him 'a person of no authority in the establishment'.[45] But Thompson could not complain to Montagu, who had appointed Birtwhistle and supported his growing authority in the establishment. He wrote instead to Darling, who supported the Cape-based commercial middle classes and was opposed to Montagu's 'family compact' which protected the interests of the merchant elite.[46] The Robben Island case was thus drawn into the wider dispute between the 'Conservative' merchants and the colonial reformers. But the lingering power of Montagu's 'family compact' delayed Birtwhistle's dismissal. Taken up by the colonial parliament, which sat for the first time in 1854, Robben Island came to represent for the victorious colonial reformers everything that was retrogressive about the autocratic regime under Montagu. Birtwhistle was dismissed and the suitability of the Island site for a modern and humane asylum was questioned.

Although many proposals for removing the General Infirmary were made in the ensuing years, nothing was done until the 1890s. This was partly because repair work on the Island was thought to be cheaper than construction of new institutions on the mainland. The chronic sick and lepers were also of not much concern to institutional reformers. But the Island site had its advantages. It allowed secure detention without the trappings of a prison, which would have offended the humanitarians. This delayed legislation for the detention of even dangerous lunatics until 1879.[47] In the 1890s, the Surgeon-Superintendent noted that because of the geographical isolation of the Island, the authorities could impose more control over the lepers than they would have if the asylum had been on the mainland, without 'giv[ing] rise to an enormous amount of ill-feeling in the country' by having harsh legal controls to prevent escapes.[48] Many of those lepers detained on the Island before 1892 were unaware they were legally free to leave.[49]

A *changing clientele*

By the 1860s, although most leper patients were still black, a greater proportion of white patients were admitted to the lunatic asylum and chronic sick hospital. This was partly a product of reforms brought about in the Robben Island asylum which improved its public image, and partly due to changing patterns of institutionalisation of the chronic sick poor in Cape Town. It was accompanied by an increasing tendency to segregate middle-class and white patients from the rest.

The long-awaited reform of the Robben Island lunatic asylum began in earnest in 1862 with the appointment as Surgeon-Superintendent of an avid supporter of the British 'moral management' system – Dr William Edmunds. Edmunds followed the methods of reformers like John Conolly in England, who wanted institutional routine, supervision and occasional physical intervention by attendants to replace the chains, whips and depletory medicines common in British asylums of the 1830s. Edmunds appointed additional staff, bringing the staff–patient ratio up to 1:12, which Conolly said was the ideal.[50] Pay increases attracted a 'better class' of attendant.[51] Better supervision over staff was effected by reforms based on Conolly's work.[52] The patients' diet scale was augmented, and lunatics no longer scavenged for food.[53] Entertainments like dances, sport and plays were introduced to restore their 'rationality'.[54]

The modernisation of the Robben Island asylum attracted more middle-class lunatics. Between 1872 and 1890, a quarter of first admissions to the Robben Island asylum were paying patients, in contrast to less than five per cent before 1872. Middle-class families, able to afford home care and reluctant to patronise any public institution but the New Somerset Hospital (which admitted some quiet lunatics),[55] had generally avoided sending their insane relatives to Robben Island, which suffered from its association with imprisonment and the scandals of the 1850s and lacked the 'comforts' required by wealthier patients.

There was an increasing demand for asylum accommodation from middle-class families by the 1860s, however.[56] With the expansion and reform of the asylum after 1862, the Robben Island institution began to resemble a modern British asylum and began to cater for the needs of a middle-class clientele. Seclusion cells, for example, built to reduce the use of mechanical restraints, provided some patients with private rooms. In 1867 a new section called 'the Gallery' was built for 'better class' female lunatics.[57] Edmunds claimed that although arrangements for the males were 'incomplete' in 1871, better-class female patients were well enough catered for.[58] Perhaps this was why the number of middle-class female lunatics increased most dramatically.

Racial distinctions had become part of the asylum's functioning by the early 1860s, but were somewhat muted under the universalist medical discourse of reform in the 1860s. The increase in middle-class lunatics at Robben Island (all of whom were white) was closely tied to the 'moral management' reforms, which ensured better accommodation and staffing and exempted middle-class patients from work. But although he was careful to keep middle-class patients apart, Edmunds moved away from explicit distinctions in treatment and allocation of accommodation on the basis of race. Soon after his arrival, Edmunds instituted 'improvements', permitting black patients to be buried in coffins instead of blankets and to receive clothing from the central store rather than cast-offs from white patients, as they had done before. The male lunatics, who had been divided into two groups along effectively racial lines in 1860, were by 1867 divided into three groups, one of which contained a racially mixed group of 'troublesome' patients. The female lunatics were similarly divided into three groups, although they had never been classified by race as openly as the men. Nevertheless, segregation of middle-class patients and some degree of racial segregation persisted.

During the 1860s there was also an increase in the proportion of white chronic sick patients admitted to the Island hospital. By this time, fewer chronic sick patients as a whole were being admitted to Robben Island as the lunatic asylum took up more of the Island accommodation and the New Somerset Hospital in Cape Town, opened in 1863 for acute cases, increased the amount of hospital provision for chronic cases at the Old Somerset Hospital. The reduction in chronic sick admissions to Robben Island was particularly marked and rapid among blacks. This was partly because after 1863 the Old Somerset Hospital tended to house more of the shorter-term pauper cases. The most debilitated and destitute of the pauper cases were probably black. Moreover, aided British immigration to the Cape during the 1840s and 1850s had increased the number of needy white immigrants in Cape Town. At a time of economic depression and tightening control over relief in the 1860s, there may have been particular concern to provide state care for destitute British immigrants. This trend towards admitting more white patients for long-term care was to become increasingly evident during the 1880s, as the number of white chronic sick admissions to Robben Island began to outstrip black admissions.

There had always been a number of chronic sick patients in the Robben Island hospital who were considered more 'respectable' than the others. A steady fifth of the chronic sick population on the Island (all white) was considered 'better class',[59] or originated from a skilled occupational background.[60] These patients were given special privileges on an *ad hoc* basis during the 1850s, but by the 1870s divisions among the chronic sick were drawn on racial grounds instead. All white patients, not just the middle-class ones, were segregated from black patients after 1876. The increase in the proportion of white patients thus went hand in hand with the increasing separation of patients by race (in the chronic sick hospital), in contrast to the muting of explicit racial segregation in the lunatic asylum.

The chronic sick hospital on Robben Island was closed in 1892 after the patients were moved to the Grahamstown Chronic Sick Hospital and the Old Somerset Hospital in Cape Town.

Two coloured female lepers in front of the corrugated-iron shack where they were allowed to prepare their own food, in the early twentieth century (Cape Archives)

The compulsory institutionalisation of all lepers

In 1892, the compulsory detention of lepers was legally enforced for the first time at the Cape. Although there had never been more than a hundred lepers on Robben Island before, the number of lepers now rose dramatically. The Leprosy Repression Act of 1891 had been promulgated in response to official and public concern that leprosy was contagious, that it was spreading, and particularly that it was spreading to the white population. There had been growing concern about the spread of syphilis and leprosy to towns and their white inhabitants during the 1880s. By the 1890s a worldwide 'leprosy scare', partly a product of growing xenophobia in the West and the expansionary pressures of imperialism, had encouraged segregatory action for leprosy prophylaxis, especially against immigrant and indigenous black populations, in America, Australia and many other countries.[61] But only a few countries opted for compulsory segregation of all lepers.

Cape doctors and officials chose the harsh segregatory option because they believed the Colony had a relatively small number of lepers, who could all be segregated to localise the disease. The threat of leprosy at the Cape was exaggerated and represented as a 'black peril' partly because of the negative stereotyping of the leper as black, a pattern which had already emerged in the early nineteenth century. At that time medical and popular aetiologies of leprosy at the Cape were connected to negative characteristics associated with the Khoi. Black culture was later to be more broadly blamed for the disease. Because a large proportion of the lepers were blacks with low social status, seen as both particularly susceptible and particularly irresponsible, segregation became politically feasible. In fact it can be regarded as part of a broader programme of denying blacks civil rights in Cape society at this time.

The lepers were not silent about what they perceived as unjust detention on the Island. They complained frequently after 1892 that they were 'imprisoned',[62] 'banish[ed]'[63] to Robben Island, 'left on the island as people who are dead', or treated worse than convicts or slaves.[64] One leper wrote in 1895:

> The first of December 1894 was a happy day ... because God had given England the power, 64 years before, to free their people [slaves] and gave England 20 million pounds and over a thousand people were freed so that men and women and children could together worship and thank the Lord. My Honour, what have we done that we cannot enjoy this right[?] We are guarded like slaves night and day by Constables ... we are now becoming impatient about this godless and sinful law.[65]

In September 1892, under the leadership of Franz Jacobs, a coloured leper from Cape Town, the male lepers mounted the first serious opposition to the Act, complaining mostly about separation from their families. They demanded table napkins and beer, table cruets and extra sugar, in an attempt to push the humanitarian veneer of the Act to an unworkable limit. They opposed the introduction of female nurses in the wards, and threatened to combine forces with the convicts, and to rape the women on the Island if not allowed access to the female lepers.[66] The response came swiftly: extra men were brought over as leper police, and Jacobs was exiled from the Island community to Somerset Hospital until he 'repented' in November of the same year.

In 1893, the female lepers struck work, saying that as the government had put them on the Island against their will, they would not do anything for themselves.[67] They refused to send all their washing to the new leper laundry, to 'assist in any kind of sanitary work; ... clean their own wards, or scrub, [or] sweep in front of their rooms ... although [Surgeon-Superintendent Impey] offered to pay them'. Impey had to employ convicts to do this work, and to clear the yard and enclosure of the 'filth which they persist[ed] in throwing there'.[68] For the women, refusal to perform institutional work was part of their argument to be treated as patients rather than as convicts, who were strongly associated with forced labour. With increases in leper numbers on the Island, and rising stigmatisation of contact with lepers, this was the first time that the patients had had to undertake a significant amount of the Island workload.

Off the Island, reactions to the promulgation of the 1891 Act were diverse. On the one hand, it intensified a minor hysteria that had been developing against lepers for some time. By the late 1880s, relatives of lepers had found it difficult to get jobs,[69] and mail steamers refused to carry leper passengers.[70] When a missionary woman visited the Island institution in about 1888, she found that other visitors refused to shake hands with leper patients.[71] After the passing of the Act, shipping companies refused to transport lepers,[72] road transport was fraught with difficulties,[73] and a special railway carriage had to be used to bring lepers to Cape Town.[74] Some families were evicted from their homes or found it difficult to get accommodation. At King Williamstown in 1894 doctors had to give certificates to black patients with leucoderma, a similar-looking skin disease, to protect them against neighbours suspecting them of having leprosy.[75]

But the enforcement of the Act also increased resistance to the identification of lepers as dangerous. Some leper cases were concealed by doctors who felt that leprosy was not contagious enough to present a danger to the community.[76] Impey pressurised the government (unsuccessfully) to modify the section of the 1884 Act that required a doctor to certify that a person was suffering from leprosy and was likely to spread the disease by being 'at large': 'Now it has happened and it will frequently happen again, that some medical men will not subscribe to the second portion of this certificate, as they are not in agreement with the hypothesis that the act premises ... [as] they think that there is no danger to the community through lepers being at large.'[77]

After Surgeon-Superintendent Impey left the Island in 1895, he began to oppose compulsory segregation openly, writing an article on the 'non-contagiousness of anaesthetic [paucibacillary] leprosy' in 1898, and supporting agitation against the detention of such lepers in the early 1900s.[78] The Medical Association concurred in 1898 that the system of compulsory segregation on Robben Island was 'not the most desirable'.[79]

Families of many lepers continued to hide them at home to forestall removal to the Island and others evaded detection by moving frequently, or absconding after being warranted for removal to the Island. Some lepers escaped from the country altogether, and hid in Lesotho. Richer lepers left for England, where the disease was rare and not notifiable.[80] The upheavals caused by this subterfuge can be illustrated by one example. In 1909, near Muizenberg station, a woman was spotted hiding behind a newspaper on her veranda by a Medical Officer of Health who happened to be passing by. He made inquiries, and her doctor admitted her affliction could be leprosy. But by the time they went to her house again to examine her, the whole family had left the area without a trace.[81] Many lepers absconded after they had been warranted but before their removal to an asylum.[82] The process was slow, as many more cases were discovered than officials had expected. By June 1899, only just under two-thirds of the 2004 cases warranted in the Colony and Transkei since 1892 had been sent to hospitals.[83]

The admission of many more lepers of varying social statuses changed the way the institution was organised on Robben Island. Paying patients were now allowed separate quarters. Systematic racial segregation of lepers at Robben Island was instituted in 1893 when there were for the first time a considerable number of white lepers on the Island. This was much later than racially discriminatory treatment for lepers (which began in the early 1850s), and racial classification of patients on paper (which began in the late 1850s). In 1854, two white lepers, Verreaux and Freeman (who were non-paying patients), were allowed to move from the general ward into separate rooms when they requested it, because, as the Surgeon-Superintendent said, they should not be 'obliged to associate with the poor coloured men, so far below [them] in civilization'.[84] The rules for the institution compiled in 1866 did not, however, prescribe racial segregation among the lepers. The *Lantern* complained in 1884 of the lack of 'strict discipline or segregation' and the consequent 'undesirable admixture of the classes' in the leper asylum.[85] In 1889, a visitor described one leper ward as 'occupied by a race part Hottentot and part Malay, with an infusion of white blood'.[86] Such mixing was seen as undesirable, but racial exclusion or separation was not formally instituted, probably because there were so few white lepers that segregation could be implemented purely on an *ad hoc* basis.

As an influx of better-class white lepers loomed in 1892, concern grew among doctors and officials about their position. In 1892, the 'Rules of the Leper Hospital' insisted first on racial segregation and then, 'if possible', the separation of lepers according to the stage of their disease.[87] In line with other forms of segregation in prisons and hospitals on the mainland at the time, the pavilion system introduced in 1893 divided white and black lepers. Racial segregation was, however, not formally provided for in legislation until ten years later.[88] Although racial segregation was by now generally accepted within the dominant classes as a 'good thing', doubts were initially raised. Before the Commission of 1894, Dr Herman questioned the system, stressing the lack of divisions among the patients:

> [Dr Herman] Apparently the whites mix up freely with the coloured patients and make friends with each other, so is there any reason for carrying out classification; is it not more apparent than real?
> [Dr Todd] No, it is convenient to have all the boys together, and all the Kafirs together and the whites together and so on ... The Kafirs keep to themselves a good deal because their language is different.

Discriminatory treatment was exaggerated as public concern for (white) lepers increased. In 1895 Cecil Rhodes donated a bath chair for the female European lepers,[89] and in about 1908 or 1909 two horses and a cart were made available for the male European patients.[90] The European lepers by 1901 got better clothes than the rest,[91] and a different diet with 'medical extras' such as tinned sardines;[92] by 1907, they got better coffins with name plates,[93] and by late 1910 free second-class rather than third-class tickets for relatives travelling by train.

The 'convenience' of the separation of patients is illustrated by the separate paths of resistance taken by white and black lepers. The white lepers do not seem to have participated in the 'revolt' of 1892, and asked separately if they might be segregated on the mainland.[94] In 1904, a deputation from the coloured lepers asked for the same privileges that the whites enjoyed: freedom of movement within the compound, extra clothing and permission to meet friends at the jetty. Both male and female white lepers asked to be separated as much as possible from the coloured lepers. They said that 'they did not want to be in the same compound with the coloured people any longer, as the coloured people had threatened them and called after them ... [They] would like a stone wall built across the compound so as to keep the coloured people quite separate ... high enough to prevent the coloured people seeing over.'[95]

The authorities resolved this problem, which was partly of their own creation, by reducing the class distinctions made within the white category and abolishing the paying system. In line with the emphasis on 'home segregation'

Staff of the leper institution, c. 1927 (Cape Archives)

for better-class whites, four semi-detached cottages for paying lepers had been built between 1892 and 1893, and by 1904 there were about ten similar cottages.[96] Some non-paying white lepers already received the privileges of the paying patients because the staff on the Island clearly felt more comfortable with this arrangement. The case of an English leper, Woodhouse, illustrates this point. He was described as respectable and well educated but came from a poor background and had a drinking problem. When he first arrived at Robben Island, Woodhouse was treated as a paying patient, given a separate room after a short time in the big white ward, and had his meals brought to him, as he was invalided. The chaplain offered to collect money from England for him so he could be treated like the other 'special' paying patients on a permanent basis. He explained that Woodhouse did not understand Dutch or the ways of the Dutch, and was 'full of nerves'.[97]

The racial division became increasingly dominant in 1904 when these 'special' paying patients were subsumed within the general white category. Those who had been paying patients retained a few privileges but all whites were now officially treated equally and paid for extras out of their own pockets.[98] Special new wards, rather than the ordinary pavilions and wards (for men and women respectively), were occupied by non-paying 'European' lepers in that year.[99] In 1910, Commissioner Magennis allocated the private quarters carefully on the basis of conduct rather than financial ability so that the occupant could be censured by removal.[100] He also refused an application for private quarters by the mortuary attendant, Jantjies (who claimed the others in his ward made offensive remarks about his job), saying that he 'was averse to coloured patients having private quarters'.[101] Privilege was thus increasingly independent of financial status within the white category.

The closure of the Robben Island hospitals

The increasing marginality and expense of the institutions on the Island contributed to their closure in 1931. The chronic sick patients were removed and white lunatics (not the criminal or dangerous ones) were gradually transferred to Valkenberg Asylum in Cape Town after 1891. White lunatics were seen to be particularly amenable to cure along European lines, for which Robben Island had been seen as unsuitable for some time. The patients left on the Island consisted therefore of lunatics (mainly black and criminal) and a large number of lepers (mainly black but with a substantial white minority). The growth of institutional provision for the sick, leprous and insane on the mainland during the 1890s coincided with an increasing emphasis on racial segregation. Racially exclusive institutions and specialised facilities created a new institutional network in which Robben Island played a minor and increasingly devalued role.

The Island institutions became ever more expensive to run because of their dependence on a significant number of white male nursing staff, whereas mainland asylums and leper hospitals began to employ cheaper female and black labour. The distinctive make-up of the Robben Island nursing staff was the result of several features of the colonial and institutional framework in which the Island operated. White nurses or attendants were initially favoured for sheltered employment in the colonies, and later as more 'respectable' attendants on the insane under the 'moral management' system. By the early twentieth century, black nursing staff were no longer employed in colonial hospitals, except where these catered largely for low-status black patients, such as the Emjanyana leper asylum in the Transkei and black sections of mental hospitals.[102] Although Robben Island now had a majority of black patients, by 1913 the practice of employing only whites on the Island staff was a 'longstanding arrangement'.[103] This 'arrangement' depended in part on the presence of a large body of relatively mobile patients, the lunatics, to provide labour for menial tasks within the institutions, and a convict station to provide additional labourers. As residential segregation became the norm in Cape Town by the early twentieth century, it was inconceivable too that the small village on Robben Island could house both black and white employees.

Men retained their importance as attendants in mental asylums on Robben Island as elsewhere, but were also to retain their position as leper attendants at Robben Island because of patient opposition to female nurses in 1892. Increasing emphasis on custody, both of criminal or dangerous (and mainly black) lunatics and of a large number of lepers reluctantly confined on the Island, helped to justify the employment of male attendants. Although Robben Island tried to attract trained staff for both the leper and the lunatic institutions, it was unable to attract trained female nurses in any numbers or the few asylum attendants and nurses who had taken the limited training opportunities available to them in the Colony. The staff was large because of the security needed for recalcitrant lepers and dangerous lunatics. With the emphasis on control, a large number of leper police were employed on the Island from 1895. In 1920, as one of six leper institutions in the Union of South Africa, Robben Island accounted for a third of all staff.[104] Although many of them were without formal training, its reliance on white males, whose salaries had to reflect their high social status, made Robben Island by far the most expensive leper colony by 1922,[105] and an expensive asylum before that.

At the same time, there were pressures for patients to be removed to mainland institutions. Valkenberg Asylum required black patients to provide institutional labour, and finally brought all the Robben Island lunatic cases over in 1921. Leprosy was declining in the Western Cape, and the maintenance of an asylum for non-African Cape lepers, which is what Robben Island had become, was seen as unjustifiable.[106] Leprosy incidence began to decline because of general improvements in diet and living conditions, but Hunter and Thomas have also argued that African urbanisation and concomitant changes such as the rise of tuberculosis decreased incidence rates.[107] Moreover, institutional solutions for the disease became less popular as the twentieth century progressed. In 1931, the League of Nations Health Organisation noted that it was 'generally recognized' that 'compulsory segregation' could be safely replaced by a more liberal 'isolation policy', which distinguished between infectious and non-infectious cases.[108] The Robben Island hospital was among the first to close, and its patients were transferred to the Westfort Hospital near Pretoria.

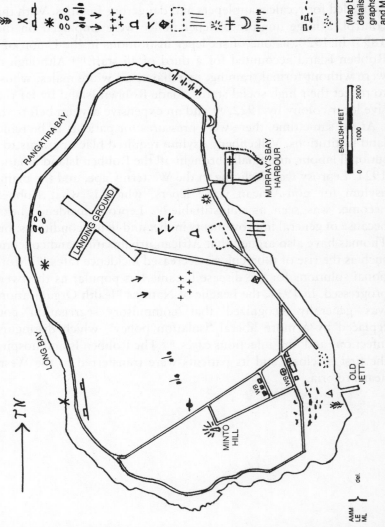

"... Fragmentary fortress, forgotten, forlorn"
— W.D. McCourt

ROBBEN ISLAND, TABLE BAY – 1945

RANGATIRA BAY

LANDING GROUND

LONG BAY

MINTO HILL

WB

WB

OLD JETTY

MURRAY'S BAY HARBOUR

N

AMM LE ML del.

ENGLISH FEET

0   1000   2000

LEGEND

🔆	Lighthouse (Charlie's Candle)
✦	BOP
WB	WAAS Barracks
⊕	Village Church (Anglican)
△	CPGI
⚹	Bakery
✕	Wreck of Liberty Ship
⬓	Searchlights camouflaged as seaside cottages
⚹	Fog siren
⦂⦂⦂	Seagulls' nests
⊶⊶	R.I. Battery (two 9.2'' guns)
→	Dummy guns
✝✝✝	Old cemetery
⌐	Tomb of Prince of Madura
Ⅴ	Arum lilies
⊕	"Naval" Church
⬚	Sub-Depot
≡	Cables for Sub-Depot came ashore here
✺	Air-raid shelter
✝	SAAF crash-boat station
☽	Degaussing Range HQ
'¦'¦'¦	Cornelia Battery (3'' twelve-pounder quick-firing guns)
⊡⊡	Village
∴∴	NE Quarters

(Map based on a *Cape Argus* map; details supplied from memory and from photographs by A.M. McGregor, L. Ellis (Edwards) and M. Laver)

Robben Island and the Military 1931–1960

Arthur Davey

Between the closure of Robben Island's leper hospital in 1931 and its conversion into a maximum security prison in 1960, the Island played an important part in the military history of South Africa. It was transformed into a fortified station and housed a large number of personnel of the armed services. This period was essentially different from the preceding and succeeding ones as there was no civilian prison or isolation hospital on the Island. The Island's dominant role as a place of banishment was relinquished while it served the military security of the country.

Robben Island in limbo, 1931–6

There was some debate about the fate of the Island once its suitability as a leper hospital began to come under scrutiny during the 1920s. In 1926 the head of the Union Public Works Department enquired of other government departments whether 'the island could be advantageously occupied' by any of them. Although the closure of the leper institution on Robben Island was indeed being considered, his circular warned that he could not say whether any buildings, equipment or material would be transferred to the department that took over the Island. This was surely the crux of any future arrangement as the extent and value of the real estate involved were considerable. Departmental policy decreed that all buildings surplus to government requirements should be sold and not retained for letting. A plan compiled by the Public Works Department in this period showed 'numerous buildings for sale' on Robben Island. The Assistant Provincial Secretary of the Cape Provincial Administration concluded after some delay that there were 'no purposes to which we can put the Island'.[1] Robben Island's fate was not an immediate issue, however, as the decision to close the leper institution was only finalised in 1930. After the last lepers were transferred to Westfort in Pretoria, a harrowing, haunting epoch of the Island's history came to a close on 14 February 1931.

Map of Robben Island, 1945 (from M.P.H. Laver, *Sailor-women, Sea-women, SWANS*, Simon's Town, 1986)

The official plan of Robben Island, revised in 1931, documented some 170 buildings and other structures. The compounds for male and female lepers, consisting of about 90 of the structures, were to be demolished because of the fear of contamination.[2] The male lepers' quarters, sturdy Victorian buildings, were set alight in January 1931. A dozen buildings, churches or residences owned by the Anglican, Roman Catholic and Dutch Reformed denominations were to remain, however. There was also a substantial amount of state-owned property in the village area, including the residence of the commissioner, medical officers' quarters and cottages for other officials (these buildings had survived from the 1840s), a drill hall, clubhouse (the old Flagstaff ward and lime kiln), post office, village school, general store, shop and 'restaurant', dairy, bakery, dispensary, laboratory and mortuary. For recreational purposes there was a cricket ground, a croquet lawn and a tennis court. A large furrow was dug next to the buildings, and when the walls still standing were demolished, the debris was tipped into it.[3]

The only remaining residents were the lighthousekeepers. An eerie quiet prevailed – tempered only by the sounds of sea and wind and the cries of gulls. However, many of the families of former staff members remembered the Island with affection. For Lawrence Green, the popular and prolific writer, who had first visited Robben Island as a schoolboy before the First World War, it too was an isle of nostalgic memory. He had returned often, and after the evacuation went ashore several times from his sailing yawl. He described the abandoned village with its deserted streets, desolate gardens and an abundance of rabbit warrens.[4]

In parliament, Harry Lawrence, one of the Cape Town members, asked whether any suggestions had been made by the public for the Island's future. In reply, the Minister referred dismissively to a few vague enquiries from estate agents and others. In response to another question, he said emphatically that it was not being considered as a place for a work colony.[5] Public interest in the future of Robben Island was muted but there was an occasional flicker of concern. In November 1934, at a meeting of the Cape Geographical Society, a speaker offered divergent options for the Island. Replanted with suitable vegetables it could become a home for sheep and goats, or it could be turned into a health resort, with hotel, golf course and tennis courts and perhaps a sanatorium, but he thought transport was an obstacle.[6]

Meanwhile, the Island attracted visitors, mainly picnickers and yachtsmen. Shooting and fishing were pastimes the Island continued to offer. The Governor-General, Lord Clarendon, went twice with a party of companions in 1932. Because of pilfering and damage to government property, however, a permit system (£1 per head) was introduced. This decreased the number of visitors. The police called in from time to time, either in the course of patrolling the fishing grounds near by or to inspect the buildings ashore. They were also required sometimes to shoot feral cats. A minor drama occurred when a stranded party of Girl Guides had to be rescued.[7]

Official uncertainty about the Island's future still prevailed as there were other more pressing concerns. When the Island was left almost untenanted in 1931 the Union of South Africa was in the grip of economic depression – part of a world-wide phenomenon. Retrenchment was the order of the day and there was no question of state funds being allocated to any offshore innovations. The Great Depression brought the Nationalist government of General J. B. M. Hertzog, in office since 1924, to the verge of collapse. The Nationalists therefore forged a coalition with their main opponent, the South African Party, in March 1933, which was followed by a fusion of the parties in the following year. Hertzog remained prime minister.

South Africa also had to contend with a possible external threat. The Japanese had overrun Manchuria, and in Germany, Adolf Hitler came to power in 1933, vowing to fight the restrictions of the Versailles Treaty of 1919. As an arbiter of peace, the League of Nations at Geneva was ineffectual. The principal defender of South Africa from any foreseeable threat by sea was the squadron of the Royal Navy based in Simon's Town. It was supported by a few coastal batteries at Cape Town and Simon's Town manned by South African Permanent Force gunners, but for the rest the external defences of the Union were weak and run-down. One of Hertzog's political lieutenants, Advocate Oswald Pirow, was assigned the portfolio of Defence and that of Railways and Harbours. Pirow, then 42 years old, was capable, vigorous and ambitious. In 1934 he unveiled a five-year plan to rejuvenate and stiffen South Africa's defence system, but it was mainly aimed at expansion of army and air force formations. As for coastal defences, he was sceptical about the likelihood of a large-scale naval attack and felt that some mobile artillery (6" guns) in conjunction with field batteries and other deterrents would be adequate to counter the odd surface sea-raider or submarine.[8]

A military role for the Island

By the mid-1930s the international situation had worsened and Robben Island began to play a role in the military scenario of South Africa. Italy, under Mussolini, launched a war of conquest on Abyssinia in 1935. Hitler, spurning the Versailles Treaty, embarked openly on rearmament and a massive expansion of the armed forces of the Third Reich. In South Africa, however, Pirow was mainly concerned with the threat of black uprisings in the African hinterland. Pirow, whose sentimental attachment to the British Empire was slight, was at heart a neutralist. He was a particular admirer of Dr Salazar, the authoritarian ruler of Portugal. Somewhat paradoxically he favoured continuation of the Union's mandate over the former German colony of South West Africa, but proposed that the Reich be compensated territorially elsewhere. It is ironic that Pirow, who increasingly espoused a philosophy alien to democratic principles, should also have planned a role for Robben Island that briefly made it one of the bastions in the struggle of the 'free world' against totalitarianism.

Pirow remarked in parliament on 17 March 1936 that he would declare Robben Island military property and fortify it with both light-calibre and heavy guns. The transfer of the battery on Signal Hill to Robben Island was necessary because it caused damage to property when fired from the hill.[9] In terms of a notice in the *Government Gazette* of 22 May 1936 Robben Island was to be 'reserved for military purposes', and members of the public wishing to visit it could only do so if they had permits signed by the Officer Commanding, Cape Command. By that time the threat of an attack from the sea had become more serious. Between 1931 and 1934 three German 'pocket' battleships had been constructed, each carrying a main armament of six 11" guns, making them potential sea-raiders of formidable power.[10] In April 1936 Pirow commented in the House of Assembly that if the main battery on Signal Hill was transferred to Robben Island it might be as well to invest in guns of sufficient calibre to deal with an attack of any magnitude. The heaviest guns in South African coastal batteries at this time were 9.2" guns of an older type than those on the new German battleships. In spite of numerous crises in the international sphere during the next few years, however, Robben Island did not become an active defensive site. Civilian visitors were still permitted. In the spring of 1937, for example, A. Dichmont, a Cape Town attorney, arranged a camp on the island for a party of schoolboys under the auspices of a church school mission organisation.[11]

In March 1939 Pirow reported on the 1934 five-year plan in parliament. He had hoped to have a 15" battery mounted on Robben Island, but with British rearmament under way it was not possible to obtain guns of that calibre. As a temporary measure he proposed an alternative. By arrangement with the Admiralty, South Africa would take over HMS *Erebus*, a monitor. Monitors were vessels of shallow draught, and in the First World War were used off the coast of Flanders to shell German positions inland. *Erebus*, which carried two 15" guns, had been built in 1916 and needed much reconditioning. That would be done in England at South African expense for about £100,000. Once in position off Robben Island, she could serve as 'a floating fort' rather than a warship and her guns would be served by army artillerists. A minefield off Robben Island could be another possible defence measure. The *Erebus* project came to nothing, however. Although the ship was refurbished and a South African crew sent to Portsmouth to take her over, she had not sailed by 3 September 1939 when Britain declared war on Germany. The British Admiralty finally retained *Erebus* for its own use.[12]

With the onset of war the safeguarding of Table Bay against attacks of surprise raiders or submarines was only one of the many concerns of the military. But coastal defences became more important after 10 June 1940 when Italy entered the conflict. In consequence, for the next three years the Mediterranean, formerly used as a direct route from the United Kingdom to Egypt, India and the Far East, became a conflict zone. Large convoys of ships carrying men, munitions and all the other accompaniments of war were diverted so as to undertake the longer voyage around the bulge of Southern Africa. Many of these convoys called at the Cape to replenish and refuel. In July 1940, for instance, a convoy which included some of Britain's largest ocean liners, adapted for troop-carrying, lay at anchor in Table Bay. The protection of such precious human and material resources from enemy action imposed a great responsibility on the South African military. Cape Town, its harbour greatly enlarged by the construction of the Duncan Dock, together with Durban and the other smaller ports, had assumed great importance as a strategic link in the war effort of the British Empire and its allies.

Japan became the third partner of the totalitarian coalition known as the Axis, on 7 December 1941. After a quick succession of conquests, a powerful Japanese fleet began to rove the Indian Ocean in April 1942, inflicting severe damage at the British-held harbours of Colombo and Trincomalee in Ceylon (Sri Lanka). A further Japanese drive westwards might have exposed South African harbours to bombardment or even landings and cut the vital sea route around its shores. Although the threat from Japanese incursions into the Indian Ocean was partly countered when British and South African forces seized control of Madagascar late in 1942, the coastal defences of South Africa had to be strengthened too. By late 1943 the international scenario had changed substantially, however. The Allies had finally won the contest for North Africa and carried the war across to Sicily and the mainland of Europe. In September Italy capitulated and Allied convoys could again sail through the Mediterranean to Malta, Alexandria and Suez. Japan had lost her earlier ascendancy at sea and her navy was locked in a struggle with resurgent United States fleets in the Pacific Ocean. The risk of Japanese forays into South African waters had thus decreased and coastal defences there receded in importance. Some of the batteries were closed down and the gunners relocated to other duties. Robben Island remained important mainly as a base for the anti-submarine vigil and the training associated with it.

The fortification of the Island

The role of Robben Island in the protection of Allied interests between 1939 and 1945 was dictated by the ebb and flow of the war. Its transformation into a 'fortified southern Heligoland'[13] began soon after the outbreak of war. This was the responsibility of the Department of Public Works, which normally undertook building programmes for the government. Its departmental head,

C. A. Celliers, was also appointed Director of Works for the Defence Force when hostilities started. In an annual report published in 1940 he explained that his department had been inundated with requests for 'urgent services'. Extraordinary measures were needed to prepare the South African coastal defences for war.

A leading role in the preparation of the coastal defences was played by John F. Craig, who had been Harbour Engineer of Cape Town since 1931 and the advisory engineer on harbours, when he had had much to do with the development of the Duncan Dock. In June 1939, aged 55, Craig was given the rank of lieutenant-colonel in the South African Engineering Corps and sent to London to confer with the defence ministry there on the general defences of the Cape in a conflict that by then appeared imminent. Robben Island figured prominently in Craig's plan, completed by October, for the Union's coastal defences. At the outset there were serious obstacles such as the lack of a proper water supply and an exposed jetty. As Deputy Director of Fortifications, Craig tackled the construction of coastal batteries vigorously. Because the South African Engineering Corps was small and had an enormous task ahead of it, it also used private constructors working under military supervision.[14]

Laying detection cables from Robben Island to the mainland as part of the anti-submarine measures taken during the Second World War in Table Bay (Naval Museum, Simon's Town)

Robben Island was soon fortified. A construction syndicate of four firms undertook the conveyance of 150,000 tons of building material to the Island. Fishing boats were hired to carry cement and other materials whilst a special landing barge was built in Cape Town to bring across loaded lorries and heavy equipment. Much was accomplished. Trees had to be cleared, roads built and ruined buildings demolished. Stone from the old structures went into the making of a compact protected harbour at Murray's Bay. Gun emplacements, underground magazines, plotting rooms and observation towers were constructed, work that was well advanced by March 1940. And, of course, quarters and other facilities for a large garrison were built.[15] At the core of the defences were two coastal batteries. The first gun to be mounted was of 6" calibre, in the Cornelia Battery. Covering the Blouberg channel, it was in position in April 1940 and a second was added in 1942. The first of the 9.2" guns, thirty tons in weight, of the 5th Heavy Battery, was installed in November 1940 and a second followed in July 1941. By 1945, a third 9.2" gun was also in position.[16] The conveyance of massive guns and mountings to the Island and their positioning on the Island were exercises in skilled ingenuity. Together with ordnance of similar calibre at the Scala Battery, Simon's Town, and the

Apostle Battery, Llandudno, these powerful guns formed the main armament defences of the Cape Peninsula.

The Royal Navy made a major contribution to the Allied cause when a degaussing range was set up close to Murray's Harbour in June 1941. A second range was later installed near Durban. When the Germans began to lay magnetic mines, more lethal as a weapon against ships than earlier types of contact mines had been, degaussing was devised as a counter-measure. It involved circling each ship with a current-carrying cable which neutralised the ship's magnetisation, and then testing the ship against electrified undersea cables. The South African naval teams who operated these ranges dealt with 4451 ships during the war.[17] A South African sailor assigned to the Robben Island installation recalled the operation vividly: 'It seemed that every ship ever launched was drawn to our island waters with the alacrity of bees to the proverbial honeypot. From sun-up to darkness we sweated in the summer heat, as grimy hulks and streamlined hulls from all eight oceans manoeuvred to and fro across sensitive cables in the Blaauwberg Channel.'[18]

Further defences were also built on Robben Island. A runway about 1000 yards long was completed in 1942. During the period when a Japanese threat was taken seriously, a small detachment of armoured cars was deployed on the Island to protect the guns in the event of a landing. To that time also belong some concrete pillboxes and rifleposts. For nearly three years the anti-aircraft (AA) defences of Table Bay had been very inadequate, but in 1942 much larger consignments of war material were received from Britain. By the end of that year, as part of a larger deployment in the Peninsula, Robben Island was to have an AA battery of four 3.7" as well as two 40 mm Bofors guns.[19] German U-boats of an improved model, with a longer sea range, also presented a threat as they voyaged southwards to disrupt traffic on the Cape route. Between October 1942 and March 1943 they took a heavy toll of ships sailing out of convoy in South African waters. New anti-submarine measures were taken at Table Bay – four long loops of detection cables were laid down. From the control station on Robben Island, the first main loop ran to Melkbosstrand and the second to Clifton. The installation was set up by a group of Royal Navy officers, who were superseded by South African operators, men and women, as soon as they were trained.

Military personnel on the Island

There had been no garrison on Robben Island during the early twentieth century except for a detachment of the Cape Town Highlanders, which had a brief stay early in 1915,[20] possibly to keep watch for signs of hostile sea-raiders. Pictorial evidence reveals that at least one field-day exercise by a part-time Citizen Force unit, the headquarters companies of the 2nd Batt. Railways and Harbours Brigade, took place in the 1920s.

In contrast to these isolated incidents, the Island was home to thousands of servicemen and women during the Second World War. Of those who served on Robben Island a few found life monotonous and bleak. One of the former artillery officers referred jokingly to its 'restful' night-life and 'lots of healthy sea-breezes (the kind you can really lean on)'. The majority, however, most of them cheerful young folk, enjoyed the camaraderie and the satisfaction of employment on useful tasks. In comparison with many other military stations and training camps, discomforts were slight, except for the occasional encounter with rough weather whilst travelling to or from the Island in the service launch, the *Isie*, or other craft used for that purpose.

The Cape Garrison Artillery, peacetime volunteers mobilised on 3 September 1939, and the gunners of the South African Permanent Garrison Artillery were the first military occupants of the Island at the beginning of the Second World War. Under the Simon's Town Agreement of 1921 (the Churchill–Smuts Agreement) the British had retained control over the naval docks at Simon's Town, but the South African government took responsibility for the land defences of the whole Cape Peninsula. In spite of the economic depression of the 1930s the coastal artillery arm was less affected by retrenchment than many other branches of the army and had well-trained gunners on its strength. It was this nucleus which provided proficient non-commissioned officers and instructors during the great expansion of the military service after the start of the war. The gunners who manned the batteries on Robben Island were mostly drawn from the coastal artillery force. A training establishment on the Island catered for coastal and AA artillery recruits until May 1942, when the AA component was detached to form part of a separate training centre at Ottery, near Young's Field. The Coastal Artillery School on Robben Island remained operational until its closure in January 1944.[21]

Other military staff soon joined the artillery forces. The South African Engineering Corps was represented by No. 16 Field Company, which had returned from East Africa in October 1941. A small detachment of it was then used in the construction of the airstrip and to fabricate a battery of dummy 9.2" guns – a ploy in the art of deception in war.[22] Chaplains, medical and hospital staff, and the military police were also resident on the Island. The operation of the degaussing range and of the later anti-submarine devices required the services of the Royal Navy and South African naval force. Civilian labourers employed in the extensive construction work were replaced by sappers of the Engineering Corps at the time of the Japanese scare. Robben Island also housed a large number of coloured soldiers.

To gain some understanding of the position of coloured servicemen, one has to understand the intricacies of internal politics on the question of war with Germany. When General Smuts obtained parliamentary backing for the Union's entry into hostilities with Germany, his support in the House of

Assembly was based on a precarious majority of 13 votes. The white population was as sharply divided as the white parliament – Smuts's coalition government faced strong opposition both from the Nationalists and from the
press that supported them. Moreover, there were extra-parliamentary forces
that engaged in acts of sabotage. There were dissident elements within the
South African Police, but the main internal danger seemed to come from the
Ossewabrandwag (OB) and its extremist wing, the Stormjaers.

The government thus proceeded cautiously and cannily, requiring no con-
scription of white males. They stressed that service in the armed forces would
be limited to volunteers. Despite war propaganda and recruiting drives, however, the military could not find sufficient white males to meet its multiplicity
of needs. Many volunteers responded, but the demand invariably exceeded the
supply. The air force, navy and medical branch absorbed numbers of recruits,
coastal defences had to be manned, reserve forces were necessary in view of
possible internal disturbances, and key installations and prisoner-of-war
camps had to be guarded. In 1940 an expeditionary force left for Kenya to
take part in an invasion of Italian-held Abyssinia. With white manpower
stretched, the government looked to the members of the Cape Corps, 'Malay
and Indian Corps', 'Native Military Corps' and to white women to act as auxiliaries.

During the First World War armed battalions of the Cape Corps had served
with distinction in East Africa and Palestine. In the Second World War the
Cape Corps was revived, but with a vital difference. In theory, its men were
not to be armed combatants, but were to be auxiliaries – drivers, cooks, bat-
men and so on. This implied inferior status and lower rates of pay, which put
a damper on recruitment, but more than 45,000 men nevertheless enlisted in
the Cape Corps. For the wartime government, the customary segregation of
troops had to be balanced against military necessity. But they also had to pla-
cate conservative elements within their own ranks and a right-wing political
opposition that vociferously opposed any suggestion of racial integration. On
Robben Island the coloured soldiers were provided with segregated living
quarters and certain other facilities in line with segregatory practices on the
mainland.

The pressing requirements of the armed forces forced the government to use
coloured soldiers in combat as well as on the home front. A scheme known as
'dilution' was proposed under which coloured gunners were trained for anti-
aircraft and coastal batteries, ostensibly so that white soldiers could be
released from local service for the war fronts. In 1941 an Anti-Aircraft
Training and Reserve Camp was established on Robben Island, close to
Murray's Harbour, at which some 2000 coloured soldiers underwent training.
But in practice some of these trainees were used as combatants. A draft of 400
of them left for North Africa in September 1941 and was followed by anoth-

er draft of 300 men. They were absorbed into the 1st and 2nd South African Anti-Aircraft Regiments and 'proved their ability and courage many times over during the succeeding months'.[23] As part of a reorganisation and reallocation of personnel, the training centre was closed in April 1942.

Women were also used as military personnel during the war. Some 14,500 women were taken into full-time service in the Union Defence Force. Until the outbreak of war, however, the Permanent Force had remained an all-male preserve, except for 19 matrons and nurses on the establishment of the Military Nursing Service.[24] The employment of white women in the army went along with somewhat greater political influence. White women over 21 years gained the franchise in 1931, and by 1939 a few had won seats in the Union parliament. During the First World War the British government had supplemented its military manpower by recruiting thousands of women after 1917 to serve in uniform in Queen Mary's Army Auxiliary Corps and similar auxiliary formations attached to the Royal Air Force and Royal Navy. There had been no corresponding enrolment of women in South Africa during that war, apart

Rangetakers from the WAAS Artillery Specialists in a plotting room (from M. H. Hill, *Look-in after 40 Years*, Johannesburg, c. 1985)

from military nurses. In the Second World War, however, a Women's Auxiliary Army Service (WAAS) and Women's Auxiliary Air Force (WAAF) were established in mid-1940. The Women's Auxiliary Naval Service (SWANS) was started in August 1943. Whilst many of these women performed clerical and other office duties that could be termed 'auxiliary', there were others who undertook more responsible and intricate tasks fully equivalent to those carried out by trained men.

In June 1941 an experimental course at Simon's Town to train women rangetakers for the coastal artillery was so successful that some of the qualified trainees were posted to the school of gunnery on Robben Island to act as instructors for a second intake. They were styled Artillery Specialists WAAS. The growing numbers of recruits to this elite group were required, somewhat patronisingly, to be 'well educated wom[e]n of a good class possessed of self-

Artillery Specialists WAAS leaving the school of gunnery on Robben Island (from M. H. Hill, *Look-in after 40 Years*, Johannesburg, *c.* 1985)

reliance'. A former commanding officer later commented on their quickness, dexterity and well-disciplined conduct.[25] During 1942 and 1943 another seven courses were run at the school of gunnery. When trained, the specialists were assigned duties with coastal batteries at the main ports, including the batteries on Robben Island itself. Over 400 out of a total of about 450 women in this branch underwent training on the Island. A particularly responsible part of their role was gunfire direction from the underground plotting rooms.[26] The emphasis on training gunners for the coastal artillery was reduced, however, as the submarine menace posed by the Germans increased and defence priorities focused on underwater vigilance and defence. The school of gunnery was closed and the WAAS artillery specialists were withdrawn in January 1944.

Women were also recruited into a special unit within the South African Corps of Signals. Colonel F. C. Collins, Director of Signals, commenting during the war on the Special Signals Service (SSS), said, 'After the war South Africans would be proud when they learnt what their sons and daughters in this branch had been doing.'[27] The SSS was concerned with the development and deployment of radar and came into being in conditions of great secrecy. Most of the research and early experimentation was undertaken at the University of the Witwatersrand and in Durban, and the first coastal set at the Cape for plotting the movements of ships was only installed on Signal Hill in May 1941. There was soon a surveillance chain of other sets covering the approaches to Cape Town, at Melkbosstrand, Blouberg, Karbonkelberg, Slangkop and Cape Point. On Robben Island a short-range set was in place by about January 1943.[28] Women were recruited in the SSS as operators. They were well educated (many of them were university graduates) and very proficient. Like the rest of the SSS, they enjoyed a certain unorthodox exclusiveness. The number on Robben Island was small, however, consisting of a team of about eight operators.

To counter the growing threat of submarine attacks, the Anti-Submarine Fixed Defence System (A/SFD) was in service from October 1942, based on long cables that came ashore near Murray's Harbour. South African naval officers and ratings were trained to operate it so that Royal Navy personnel could be replaced. In spite of resistance by high-ranking army officers, an auxiliary naval service for women was established in October 1943. It was elitist in composition and had a limited establishment of about 260. Smart naval uniforms conferred a certain cachet on their wearers. The South African Women's Auxiliary Naval Service (SWANS) had a commendable record, and women operators assigned to technical duties 'seemed to possess a particular aptitude for the operation of delicate instruments'.[29] The first detachment of SWANS arrived on Robben Island in November 1943. The SANF Sub-depot on Robben Island was the establishment where all A/SFD personnel were instructed, including women trainees. The SWANS were also employed on visual watchkeeping duties. Groups of them were trained on the Island until 1945 for later duty at other naval sites or on the Island itself. In the last phase of the war SWANS participated in the training of South African and British officers for service with the fleet in Far Eastern waters.[30]

Robben Island was never required to fire its guns in anger and so shared the fortunate lot of that far older fortification, the Castle at Cape Town. The coastal defence system was costly and has been likened to 'an individual who has to pay heavily for household insurance against a fire which never occurs'.[31] With hindsight one may conclude that the coming of a Japanese invasion fleet was less likely than was thought at the time. But the U-boat factor had to be taken seriously – 81 ships were lost to enemy action in or close to South African waters.[32] Although about a dozen of these vessels were victims of torpedoes or mines close to the Cape Peninsula, no direct attack was ever launched on the congested shipping in Table Bay harbour or roadstead. On occasion submarines ventured towards it, notably on 6 October 1942 when U-172 lay at periscope depth between Robben Island and Green Point.[33] The defences of Cape Town, of which the Island was a prominent component, acted as a deterrent. The degaussing range and the training schools for gunners and anti-submarine operators were important elements in the Cape defences. In the Island's chequered history this was perhaps 'The most constructive phase of its existence'.[34]

After the war

By the end of the war in Europe in May 1945 many of the activities on Robben Island had been scaled down, together with a reduction in the numbers of the garrison. Once the final phase of hostilities in Asia was over in August, the Island's future had again to be determined. There was some speculation about the prospects awaiting a well-equipped 'boom town' and its facilities.[35] In the meantime a military 'care and maintenance' squad looked after the buildings. In parliament the Rev. C. F. Miles-Cadman, who had served on the Island as an army chaplain, asked what the government's plans were. General Smuts replied on 16 April 1947 that the Island was to be the headquarters of the coastal artillery, 'the heart of the defences of this city'.[36] The defences of the Peninsula and surrounding areas would be based on it too. In fact, the Island had already been launched into the next chapter of its life.

It was tranquil on Robben Island, as yet virtually untouched by the harsher aspects of the policy of apartheid introduced by the Nationalist government in 1948. One of the signs of increasingly racist government policy, however, had been the disbanding of the Cape Corps in June of that year and, instead, the general employment in the Defence Department of 'unattested Non-European labourers'. On Robben Island the Coastal Artillery School recommended activities from 1 February 1946 under the command of Major L. T. Klootwyk. Gunners of the Permanent Force and their families were the first main post-war occupants and, of course, provided some continuity. A new primary school was established and pupil enrolment increased from 31 in mid-1947 to 57 at the start of 1952. It was a parallel medium school with instruction given in English and Afrikaans up to Standard 6.[37] With its school, library, power station and waterworks to serve civilians and the military, Robben Island again had a stable community life. Villagers could count among their blessings low rentals, the absence of crime, and freedom from the mainland's traffic ordinances. However, the water supply of the Island caused some concern as a hydrographic survey in 1956 showed that the water table had dropped. Three years later it was reported that four of seven boreholes had dried up.

The Island was more accessible than it had been in wartime, and the military authorities permitted many visits by civilians. The Boy Scouts had the use of a disused building for a camp in 1947; a party of 32 final-year civil engineering students of the University of Cape Town were received as guests in 1956 to conduct a topographical survey of part of the Island; and former residents were present at the unveiling of a plaque at the Anglican church to commemorate eight Robben Islanders who had lost their lives in the Second World War. There was quite a strong sense of origin and place among the one-time residents, and some two hundred of them formed an association on the mainland in 1957 and collected mementos for a small museum. A feature of that year was a successful 'open day' when 1160 visitors came over to the Island.

In 1951 the South African Marine Corps was created, absorbing the Permanent Force coastal and anti-aircraft gunnery units and ushering in an organisational change. It had a strong reputation for professional efficiency, but it was dissolved in October 1955 and its functions were transferred to the Navy and the School of Anti-Aircraft Training at Young's Field. By that time long-range coastal guns had become obsolete in an era of rocketry and guided missiles. Nevertheless the Robben Island batteries undertook firing practice with live ammunition on occasion until 1956 – for instance in 1951, when advance notice was given of firing by the Heavy Battery (called the De Waal Battery from 1952) and the Cornelia Battery. Residents were advised to leave their windows open![38] In 1956 a Citizen Force battalion, the Cape Town Highlanders, staged a combined sea and air exercise to seize key points, and apparently this 'invasion' of the Island was regarded as a success.[39]

The South African Navy was the third and last Defence Force tenant of Robben Island and successor to the Marine Corps as custodian of the guns of the De Waal Battery. A training establishment for Citizen Force sailors and a stores depot were set up. The shore station was designated *SAS Robbeneiland*, with responsibility for towing targets, rescue work and daily trips to Cape Town harbour.[40]

A fateful decision was taken in 1959 that brought the 20-year stay of the armed forces to a close. On 13 May, C. R. Swart, the Minister of Justice, announced in the House of Assembly that Robben Island would be taken over by the Prisons Department as a maximum security institution. The South African naval facility there would be withdrawn over a period and relocated at Simon's Town.

A Cape Town newspaper commented discerningly that most of the ties with the city would now be cut. Yachts and fishing boats would be obliged to give it a wide berth. A columnist of the *Cape Argus*, who mentioned that fishing interests had coveted the Island, thought that even smelly fish factories would have been preferable to 'Blackie' Swart's 'Alcatraz'. However, the public reaction was muted. The Mayor of Cape Town said that he had heard of no protests and he did not think Capetonians minded its becoming a prison. In 1960 the *Cape Times* again referred to problems of restricted access, which included the annual Muslim pilgrimage to the *karamat* (shrine) there. Major P. van der Byl, MP for Green Point, was allowed to go ashore on the Island under the new dispensation, as it fell within his constituency and he was canvassing support in the referendum among white voters in 1960 to determine whether South Africa should become a republic. He recalled an occasion almost thirty years earlier when he had been there with Lord Clarendon to shoot rabbits.

In the literature on Robben Island the long haul between 1931 and 1960 has usually been ignored or brushed aside. Totally different in character from the era of the lepers that preceded it or the era of the political prisoners that was to follow, it has its own rich historical texture.

Resistance on Robben Island
1963–1976

Fran Buntman

Resistance and anti-apartheid politics in South Africa, it is generally thought, greatly diminished in the aftermath of the Sharpeville massacre of 1960 and the Soweto uprising of 1976.* One useful way of thinking about Robben Island[1] from 1963 to 1976 is in the light of these dark days of struggle. On the one hand, the establishment of Robben Island as a political prison was a consequence of state power and repression, and the ability of the National Party government to suppress most of the opposition in the country. On the other hand, Robben Island was an important area where resistance against oppression and struggles against apartheid were both continued and extended, often under the most difficult conditions. It is with the serious and intense political struggle against apartheid – continued within Robben Island prison – that this chapter is concerned.

POLITICAL CONTEXT

The African National Congress (ANC) was founded in 1912. From the late 1940s and particularly in the 1950s it became increasingly militant in its opposition to the racism that came to define the country. In part the ANC's regeneration was a response to the first steps taken to implement apartheid, after the electoral victory of the National Party in 1948. Growing opposition was met with ever greater repression by the government.

The ANC was not, however, the only organisation that opposed apartheid. Within the ANC a split developed and the Pan Africanist Congress (PAC) – an organisation with an Africanist ideology as its name implies – emerged in 1959. Both organisations were to re-evaluate the nature of South African politics and the strategies called for when, on 21 March 1960, police fatally shot 69 residents of Sharpeville, mostly in the back, as they were protesting against the pass laws. It was a turning point in South African history. In the wake of the massacre, the government was to ban both the ANC and PAC, and they in turn were to adopt armed struggle.

Organised oppositional violence soon began. After Sharpeville, the ANC and PAC 'both produced insurgent offshoots. These were both dedicated to revolutionary transformation of society, and both were prepared to employ violent measures to attain this.'[2] The two organisations were uMkhonto weSizwe, the ANC's military wing, and the PAC-oriented Poqo movement. The relationship between Poqo and the PAC was complex. Tom Lodge describes Poqo as 'inspired by the PAC', and notes that in some ways members directly identified with the PAC, although in other ways Poqo represented a departure from that organisation.[3] Whatever the differences between Poqo and the PAC, the two appear to have been treated as one group on the Island, both within the prisoner community and by the state. The divisions within the PAC nationally and those between the PAC and Poqo were no doubt crucial to the divergences within the PAC on Robben Island.

The early 1960s saw a rapid increase in legislation designed to suppress most opposition to apartheid and all violent protest. The laws and the opposition to them created a new phenomenon in South Africa: political prisoners en masse. Hundreds of prisoners, all black men, were sent to Robben Island. By the mid-1960s, the National Party government had in the short term quelled much of the dissent, both violent and non-violent. This ushered in a period of relative political quiescence until the Soweto uprising of 1976. There was, of course, sporadic resistance, including important strikes by workers in Durban in the early 1970s, and the growth and increasing influence of Black Consciousness. But in general, within the country, levels of repression and fear remained extraordinarily high during the 1960s and 1970s. Once prisoners on the Island were released they were often banished, banned or otherwise harassed. This limited, but did not necessarily stop, their continued activism when they emerged from prison.

By 1963 and 1964 hundreds of men from around the country had been sent to the Island for furthering the aims of the ANC and PAC, and engaging in organised acts of violence and sabotage against apartheid. (In many cases they had, however, only got as far as planning armed opposition.)[4] The most famous trial of the period was the Rivonia Trial, which began in late 1963 and ended in June 1964. At the trial senior ANC members – Nelson Mandela, Walter Sisulu, Govan Mbeki, Raymond Mhlaba, Ahmed Kathrada, Andrew Mlangeni, Elias Motsoaledi and Denis Goldberg – were sentenced to life imprisonment. With the exception of Denis Goldberg, who was white, they were sent to Robben Island.

Initially, most of the prisoners on the Island were members and supporters of the PAC and Poqo. In time, more and more ANC adherents arrived, including some members of uMkhonto weSizwe. The former prisoner Natoo

Rivonia Trialists, clockwise from top left: Nelson Mandela, Walter Sisulu, Andrew Mlangeni, Elias Motsoaledi (Mayibuye Centre)

Babenia has noted that 'When we arrived [in March 1964] there were only eleven ANC chaps on the island. We brought the number to fifty one. Within six months of our arrival there would have been well over eight hundred of us ANC.'[5] Over time the numbers evened out, and eventually the ANC outnumbered the PAC.[6]

In addition to the PAC/Poqo and ANC prisoners, who together formed the overwhelming majority in the prison, there were non-political prisoners and prisoners from other political organisations. Eddie Daniels was the sole representative of the Liberal Party on Robben Island. The National Liberation Front (or Yu Chi Chan Club) had seven men on the Island. Later on, in 1972 members of the African People's Democratic Union of South Africa (APDUSA), which had been affiliated to the Non-European Unity Movement (NEUM), came to the prison. In 1974 Mosibudi Mangena was the first Black Consciousness prisoner to arrive; many more Black Consciousness adherents followed him, especially in the wake of the 1976 uprising. Throughout the whole period under consideration numbers of political prisoners declined.[7] While in the early years there were 'well over 1000 political prisoners', in 1974, for example, the political prison housed 399 inmates.[8]

Overview

The story of Robben Island as a political prison begins properly in 1962.[9] This was when the first political prisoners, overwhelmingly (if not exclusively) Poqo and PAC supporters, joined the non-political prisoners already on the Island. (The non-political prisoners were probably there from 1961, as the South African Prisons Service officially took control of the Island on 1 April 1961.)[10]

There is not much information about the early days when political prisoners began inhabiting the prison. D. M. Zwelonke commented that the first prisoners 'really had it tough'.[11] In part this is supported by the experiences of Nelson Mandela, who was one of the first political prisoners on Robben Island; he spent two weeks there before the Rivonia Trial.[12] According to his long-time cell mate, Michael Dingake, Mandela remarked that 'In those days … the conditions were mixed. Bad and not so bad.'[13] One of the main reasons for the adverse conditions was the presence of two notorious members of the Prisons Service, the Kleynhans brothers, who terrorised the prisoners. But, at least in 1962, there were also coloured warders who mitigated some of the hardships and abuse. By 1963, these coloured warders had been removed. From then on, all warders and prison personnel were white, and all the prisoners were black (African, Indian and coloured). Neville Alexander, who was

Rivonia Trialists, clockwise from top left: Govan Mbeki, Raymond Mhlaba, Denis Goldberg, Ahmed Kathrada (Mayibuye Centre)

on the Island from 1964 to 1974, argues that because of this Robben Island
acquired a 'peculiar status', in that state policy sought to heighten racial prej-
udice and abuse of prisoners.

> It is important to understand clearly what this 'peculiar status' of RIP
> [Robben Island Prison] is and what it entails ... RIP must be the only
> prison in the country where in spite of a[n] ... exclusively Black prison
> population, the staff is exclusively White. This undisguised recourse to
> the racial prejudice of the Whites as a reinforcement of the maximum
> security measures ... is one of the major factors in the hardships suffered
> by prisoners at RIP.[14]

Indeed, prisoner after prisoner has identified the behaviour of the warders as
one of the most important reasons for the appalling conditions and brutality
of the early years.[15]

In addition to the deliberate and exaggerated racism of the prison, whose
white warders had been taught to demonise their black charges, criminal or
non-political prisoners were also apparently used to brutalise and terrorise the
political prisoners. Accounts differ significantly as to the role of the non-political prisoners in making Robben Island a 'hell-hole'. Moses Dlamini suggests
the criminals were an essential part of the terror of the early years. They were
members of vicious and notorious gangs, who were 'hand-picked by the
enemy from the most notorious maximum [security] prisons of South Africa
to come and demoralise and humiliate us with the assistance of the uncouth,
uncivilised, raw Boer warders so that we would never again dare to challenge
the system of apartheid colonialism'. According to Dlamini's account, the
gang members were removed from the Island in 1965.[16] When they left there
was an immediate sense of space being opened up, which permitted 'a blos-
soming of cultural activities throughout all the cells in the Island'.[17]

The early years, until approximately 1966, were exceptionally harsh for the
political prisoners. What triggered the gradual improvement of conditions was
a mass hunger strike by almost the entire prisoner population of over a thousand men. Slowly, brutality decreased, food improved, and cultural, academic
and political activities could be organised by the prisoners. There was a regression in conditions, however, in the early 1970s, with the arrival of a new
Commanding Officer, Colonel Badenhorst, when a reign of terror was re-
established.[18] After Badenhorst left the Island in 1972, conditions once again
began to improve slowly. In summary, Alexander explains the overall pattern
of regression and improvements as follows:

> At RIP itself the years 1962–1966 were years of hell ... From 1967
> onwards, any objective observer would have to admit that major

improvements ... were made ... Thus the general picture that emerges is one of extreme harshness and physical pressure on prisoners from 1962 until December 1966 with a peak of inhumanity and brutality in 1962–1963 and again from August 1966 onwards ... Then from 1967 until 1970 inclusive there followed a period of relatively civilized treatment and a much more relaxed atmosphere. 1971–1972 saw a relapse with the harshest treatment concentrated in the first nine months of 1971. From 1973 (April) onwards all overt physical pressures were eliminated, treatment became relatively humane again but ... other problems were manufactured by officialdom in order to harass the political prisoners.[19]

Conditions in the prison were always a product of the interaction between state designs and prisoner struggles for improved treatment. The state could and did worsen or improve conditions as it saw fit: 'there was no linear progress [but] instead a deliberate zig-zag policy.'[20] The arbitrary change of conditions for the worse had a very destabilising effect on the prisoners' lives. 'This pendulum policy', noted Alexander, 'represents an extreme injustice and is a source of insecurity that plagues prisoners, who never know when things will revert to "normal."'[21]

But what were these hellish conditions, and what was 'normal'? To answer these questions one must examine the conditions on Robben Island in the 1960s; many of them prevailed still in the 1970s, and some even in the 1980s. As this chapter argues, combating the physical conditions that threatened the survival of the prisoners was the primary form of resistance in which the prisoners had to engage before they were able to extend their struggle to personal development as individuals and to political renewal for organisations. The nature of the prison, the conditions first encountered there, and how these were improved need now to be examined.

FIRST STAGES OF STRUGGLE

The prison and its population

Within the political prison, which was largely built by the inmates in the early 1960s, most prisoners were housed in the general sections. A few were housed in a single-cell section, which is often identified as the 'leadership section'. (It was of course the state that defined who was to be in this section.) Although the composition of the single-cell section changed over the period 1964–76, it included amongst others the ANC's Rivonia group (Nelson Mandela, Elias Motsoaledi, Govan Mbeki, Ahmed Kathrada, Andrew Mlangeni and Raymond Mhlaba),[22] the PAC's John Nyati Pokela and Zephania Mothopeng, the NLF's Fikile Bam and Neville Alexander, Eddie

Daniels of the Liberal Party, and Sonny Venkatrathnam and Kader Hassim of APDUSA. There were other men, widely considered as leaders, who were not in the single-cell section – among them Harry Gwala of the ANC and Johnson Mlambo of the PAC.[23]   Although Andimba Toivo ya Toivo of SWAPO was in the single-cell section, the Namibians were for the most part housed in a separate portion of the general section.[24]

The single cells were meant to house, as the name suggests, individual prisoners. Here the men had far less (legal) contact with their fellow prisoners, and were locked in their cells for much longer hours, than the men in the general sections. These different sections were designed to separate the prisoners and prevent contact, especially that between the single cells and the rest of the prison. But the prisoners soon found ways to overcome the divisions, and there was always communication, although it was often slow and interrupted because of the illicit methods that had to be used. One common method was to wrap messages in plastic and put them in the drums of food which all had to go through to the kitchen serving the entire prison.[25]

Not only was prisoner life structured by the physical divisions which the state imposed or by the ideological divisions of the various liberation movements and groupings in South African politics. Over time, an extensive committee structure evolved amongst the prisoners, to regulate the relations and activities, between and within organisations, that formed the substance of prison life. As with life outside prison, there were differences among prisoners – which were occasionally the basis of division – along lines also of ethnicity, region and generation.[26] Although the state tried to exploit some of these divisions, it seldom succeeded. Fikile Bam has noted, for example, that at one point he was put in a cell where he believed the authorities had deliberately mixed Pedi-speaking men from the northern Transvaal, who were predominantly ANC supporters, and Xhosa-speaking men from the opposite side of the country, who were predominantly PAC supporters, in order to precipitate fights and tension.

> It was a deliberate policy of ... the prison authorities that as long as ... we were fighting amongst each other, their task was much easier of breaking us. And sometimes it did happen. But as a matter of fact it wasn't that regular that it happened. In this particular section, the relationships were just wonderful and I made friends with both groups. And you know, in fact, [we] spent a lot of time learning each other's languages, and didn't care much about their differences.[27]

Indeed, although Dlamini and others regard the state's use of criminal prisoners to undermine the political prisoners as partly successful, most former prisoners believe that the criminals were removed because the politicals had begun to politicise them and even recruit them into their organisations. According to Neville Alexander, the state also realised the non-political prisoners helped the political prisoners to get access to newspapers, and kept them up to date with the news, despite the fact that newspapers and radios were prohibited.[28]

Conditions

Racism overtly and covertly defined much of prison life. As has been mentioned, prisoners were all black and warders all white, and racial slurs cast by the latter were the hallmark of daily life for prisoners, at least in the early years.

Apartheid logic ensured that prisoners of different races ate different food.[29] Supposedly, this was an attempt to cater for the traditional or cultural norms of the different races. However, 'culture' had nothing to do with the diet: this was based on racial discrimination. For example, the 1970 *Survey* of the South African Institute of Race Relations noted that white prisoners were fed four ounces of mealie meal or mealie rice per day, while coloureds and Indians were given fourteen ounces and Africans twelve ounces. Similarly, while whites were given seven ounces of meat or fish every day, coloureds, Indians and Africans were only allowed meat or fish four times a week – six ounces for coloureds and Indians and five for Africans.

Yet the racially discriminatory diet failed to create divisions between the prisoners. Because Robben Island's community was 'politically conscious and enlightened', the diet had only 'irritation value'.[30] Still, it was opposed for the racism it was. In the single cells there were enough non-African inmates for the better food given to coloureds and Indians to be fairly divided amongst all, in violation of the prison rules. This could not be done in the general sections where Africans were by far in the majority.[31] Apart from the issue of racism, the insufficient quantity and poor quality of food were always a cause of complaint on Robben Island.[32]

Food also had the potential for being a fiercely contested weapon. On one hand, refusing food by means of hunger strikes was perhaps the most powerful weapon of the political prisoners.[33] On the other hand, until 1973 one of the methods warders would use to punish prisoners was to withdraw their meal 'tickets' and thus force them to go without food for a day. The cry of *drie male*, or 'three meals', was an arbitrary edict imposed with regularity by warders when they felt that a rule had been broken or that a prisoner should be punished. Prison regulations allowed that a prisoner who acknowledged culpability for a minor infraction might be deprived of between one and three meals (all on one day) by any officer with at least the rank of Chief Warder. In theory, if the prisoner did not admit guilt, he would be charged in a prison court or higher body. In practice, however, 'it was physically risky for almost all prisoners in 1962–4 not to "accept" meal-stops.'³⁴ The regulations were often abused by the authorities, and 'there have been many instances where head-warders, and even ordinary warders, have had prisoners locked up without food for a day (and even longer) without so much as referring the matter to the head of the Prison, let alone taking the prisoner into the presence of the Head'.³⁵ Only later, when political prisoners sufficiently challenged the power relations in the prison, were they able to refuse meal-stops. This invariably meant hiring lawyers for what were usually trivial cases, and not all prisoners were in a financial position to do so.

It is difficult, and perhaps even inappropriate, to make a distinction between overt or explicit examples of racism as described here, and the pervasive racial hatred that informed the way the prison was run more generally. Indeed, during the early years, extreme brutality characterised by actions meant to humiliate and undermine prisoners became intrinsic to Island life. Three examples of these attempts at systematically brutalising and humiliating prisoners can be given. Firstly, a daily feature of prison life was the *tauza*, which officials claimed was meant to prevent prisoners smuggling objects on or in the body. Indeed, the non-political prisoners proved incredibly adept at smuggling, even within the body's orifices. Dennis Brutus, for example, writes of knives that 'suddenly flash – produced perhaps from some disciplined anus'.³⁶ In the *tauza*, the prisoner had to strip and, once naked, jump around to dislodge any concealed object. He would end the 'dance' by bending over naked to expose his rectum to the warders. Dikgang Moseneke recalls this perverse ritual:

> Few things can be as degrading as that [the *tauza*]. With time, I suppose, your sense of propriety gets weakened, you become less sensitive to it. But the truth is, this is one single harrowing thing that I had to go through each time. I was 15, and I was with people a little older than me ranging to 60 or 65. And being a product of the conservatism you would find in African society, and where age remained a very important factor ... and therefore it was just a difficulty; every day you'd just have rows and rows of adult people who stand there stark naked, and they're made to *tauza*, and then they move around and they pick up their clothes at the side. And this whole process would be done by the warders who would be manning us ... Somehow they seemed to have enjoyed it. They seemed so totally depraved, that they could live with this comfortably and find nothing wrong with it.³⁷

Perhaps the most brutal aspect of day-to-day life was the hard labour the prisoners performed, and the abuses associated with it, especially in the early years. Most prisoners would work in the quarries, quarrying lime and stone, or chopping wood, crushing stone, 'making or repairing roads with pick and shovel', or dragging seaweed from the beaches and the sea.[38] A very small number of political prisoners were allowed to work in more productive and less physically draining jobs, in the hospital, kitchen or offices. Until the early 1970s, most of these jobs were given to the criminal prisoners. Soon after arriving on Robben Island in 1964, Natoo Babenia was sent to the quarry as part of a 'quarryspan'. Before prisoners could begin work in the quarry, a dyke had to be built. Rubble had to be dumped into the sea to make a wall, and wheelbarrows were used to cart this gravel.

> Us new drafts were told to take the wheelbarrows with spindly, creaky steel wheels ... We had to push the barrows through the line of the Kleynhans warders. As we moved along, each of them would let fly with the baton. At the end of the journey was a small incline where Karnakemp [a warder][38] waited for us ... Baton flying around, he would scream 'Ek's nie jou Sir nie, ek is jou Baas!' ... [I am not your Sir, I am your Master!]
>
> Once you passed Karnakemp we had to tip the stones into the sea and go back for more. The 'Big Fives' [a prison gang] would be waiting. Come slowly and they would leave their spades and beat us. Or they would overload the wheelbarrow so you could hardly push it. Shits like Teeman and Meintjies would then run to Jan or Piet Kleynhans and say 'Baas! Baas! Daai kaffirtjie wil nie werk nie!' [Master, that little Kaffir won't work.] Piet and Jan will then sit on the wheelbarrow and ask us to push. If we tried and the wheelbarrow fell from our grip they would fall on us with their batons shouting, 'Julle wil ons seer maak! Julle wil ons dood maak!' [You want to hurt us, to kill us.] We'd then get our cards taken away for [a] three meal stop.
>
> As time went, the warders got us to push faster. Inevitably you would push the wheel into the ankles of the comrade in front. Karnakemp, the sadist, liked to see this ... [39]

Individual prisoners could also be singled out for abuse. An often-cited example is that of Johnson Mlambo, who was buried in sand up to his neck and then urinated upon.[40]

> Mr Mlambo, a twenty-year-stretch man, a short man, was made to dig a pit big enough to fit him. Unaware of what was to follow, he was still digging on when he was suddenly overwhelmed by a group of convicts. They shoved him into the pit and started filling it up ... When they had

---

Prisoners breaking stone in the courtyard of Robben Island Prison (Mayibuye Centre)

finished, only Mlambo's head appeared above the ground. A white warder, who had directed the whole business, urinated into Mlambo's mouth. The convicts tried to open his tight-locked jaws, but could not ... The warder pissed and pissed; it looked as though he had reserved gallons of urine for the purpose ... When the warder had finished ... vicious blows of fists and boots rained around the defenceless head sticking out of the ground.[41]

Resisting the oppression

These details of conditions and treatment are merely an indication of how harsh and dangerous life on the Island was at many points in the decade after 1962. One could also comment on the frequent lack of medical care, or the harmful nature of the work itself, amongst a litany of violations of the rights and humanity of the men on Robben Island.[42]

But Robben Island is known as much as a 'university' as a 'hell-hole' – with good reason. For many, perhaps most, of the political prisoners, the period of incarceration was used to advance their personal and political development, as individuals and as members of organisations. Yet how was this possible?

Although there was very little space for personal or political growth in the harsh conditions already described, this is not to say there was no political life or academic study in the early years. Harry Gwala, for example, commented that 'political education did not depend on the harshness of the authorities. It was a matter of do or die. It was underground work. We were subjected to underground work before we went to prison. Prison was a continuation of that, so we had no problem with the restriction imposed on us [in prison].'[43] For most people, however, mere survival and the slow improvement in conditions were necessary prior steps before the Island could be turned into a 'university'. '[I]n the first instance,' Jacob Zuma has noted, 'we had to struggle to correct ... the prison conditions, which were appalling.'[44] Dikgang Moseneke similarly remembers that 'there was no time then to focus acutely on political matters; strategies were directed at dealing with these conditions, and therefore were strategies of survival, and which inevitably would bring greater cohesion, between both the ANC and the PAC.'[45]

Arguably, the most important reason for improvement in conditions was the resistance of the prisoners themselves. Many, if not most, political prisoners resisted the reign of terror conducted by prison officials and criminal gangs. Given circumstances like these, they had to concentrate on survival before they could attempt to organise collective protest aimed at reform. Furthermore, there had to be sufficient changes in conditions so that, however minor and partial these improvements might be, they could open some sort of space for large-scale and effective resistance.

Exactly what these openings were is to some extent a matter of speculation and perception.[46] In the first place one needs to stress the important played by released prisoners in highlighting the plight of their still-incarcerated comrades. Many of the prisoners' sentences, especially those of Poqo members, were comparatively short. When their terms ended in 1965–6, some of the prisoners first to be released began exposing conditions on the Island.

> There has been very little said about those who left the Island during that time [the 1960s] who were mandated to go and speak to institutions like the United Nations, Amnesty International, Red Cross, to make representations, explain the reality of the situation on the Island ... It has to be known that today the Island is what it is ... as a result of bitter struggle on the part of those who were there ... [47]

Dennis Brutus, for instance, testified in the late 1960s about prison conditions before the United Nations Special Committee on Apartheid. His testimony was also used in various publications, including those of the International Defence and Aid Fund.[48] Neville Alexander's *Robben Island Dossier 1964–1974* was originally written in secret to publicise the plight of the prisoners. The need to expose conditions was an ongoing imperative. Alexander notes that 'it was an unspoken injunction understood by all prisoners who were released from the island that one of the most important contributions they could make to the well-being of those they left behind was to let in the light of public scrutiny on the goings-on in that prison.'[49]

International attention was increasingly marshalled to focus on conditions on Robben Island. Mary Benson, who was involved in creating international pressure against apartheid, has argued that the incarceration of the Rivonia trialists heightened international attention on South Africa in general, and Robben Island in particular.[50] Harry Gwala has similarly noted that 'the limelight which had fallen on Rivonia [was then] transferred to Robben Island.'[51] Another important dimension of international attention and pressure was the scrutiny of the International Committee of the Red Cross (ICRC). The first ICRC visit to Robben Island occurred in 1964. It is possible that this made the government increasingly aware of the possibility of international concern and pressure. The ICRC also challenged general maltreatment of prisoners on Robben Island. Mlambo is one of the Islanders who credit the ICRC with helping to improve conditions in the prison.[52]

Another reason for the amelioration of conditions was a series of articles published in June and July 1965 in the *Rand Daily Mail* on prisons in South Africa. These were based on the testimony of Harold Strachan, who had himself been imprisoned. Although none of the Robben Islanders in interviews have mentioned the Strachan exposures, the timing of the articles and the comments of Hugh Lewin and others seem to suggest they were important in improving prison conditions in general.[53]

Helen Suzman is also widely credited for her work to end ill-treatment of political prisoners. Alexander writes:

> She is the one member of the South African Parliament whose name is inextricably linked with the only systematic attempt to get international-al standards implemented in the prisons in general and on Robben Island in particular. Her staunch insistence on the application of ... humane provisions ... became quite literally a bridge of survival and of sanity over which most of us could walk out of imprisonment without having been too deeply scarred and disfigured.[54]

Similarly, Harry Gwala, in explaining why conditions changed, emphasised, on the one hand, 'the struggle waged by the prisoners themselves' and, on the other hand, 'the visit[s], in particular by Mrs Helen Suzman'.[55] None of these changes would have had much effect unless the prisoners had taken up the opportunities presented. Suzman herself has emphasised the role of the prisoners in improving conditions. 'The fact that they were strong, and they were united, and they were organised and they were informed – that was important.'[56]

The first major hunger strike by prisoners took place in 1966, and marked a turning point in conditions on Robben Island. Dlamini explains the events that led up to the hunger strike: first of all, there was the fall from power of a prison gang, the Big Fives, and the prison officials who supported them. The second event was the removal of most or all of the criminals in January 1965 and the subsequent beginnings of a cultural rejuvenation among prisoners. The next moment was the change in attitudes of the prison official hierarchy, who acceded to a whole set of demands. Finally, after an abortive hunger strike by 18 youths in April 1965, a major strike was planned and held a year later. [57]

> After the failure of the last hunger strike by PAC comrades in April 1965, we analysed our mistakes and prepared for another one. There had been mass mobilization since then, preparing all the comrades in all the cells for the need for a hunger strike in order to bring about far reaching reforms in the whole prison machinery. It was necessary mostly because about half of the political prisoners were doing five years and less, and when the long-term prisoners remained, they would all have to carry the burden. We had to help our comrades before being released ... The aim of the hunger strike was to improve, first, the food situation, then the clothing and shoes, followed by the working conditions, the punishment at work for having failed to satisfy a certain quota, the

treatment by warders, *tauza* and many other grievances which we had often raised with the prison authorities since 1963 to no avail.[58]

Another example of resistance before 1976 was the legal action Sonny Venkatrathnam and Kader Hassim brought against the prison authorities in 1973: they challenged the right of warders to place prisoners in solitary confinement without a hearing and to withdraw a day's meal arbitrarily. They also insisted that study and recreational activities were rights; the prison authorities, however, asserted that these were privileges. While they were successful in the first challenge, the Supreme Court upheld the distinction between rights and privileges.[59] Like most events in prison, this challenge is revealing of the conditions prisoners faced, of the approaches that could be taken to the situation, and of the consequences and implications of resistance.

Venkatrathnam has explained the situation which caused the protest to begin. Whenever he waved hello to someone in another block (but in the same section) as they were going to breakfast, the warder would promptly take away three meals. Furthermore, 'there was no library. We could not borrow books. They would not allow us to study ... It was ... intolerable if you were accustomed to being a reading type of person.' The environment was very tense, as the warders hated the prisoners, having been told they were terrorists. And to make a complaint, one had to apply for permission to do so, and then only on Sunday during inspection.[60] Venkatrathnam and other prisoners in his section therefore decided to draw up a petition. Paper was denied to them, so they used brown cement bags.[61] In addition, they decided not to request permission to make these complaints and demands.

> We wrote this two-page petition to the officer in command on Robben Island, addressing a whole lot of things. About the right to have a handbook [i.e. the prison regulations]. We said we had rights and obligations. And we wanted the right to study, we wanted an interesting prison library. We wanted recreation time. [We] complained about the food, the attitude of warders. We said we needed the right to legal representation. There must not be this arbitrary punishment. Even if it is an administrative [procedure], we still needed legal representation.

The petition was handed over to the authorities on Sunday morning, and on Monday, in consequence, Venkatrathnam and Hassim were put into solitary confinement.

> Solitary confinement on Robben Island was a pretty grim affair. [The cell] ... was no bigger than the toilet ... and [it was] damp, dark, cold. No flush toilet, just a squat hole there for you and a little water. That is

all. You get about fifteen minutes to go and have a wash in the morning and that's it. Otherwise you spend almost 24 hours in that cell alone.

They had begun to despair of the situation improving but were able to smuggle out letters to their lawyers, explaining their predicament. The lawyers in turn knew they had no legal right to intervene, and so they instructed the wives of the two men to bring urgent court applications. This enabled the lawyers to come to the Island to take proper instructions from them. Venkatrathnam concluded:

> Basically we won. Ninety-nine per cent of our application came through ... I think life on Robben Island changed dramatically and permanently since that day. Not only for ourselves, but I think for the whole population of Robben Island. Because since that day no prisoner was arbitrarily sentenced to three meals [or] solitary confinement. Every time they had to charge a prisoner for anything they had to formally serve him with a charge sheet ... [For the first time now] they gave us the prison regulations [which Venkatrathnam emphasised as one of the biggest victories].

According to Venkatrathnam, their application to the Cape Supreme Court 'changed the power relationships between prisoners and warder tremendously'. He also considered it a challenge to the prevailing means prisoners used in struggling for improvements in the prison. He had heard 'through the grapevine that Nelson [Mandela] ... felt that we did the wrong thing' in launching the application, and that his preferred strategy was negotiation.[62] Alexander, however, credits the application and subsequent legal judgment with making a significant contribution to improving life in prison.[63]

Apart from illustrating the different forms resistance took against abuse, this protest is illustrative of an important theme: that external attention on the prison was often vital to the success of prisoners' struggles. On several occasions in fact hunger strikes were specifically timed to ensure that visitors would learn of them, and thus outside publicity could be organised.

This quest by the Robben Islanders to improve the appalling circumstances of their lives was a critical precondition of their being able to do more than 'merely' survive prison. In this regard, the real achievement of the political prisoners can be pointed up by contrasting their struggle with that of most criminal prisoners. The non-political prisoners sought firstly to survive prison, and secondly to improve the conditions of their existence. Hence they would smuggle food, work with the warders, or join gangs to provide protection and find ways of improving conditions. While all of these acts represent a form of resistance, they do not attempt to challenge power relations fundamentally, either within the prison or in the broader society. In contrast, the political prisoners sought not just to protect themselves, but to resist in such a way as to challenge some of the power relations inside the prison, and to use their incarceration to challenge the power relations of apartheid South Africa outside prison once they were released. It is to these forms of resistance that this chapter now turns.

Two important provisos need to be stated, however. Firstly, the different dimensions of resistance – overcoming basic material deprivations and ending physical abuse, the struggle for education and a sporting and cultural life, and the attempt to organise politically – were all interrelated. Secondly, while ensuring survival and humane conditions of existence was a fundamental precondition of more far-reaching resistance, it is important to recognise that improvements were not linear, and prisoners constantly had to resist regression in their treatment and struggle for improvements. The Badenhorst regime of the early 1970s and the regression it represented have already been mentioned. The potential and actual loss of rights and 'privileges' was a constant factor in Island life, and thus required constant struggles by the prisoners.[64]

RESISTANCE BEYOND SURVIVAL

In theory, imprisonment is meant to rehabilitate a prisoner, who has invariably broken not only laws but social codes and mores in a society. In the case of political prisoners in South Africa, the state had little hope of 'rehabilitating' them. This would have involved a renunciation of the anti-apartheid struggle and an acceptance of the racist perspective of their gaolers. Moreover, much of the treatment meted out to the political prisoners showed that the state was not only unconcerned with rehabilitation, but was focused on retribution. Once physical abuse was no longer a defining feature of daily prison life, retribution and punishment continued to operate through the negative psychological effects of imprisonment itself, combined with persistent harassment by the authorities. The state could and did make life difficult for the prisoners, interrupting or preventing academic education, censoring letters and visits, and denying news and newspapers. Determined to resist the state's attempt to destroy them mentally, the Islanders began to extend their cultural, academic and sporting activities.

> Before, our enemy had been physical cruelty, now it was boredom, isolation, the psychological decay of an endlessly unproductive and confined existence; so the [mini-Olympic] Games [among other endeavours] were an important way of getting ourselves mobilized, using our inner resources to smash the routine and monotonous futility of prison life.[65]

Academic education

Political prisoners on the Island developed and sought to live by a code of conduct. This code called for prisoners to maintain their commitment to a changed society, ensure non-collaboration with the authorities, and find and make positive things from their imprisonment. This demand for self-improvement can be seen in the value placed on academic education. As Babenia noted, 'If you do not watch out, prison can put your brain to death.'[66] Academic study was valued on three grounds. Firstly, it was important in maintaining morale. Moseneke, who graduated from Robben Island with a school-leaving certificate and BA in Political Science and English, commented: 'Many people have emerged to survive Robben Island largely because of their studying. It is one single thing that really keeps you together.'[67]

> Without study privilege, many of the prisoners would have atrophied intellectually and bouts of demoralization might have superseded the general buoyancy of the community. Studies to a large extent played some diversionary role. It is true the majority of prisoners did not enjoy the formal privilege of study while they were in gaol for a number of reasons, the principal one being lack of funds. Informally, no prisoner who had an interest in learning failed to benefit from the intellectual atmosphere that prevailed. The privileged students took risks, 'abused' their study privilege to help their less privileged fellow inmates.[68]

Academic education was also valued for its contribution to the community as a whole. Islanders sought to increase the educational standards of all prisoners, and formal and informal education was conducted across organisational lines. One of the key areas of this effort was the attempt to ensure no man left the Island without being able to read and write if he came there illiterate. Mbatha, Moseneke and Babenia all refer to the highly successful literacy campaigns held on the Island in the 1960s.[69]

> In a matter of three to four years we had actually wiped out illiteracy on Robben Island. Completely. Everyone could read and write, at least in his mother tongue. As we moved on, we issued little wonderful certificates for every step that he would have passed, the heading always being 'The University of Robben Island'.[70]

Apart from literacy, there were also classes on a range of subjects from history to biology, and at all educational levels. Very often these classes were held in the quarry while prisoners worked.[71]

Academic education was also seen as the basis of a sound political educa-

TOURS TO ROBBEN ISLAND

Following the recent handover of Robben Island to the Department of Arts, Culture, Science and Technology, the newly established Robben Island Museum is conducting daily tours to the most symbolically significant site in South Africa.

The Robben Island Museum

"While we will not forget the brutality of apartheid we will not want Robben Island to be a monument of our hardship and suffering. We would want it to be a monument reflecting the triumph of the human spirit against the forces of evil; a triumph of freedom and human dignity over repression and humiliation; a triumph of wisdom and largeness of spirit against small minds and pettiness; a triumph of courage and determination over human frailty and weakness; a triumph of non-racialism over bigotry and intolerance; a triumph of the new South Africa over the old."

Robben Island is 5,4 kilometres long and 1,5 metres wide. It between 15 and 30 minutes to walk across the breadth of the island two hours to walk right around it. The island is separated from the main 9 kilometres of sea. It takes 30 to 40 minutes to reach Robben Island by Cape Town harbour.

The lighthouse built in 1804

Minto Hill – the highest point on the island

Van Riebeeck's quarry

Graveyard

The Anglican Church 1841

The old male leper church, built in 1895.

The guest house – this used to be where the commissioner of the island lived

Old Victorian building – today the island school

The old leper morgue now used as a bank

Correctional services facility

Faure jetty

Map adapted from the book Dreaming of Freedom – *The story of Robben Island* SACHED BOOKS/MAYIBUYE BO

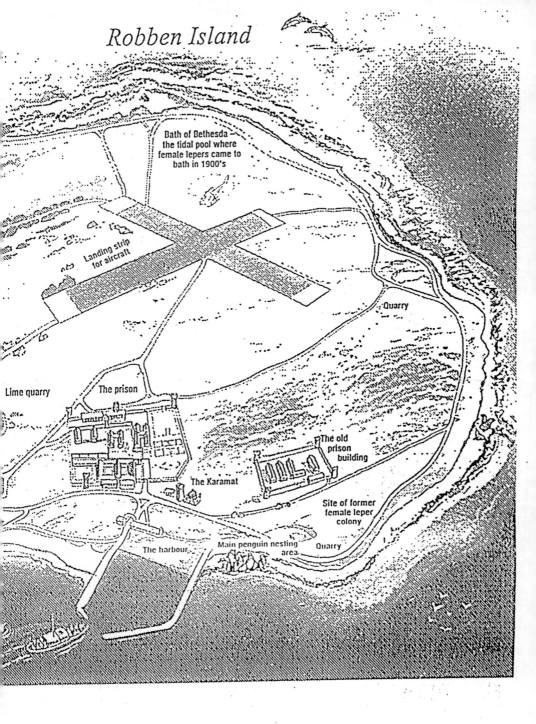

Robben Island

Bath of Bethesda —
the tidal pool where
female lepers came to
bath in 1900's

Landing strip
for aircraft

Quarry

Lime quarry

The prison

The old
prison
building

The Karamat

Site of former
female leper
colony

The harbour

Main penguin nesting
area

Quarry

TOURS TO ROBBEN ISLAND

Tickets are sold from the Embarkation Point on Jetty 1 at the V&A Waterfront, directly in front of the extension to the Victoria Wharf and can be purchased between 8h00 and 17h00. Tickets are limited and are available on a first come first served basis. For further information, please call (021) 419 1300. (Office hours)

Ferries depart promptly at the times indicated. Please ensure that you arrive 30 minutes before departure.

THREE TOURS PER DAY. TOUR TIMES AS FOLLOWS:		
	Depart Cape Town	Arrival Cape Town
TOUR 1:	09h00	12h30
TOUR 2:	11h30	14h30
TOUR 3:	13h15	16h45

Adults: R80 • Pensioners/students with ID R50
Children (4-17) accompanied by an adult: R25
Children under 4: Free • School Groups: R20 per student

Please Note:
- Group tours to be accommodated by special arrangement.
- Special rates are available on written request.
- Physically challenged visitors should inform the booking office prior to their visit.

The Robben Island Museum and their servants and agents will not be responsible for and shall be exempt from all liability in respect of any loss, damage, injury, accident, delay, or any inconvenience to any person or his/her luggage or any personal property whenever the same shall arise from or be occasioned irrespective of the negligence of the Robben Island Museum.

tion. In recalling the political theory classes that he and Stephen Dlamini started on the Island, Harry Gwala explained that people who were illiterate could
not understand the abstract concepts they were teaching and using. 'So we
organised … literacy education.'[72]

Constraints on academic education

The issue of academic study highlights the important point that has been

Certificate awarded to Natoo Babenia in March 1973 (Mayibuye Centre)

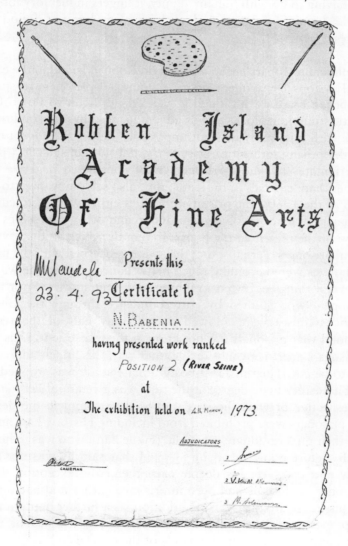

made: that though there was an undoubted and enormous improvement in
conditions on Robben Island over the years, it 'still [remained] a prison'.[73] The
inmates were constantly vulnerable to their gaolers' edicts and controls.

> That the form of psychological torture did not work as expected does
> not imply that it did not work at all. The fact that I underline it so
> much, means that I am still smarting under its effects. The common
> characteristic of torture whether physical or psychological is that it is
> painful to every sensitive victim. The psychological pain is more painful
> for, having to do with human dignity, it lingers in memory long after the
> physical pain has gone and as long as it has not found equitable
> redress.[74]

When political prisoners began arriving on Robben Island in the early 1960s
the official Prisons Department policy encouraged prisoners to study. Many
prisoners began to study, although it was very difficult to do so because of
bureaucratic stumbling blocks and disadvantageous physical conditions. If one
could cope with this, study was not impossible. Before the advent of political
prisoners the prison authorities, it appears, did not consider it a problem to
encourage inmates to study. Prisoners were considered negative social elements rather than 'enemies of the state'; they also seldom wanted to study. But
by the end of the 1960s, the prison authorities either wanted to cut down on
their bureaucratic load (involving censorship and other 'necessities' of organising study) or they resented the boosts to morale which study privileges gave
the political prisoners. Perhaps, too, they were concerned with the fact that the
political inmates were becoming much better educated than the warders.

Thus, several things occurred to inhibit and limit studies. Prior to 1968 or
1969 prisoners who studied by correspondence through the University of
South Africa (Unisa) were allowed to pay only half of the regular fees.
Dingake notes that prisoners did not know if this was due to Unisa's concern
or to a Prisons Department subsidy.[75] Either way, this 'much-appreciated subsidy' was to be cut. Then in 1969 postgraduate study was stopped. Whoever
was doing a postgraduate degree at the time was given until February 1970 to
finish, irrespective of when he was supposed to complete the degree. Soon
after this, prisoners were prohibited from including History, Law and Political
Science in their undergraduate curricula. (Fikile Bam, who was in his final year
of an LL.B. before going to prison in 1964, has said he was not allowed to
study Law and complete his degree even then. The exception was Nelson
Mandela, only because he had been imprisoned earlier and had already been
given permission to study Law.)[76] In addition, as a further limitation on study,
censorship increased tremendously, and restricting the use of the library
became 'a punitive weapon in the hands of the officials'.[77]

Sport and recreation

The prisoners were acutely aware of the need to protect their physical and mental health.[78] Sport was a key means of doing so. Steve Tshwete notes that 'Sport was very important on the Island. It relieved the tension and anxiety about family, about home and about survival in prison itself.'[79] Furthermore, although when sport was first authorised in 1967 there was some division on political lines, in general sport was a means of uniting people irrespective of ideology or affiliation.

Sport was also one of the areas in which people learned or shared organisational skills, and in which collective norms were established and put into practice. Over time a complex network of sports bodies emerged, with detailed constitutions governing the rules and organisation of sport. The extensive documentation of the sports (and other recreation) committees is indeed remarkable.[80] For example, the following excerpt from the 'Robben Island Political Prisoners Recreational and Cultural Committee' (hereafter referred to as the 'Recreational Committee') suggests the formality, careful thought and extensive work that went into its constitution. Section 9 (of a 16-section constitution) dealt with the Misconduct and Protest Committee.

> MISCONDUCT AND PROTEST COMMITTEE
> (a) To settle disputes arising within the Assoc[iation], there shall be set up a MPC of five (5) members elected at the Special General meeting for 1 year of office; 7 (a) [which dealt with meetings of the various levels of the Association] shall apply *mutatis mutandis*.
> (b) All matters of 'misconduct and protest' nature shall only be discussed by the MPC. Reports of misconduct and/or protest shall be submitted in writing to the secretary of the Assoc. who shall forward it to the MPC.
> (d) When a member(s) of the MPC is/are a party to the matter under jurisdiction, such member shall recuse himself ...
> (e) When the presence of the members of the MPC is considered by the MPC to be prejudicial to the interest of one of the parties concerned, such member(s) shall duly recuse himself ... [81]

Most of the minutes dealing with sports club administration were just as meticulous, whether the issues were apparently mundane or serious. It was not just the structure of the sports and recreation committees that was formal, but the very discourse in which the administration of sporting affairs took place. The rationale, it seems, was that if the prison authorities did not accord them the respect they deserved, the prisoners would at least respect each other, and ensure that sporting passions did not overwhelm decent behaviour. Thus, minutes and correspondence almost always referred to a community member as

MAFUBE — LAWN — TENNIS — UNION
ESTABLISHED 1973 A.D.

I. NAME

The name of the body shall be Mafube Lawn Tennis Union herein referred to as Mafube / Union "MALTU"

II. AIMS AND OBJECTS

(i) To organise and promote the game of Lawn Tennis among the inmates of Robben Island Prison

(ii) To interprete and teach the rules of Tennis.

(iii) To arrange friendly and competitive games among its affilliates and the inmates in general.

(iv) To organise and stage Variety and Exhibition matches among the inmates

(v) To engender and develop the sporting spirit among the inmates.

(vi) To pledge its allegiance to the SPORTS CO-ORDINATING COMMITTEE as the sole liason between the Union and the authorities on ALL matters pertaining to the Union

(vii) To elect a TENNIS PLAYER of the year and a SPORTSMAN of the year. The Sportsman of the year may be elected in conjunction with the other organised sports bodies.

III. OFFICE BEARERS.

(i) The Union shall elect an EXECUTIVE COMMITTEE, which shall be the SUPREME ADMINISTRATIVE ORGAN OF THE UNION.

(ii) The elected Executive Committee shall consist of FIVE (5) officials elected at the ANNUAL GENERAL MEETING. (A.G.M.)

(iii) Election into office shall be open to all members of the affilliate clubs on the bases of merit, competency, ability and enthusiasm.

(iv) Any incompetent member of the Union Executive Committee may be voted out of office by ⅔ majority of club delegates at a G.M.

(v) Under no circumstances shall Executive office be used, severally or jointly, to secure advantages of any individual or club.

(vi) The following offices shall be elected:

(a) PRESIDENT OR CHAIRMAN   (d) RECORDING SECRETARY

(b) VICE PRESIDENT OR VICE CHAIRMAN   (e) TRUSTEE

(c) ORGANIZING SECRETARY

(vii) This Executive shall be wholly responsible for its administrative duties to the GENERAL MEETING.

Constitution of prisoners' tennis union (Mayibuye Centre)

'Mr'. The following minutes of 6 February 1972 of the Ixhalanga Rugby
Football Club are emblematic.

> INFORMAL EXECUTIVE MEETING – 6th February, 1972
> Venue: Behind Cell 'E3' and 'C1'
> Time: Exercise time in the Morning.
> The Chairman declared the meeting open. The Executive was more
> concerned about the consequences of the friendly match staged by Egala
> RFC and our club. The unsportsmanlike and ungentlemanly conduct
> showed by some of our players was discussed. The names of Messrs A.
> Suze and Pole were mentioned. Mr. A. Suze left the field in the midst of
> the play without informing his captain. All the members of the
> Executive deprecate such unbecoming behavior, saying it was lowering
> the dignity of the Club. They felt a stern action should be taken against
> Mr. Suze's conduct in the field.
> Mr. Pole enlightened the Executive about the incident of his with Mr.
> Henge outside the field, where it was alleged that there was an exchange
> of words nearly accompanied by shots [sic]. He realised the mistake he
> committed and apologised.
> The Executive further discussed an incident which resulted to injury
> of Mr. Matsiliza who was playing a Full Back. They felt that a strongly
> worded letter should be addressed to Gqala RFC enlightening them
> about the disappointment our Club found itself in because they never
> expected such rough play in the field. But on second thought they felt
> that they should await for a letter of apology from Gqala.
> The captain Mr. Ndibi called, gave a report about the match. He was
> also greatly concerned about Messrs Suze and Pole's conduct in the
> field. He said he found them on certain occasions addressing the refer-
> ee without his knowledge.
> Mr. Suze called because he wanted to have an interview with the
> Executive. He told the Executive that he had come to a decision that he
> was no longer to play but to remain just as a member of the Club. The
> reason was that he found Rugby not suitable for his liking. He time and
> again quarrelled and that was something he did not like. He mentioned
> his quarrel with Mr. Masuku in the cell. The Executive found it could
> not discuss the matter but only to take it to the Council. The chairman
> declared the meeting closed.[82]

The records of the sporting and recreation committees are one of the few
ways one can have access to the prisoner community's perception of life on the
Island at the time. Unlike interviews or prison memoirs, these records were
produced on the Island in the course of daily life, for the use of the prisoners

themselves, not for an outside audience. One of the most interesting and important things that emerge in the documentation is the concern with the vulnerability of the community, either in itself or in terms of the state of sport. Thus the chairman of the Makana Football Association (MFA) of the time, John M. Ramoshaba, raised various issues of concern to the MFA annual general meeting.

> (1) The mental, moral, spiritual stability of the inmates is not regarded or seen by others as depending on strong and healthy bodies, and good relations between persons and groups.
> (2) The will to play is dead in many of the inmates.
> (3) Soccer is being dealt a blow because many soccerites [*sic*] and fans either live in the past of the Island soccer or a future of soccer far removed into the future away from the Island. The present as far as they are concerned is either of no account or nonexistent.
> (4) Any organised group performs better and more harmoniously, if the procedural aspect of its affairs is strictly adhered to. Random and loose handling of affairs can never be a blessing.
> (5) Discipline has plainly become painful to others. Thus any irregularities in behaviour displayed by any member of any football club on the field of play or off it or any disregard to apply discipline by any responsible body connected with soccer, manifests in all starkness the unmerciful blows dealt such a healthy, attractive and beloved game: 'soccer'.[83]

What comes across in the hundreds of sports club minutes and letters is the fragility of the community – how easily tempers flared, how important sport (as well as other forms of recreation, including culture) was in maintaining morale and relieving tension, and yet how difficult it often was to maintain sporting standards, both in the administration and in the games themselves.

Former Islanders often speak of the positive things that were gained from their years on the Island: the community that was forged, the lessons learnt, and the personal and organisational growth experienced. Bam, for example, has said he did not regret the experience, and Dennis Brutus writes: 'It is not all terror/ and deprivation,/ you know;/ one comes to welcome the closer contact/ and understanding one achieves/ with one's fellow men,/ fellows, compeers'.[84] Especially in regard to the period after the early 1960s, one may be misled into understating the enormous difficulty prisoners faced of keeping any semblance of normality in their psyches. The determination with which prisoners forged meaning in their lives in prison was a remarkable act of resistance, a refusal to let the state destroy their minds, bodies or souls.

The world of sport and cultural life on Robben Island cannot be separated from other spheres of prison life. This was especially true of the organisational training that the recreation arena provided. Michael Kahla, in his Chairman's annual report to the Prisoners' Record Club of 30 August 1974, writes of the challenge that faced him and his committee; he was the only member left of the first executive.

> Gentlemen ...
> On our assumption of office we were faced forthwith with the task of having to organise and overhaul this club – to endeavour to serve you to the best of our ability – to satisfy that diversity of tastes in this most abstract of all the arts – music. To show that this is no mean task we were flooded with a barrage of complaints, suggestions and requests. We welcomed all these, and interpreted them as a sign of life – the beginning of an education in Music.

The annual report that follows outlined the tasks, difficulties and challenges that developed: disagreement among the prisoners as to the process for choosing and playing records, the warders' obstruction of their procedures, and concern about protecting and enlarging the record collection. Whatever the pressures he and his team were under, Kahla apparently felt he had gained more than lost in his community service. He ended his report with the following comment: 'Finally, I wish to express my deepest gratitude to you all for having conferred this office upon me. You have given me a schooling in administration, patience and understanding that no formal school could have given. I thank you all.'[85] Indeed, this is the general impression one has in reading these documents; that the recreation and sporting committees were an invaluable tool for teaching new, or honing old, organisational skills. As such, they contributed to the quality of life within prison, and the preparation for life outside prison, by developing individuals and their organisations.

Before exploring the overtly political dimension of life on the Island, we need to underscore the fact that resistance to overt abuse and resistance to the more insidious boredom, depression or monotony of prison life were inextricably linked. In calling for a recognition that the Island should not be recorded simply as a site of oppression and persecution, but as the site of a multidimensional resistance, we should not lose sight as well of the repression and oppression, the pain and the torment. Natoo Babenia describes his reaction to the abuse suffered in the episode at the quarry, quoted above.

> As we dashed around 'Zed' gasps to me, 'Natoo, they are going to kill us!' I had tears in my eyes and was limping with only one sandal. Riot, just behind me, was also crying. It was such a quick glimpse into tragedy and three comrades' honest sharing of emotions, but next moment we heard Piet [Kleynhans, the warder] shouting, 'Wat doen daai twee

koelies daar?' [What are those Coolies doing?] Quickly we took up our wheelbarrows and went our separate lonely ways.[86]

Vulnerability such as this makes it clear that the political struggle also had profound personal and human costs, effects and implications.

FURTHERING THE AIMS OF BANNED ORGANISATIONS

There is probably no greater form of resistance for a political prisoner than to continue political organisation and political struggle while imprisoned or as a result of imprisonment. This was a prime achievement of the Robben Islanders,[87] and it was effected in a number of arenas and through a number of methods. A primary means of continuing political resistance was through political organisation and affiliation to movements and organisations. Crucial to this endeavour was the illegal collection and dissemination of news. Another important factor was the structures and processes that mediated relations between political movements. Finally, struggle was extended through explicit and implicit training and preparation for continuing political activism upon release.

Organisations and structures

Political organisation on Robben Island was of course influenced by the national context from which the prisoners had come and by the state and history of the political movements in the country at large. At least three factors affected the differences between the ANC and the PAC as regards organisation on the Island. First, the ANC was a far better established body, whereas the PAC had only been created in 1959. There was therefore a greater fluidity in the PAC's composition, which was perhaps most apparent in the fact that the Poqo movement to some extent saw itself as part of the PAC, and vice versa. Secondly, the ANC set up its armed wing, uMkhonto weSizwe, with relative speed, and it had a growing (if uneven) military impact, especially from the late 1970s. It proved a point of organisational reference and pride within prison and increasingly within South Africa, especially in the wake of the 1976 uprising. In contrast, the PAC's armed wing, the Azanian People's Liberation Army, was slow in being established, and then was fraught with internal conflict and desertion at least until the early 1980s.

Lastly, the ANC had the very dubious advantage (at least as far as Robben Island politics was concerned) of having most of its national leadership imprisoned together, and for life sentences. In contrast, the PAC on the Island was often wracked by divisions that developed as prisoners aligned themselves with various regional leaders: a national leader like Zeph Mothopeng was on the Island for a relatively short period only. Perhaps, too, the involvement of the state in 'creating' or furthering leadership played a role: long-term PAC prisoners like Johnson Mlambo were kept in the general sections rather than in the single-cell section generally considered for 'leadership'.

The most senior structure of the ANC on Robben Island was the High Organ. This was initially composed of the four prisoners who had been members of the ANC National Executive Committee at the time the ANC was banned; these were Nelson Mandela, Walter Sisulu, Raymond Mhlaba and Govan Mbeki. From time to time they co-opted others on to the committee, such as Ahmed Kathrada.[88] Within the general sections of the prison, the ANC soon organised around the Disciplinary Committee, or DC.

> Right from the beginning we had what was called a Disciplinary Committee. Until the ANC leadership arrived, the 'DC' was the top ANC body on the Island. They were appointed by a senior ANC comrade. In the early days there were five on the 'DC': Curnick [Ndlovu], Billy [Nair], Phillip Matthews, [Andrew] Masondo and Jeremiah Francis.[89]

The role of the DC was to monitor and mediate the potential and actual tensions amongst the men, both within and between organisations.

> The 'DC' would meet regularly and discuss various things amongst themselves, like the conditions, the attitude of the PAC towards us and, say, food. And, very importantly, if something happened in one of the cells, like if two chaps fought, it would go to the 'DC'. The 'DC' would resolve the issue and reprimand the fellows. Times were hard and people would easily lose their tempers, often over the most small, inconsequential matters.[90]

By the mid-1960s, these structures had been enlarged. A new position of Public Relations Officer was instituted, as well as group leaders in each of the four sections of a prison cell. Below this were smaller organisational cells[91] of about four people per group. In turn, each cell would have a leader who would liaise with other cell leaders in the group, and the group leader would interact with other group leaders, combining with them to form a committee.[92] There were also organisational cells amongst the single-cell prisoners.[93]

Of course all this political activity violated the prison rules, and therefore had to be kept as secret as possible. This was one of the reasons why groups were small; 'if the warders found you meeting in big groups, which was very difficult anyway during those early years, the warders would accuse you of having a political meeting. You lose three meals.'[94] Long-term punishments for political activity were also used. Curnick Ndlovu noted that communication

between sections and especially with leaders in the single cells was essential
but dangerous. People would be 'victimised in such a way that if they catch
you with any document then your studies are going to be taken away for the
whole year ... They would even cancel when your exam papers are there.'[95]
Apart from being monitored by the warders, the political prisoners were also
spied upon by some of the common-law prisoners, as well as by informers
from within the political community. 'There are informers on Robben Island
too,' notes Alexander, 'men who for diverse reasons have left their organisations (or been expelled) and are collaborating with the authorities.'[96] The
security police also monitored the prison – in the case of Mac Maharaj, going

Nelson Mandela and Walter Sisulu, photographed in 1966 in Robben Island
Prison (Mayibuye Centre)

Raymond Mhlaba (right) and Govan Mbeki (below), members of the ANC's High Organ on Robben Island (Mayibuye Centre)

through his letters and listening in on his visitors in an attempt to identify secret messages.[97]

According to Johnson Mlambo, the PAC did not really have a structure on Robben Island in the early 1960s.[98] Mlambo explains this as a consequence of the presence of competing regional leaders from around the country that came into the prison. But with time there was a push towards centralised and common leadership. This was helped enormously with the arrival of Zephania Mothopeng in mid-1964. Soon after his arrival, however, he was removed to the single-cell section, which again limited the unifying influence he might have. This was further reduced when he was transferred from the Island a year later. In turn John Nyati Pokela, also a national PAC leader, was imprisoned on the Island in 1967. According to Mlambo, he too played an important role in developing the PAC on the Island, especially in the area of political education, although he was in the single cells. By the early or mid-1970s, 'we had a committee in charge of the PAC in the main section and that committee functioned of course under the leadership of Pokela. He was in the single cells but the committee was in the main section.'[99] The committee in the main section – which had different names at various times, including 'administrative committee' and 'coordinating committee' – was made up of about five people, who were elected to that position. Furthermore, PAC members within prison cells would have a representative who was the link between their cell and members in other cells.

At times, PAC unity was achieved at considerable cost. It was a widely accepted article of the political prisoners' code of conduct that prisoners should not benefit themselves at the expense of comrades or at the expense of organisational unity. There were, however, certain political prisoners who worked with criminal prisoners to smuggle food, which meant that there was less food for the political community as a whole. This of course led to divisions, and also worked against PAC and ANC unity vis-à-vis the authorities. 'Us politicos felt that smuggling was bad. For when you smuggled, or as others would have it, stole from the kitchen, you were taking food away from your comrades.'[100] The problem of smuggling appeared to be greater among certain PAC followers (and the non-political prisoners), and therefore had to be tackled by that organisation. This was to cost Johnson Mlambo his eye, as he elaborates:

> In 1967 ... we took this particular stand within the PAC that we are going to try and stop people receiving special treatment and the like. Because they are humiliating us, and it is in our interests to stop this ... In the process of trying to stop ... that, we discovered someone had received some special dish and we were trying to take it away and dump that food in the toilet. Whilst we were struggling to get that dish away

from him, he, together with a few who went along with that, actually put ... his finger into my eye socket and that is how I lost my eye.[101]

The problem and practice of smuggling food only really ended, however, when the political prisoners finally won their struggle to have fellow politicals rather than criminals prepare their food. This happened in the mid-1970s.

Internal divisions were not unique to the PAC. The ANC had divisions too. Some of these reflected long-standing ideological tensions within the ANC, such as those between 'nationalists' and 'communists'. Another source of tension was between leaders and the more mass-based membership, a form of tension in this case exacerbated by the limitations prison imposed on communication. 'There was the possibility of democracy in all of these structures. But there was also the chance for top-down telephones. Sometimes we would talk back to the leadership and tell them they are talking nonsense. Or it could work the other way around.'[102]

Perhaps the disagreement that had the potential of being most dangerous to the ANC was that between Nelson Mandela and Govan Mbeki. The primary or at least initial reason for the conflict was over the question whether it was acceptable for the ANC to support participation in apartheid structures as a strategic measure. Nelson Mandela (with Walter Sisulu) believed the question should be debated with an open mind to participation. Govan Mbeki (with Raymond Mhlaba), on the other hand, militantly opposed any reconsideration of the 1962 ANC Lobatsi Conference resolution that called for a boycott of apartheid institutions. Not surprisingly, other accusations and further acrimony developed out of this disagreement. André Odendaal writes:

> Mandela and Mbeki represented 'polar opposites in attitudes and opinions', according to the memorandum which was sent from Robben Island to the movement in exile. The personality clash and political impasse between them lasted for several years, 'at times reaching extreme tension and bitterness'. Allegations abounded, including one that some members were abandoning the armed struggle and another that some were fomenting racial discrimination. Mandela's status as the most senior ANC leader on the island was also called into question.[103]

The long period of crisis, from the late 1960s to the mid-1970s, was eventually resolved when new members were included in the High Organ. Various other suggestions and measures, such as criticism of the men at the heart of the conflict, the reinstatement of the four men on to the High Organ, and a reaffirmation of Mandela's leadership, also helped to bring the crisis to an end.

News and political education

Whatever the organisational differences that existed, political education was a concern shared across the political spectrum in prison. Indeed, while academic education is considered to have been important, political education lies at the heart of ex-Islanders' reflections on their incarceration and of the identification of the Island as 'university'. Thami Mkhwanazi, for example, wrote that 'I had first heard the Island described as the University of Revolutionary Politics by a security policeman during my interrogation. He said I had been caught because I was an amateur – and soon I would be sent to "the university."'[104] Political education was understood broadly to include news analysis, seminars, research, debate and discussion about politics. Furthermore, living on Robben Island was itself a form of political education because every action was self-consciously considered in political terms.

The precise structure of political education varied from time to time, from section to section, and according to organisational affiliation. In general, the education committee of an organisation decided upon the content and implementation of political education. Jacob Zuma describes his experience:

> A group of us who came from Durban [had been involved in political education there] ... SACTU [the South African Congress of Trade Unions] in particular developed a culture here in Durban of political education which we called labour theory discussions ... About five of us who had attended those political discussions here [in Durban] found ourselves on Robben Island ... and felt we needed to have some political discussions among ourselves [on the Island] to revise what we used to discuss [before prison]. We ... began ... political lectures for everybody during lunch-time, which was an hour, we used that [time] to revise and discuss if there were news items ... So when we were joined by particularly Comrade Stephen Dlamini, who was our leader, [and] Harry Gwala ... [who] was actually our political instructor outside ... we started having discussions with them every day at lunch-time and we were gradually joined by other people, whoever was interested. Revising political lectures or discussions that we'd had over the weekend, analysing news items, discussing about labour theory in particular and enriching our knowledge, that became in fact the nucleus of the culture on Robben Island, the culture of political education.[105]

From a PAC perspective, Mlambo has noted:

> But there were many things we also learnt. Some of us were totally inexperienced and we learnt a little more from some of our leaders ... Uncle Zeph [Zephania Mothopeng], who was the second president of the

Zephania Mothopeng, PAC
leader on Robben Island
(Mayibuye Centre)

PAC, after Sobukwe ... was always bombarded with questions. 'What were we going to do with the Europeans when we were free?'[106] That question was a perennial one. He would give a talk enlightening us on this or that aspect – and, by the way, it was illegal to even have those political discussions. You would be charged for holding meetings ... [107]

One important source of information was the leaders. The political writings of people such as Sisulu, Nair and Mbeki were circulated (illegally) in the prison for use by the inmate community.[108] Leaders were also looked to, to provide information that was otherwise unavailable:

When I arrived in the single cells section, ANC members were discussing the history of the ANC. Needless to say we had no written guides, but Comrade Walter Sisulu, who led the discussions, was a walking history of the organisation. Comrade Walter's memory was phenomenal. Not only did he remember events, and the names associated with them, but also the circumstances under which they occurred.

Political discussion was prohibited on Robben Island: it flourished notwithstanding.

After the history of the ANC, which took a vast period because of its richness and the complexity of its evolution, other topics were tackled: nationalism, Marxist theories, and current national and international

topics. Consensus was never the object in discussions of a general political nature. The aim was to learn from each other. [109]

An important part of political education was the need to apply party principles and ideology to the world of political activity outside. To do that, prisoners needed to follow national and international news. But this was entirely
forbidden. So a fundamental aspect of resistance became the struggle to get
news. Formal representation was consistently made to the prison authorities
and visitors like the International Committee of the Red Cross and Helen
Suzman for the right of prisoners to read newspapers. On a day-to-day basis,
however, the real struggle lay in obtaining news by an array of illicit means.[110]
At times the struggle for news was a source of competition and even antagonism between the liberation movements, but more often there was cooperation
between them on sharing the news that had been obtained.

Inter-organisational relations
One of the remarkable achievements of the men imprisoned on Robben
Island was that there developed, with some notable exceptions,[111] a high
degree of cross-organisational solidarity and unity in terms of attitude towards
the authorities, and in establishing a shared set of mores and rules to govern
life on the Island. Experience of gangs in common-law prisons and among the
common-law prisoners on Robben Island made it very clear that in the
absence of unity vis-à-vis the common enemy, the state and the prison authorities would quickly use a divide and rule strategy.[112]
While relations between organisations had ebbs and flows, it does appear
that there was generally a high level of cooperation, especially with respect to
the state. Unity was always a particular imperative in protest action like
hunger strikes. In cases like these, representatives of organisations from the
general sections would consult each other to reach agreement on the appropriate course of action.
The relations between organisations in the single cells were more formal.
Helen Suzman notes that Nelson Mandela was chosen to represent the prisoners in the single cells, despite their different affiliations. 'Neville Alexander
said, "Don't waste time speaking to us, go to the end and speak to Mandela,"
which I did.'[113] Fikile Bam speaks of being 'particularly flattered when I was
chosen as the first chairman of the Prisoners' Committee in our section at a
time when the groups [political organisations] were really difficult to deal
with.'[114] In time, that committee evolved into Ulundi, a formal committee on
which each organisation in the single cells had a representative: the ANC, the
PAC, the Liberal Party (represented by Eddie Daniels), SWAPO (represented
by Toivo ya Toivo), the NLF/NEUM group, and later APDUSA. According to
Sonny Venkatrathnam, Nelson Mandela chaired this committee for many

years, and as such represented the community to visitors from the International Committee of the Red Cross. Then, with Venkatrathnam's own removal to the single cells as a member of APDUSA, and the arrival of the first Black Consciousness members on the Island and within single cells, a 'kind of alliance' was formed, and he now became chairperson of Ulundi. 'And I said, "What, is Nelson going to serve under me?" ... There was a lot of power ... in the sense that you were the spokesperson. You had to meet with the prison department and the visitors ... And a number of things happened during this time because of this change. The ANC were getting jittery about their position there.'[115]

Notwithstanding his criticism of certain political practices on the Island, Venkatrathnam has also emphasised the human dimension of personal friendship, solidarity and mutual care. 'Despite the kind of alliance that was formed [between various groups in opposition to ANC control], the relationship between individuals on the Island did not change. My closest associates in the single cells were ANC people.' Furthermore, there was an equality between the prisoners that no doubt did much to underscore the camaraderie.

> One thing I experienced on Robben Island was the spirit of camaraderie, [a] tremendous spirit of camaraderie. This is one of the greatest things about Robben Island that I still think of fondly, is that when you are depressed, people will realise it quickly and come and try and knock you out of this feeling. If you are ill they will hang around you, even clean you ... We could talk to anybody as equals. That was the other great thing [on the Island]. Whether it was Nelson or any of the young chaps, there was no position [of inequality] in the single cells at least. Everybody was treated equally. Even in terms of work – you know we organised our own work schedule – if it is this group's turn to wash the toilets [everyone from] Nelson to the youngest guys will join in and help do it. The point is there was always absolute equality in terms of where prison life was concerned. In terms of organisation it was another matter. In the organisation was leadership ... but as prisoners it was absolute ... I have never experienced such camaraderie [as I did on the Island] in all my life, and you cannot possibly get it outside prison.[116]

Whatever the formal status of the relations between organisations, personal friendships often blossomed between members of different movements. One of the ways prisoners reduced ideological antagonism was to steer clear of discussions that would bring up political differences. Prisoners would generally avoid discussing ideological questions with those of another group, and maintain an attitude of tolerance for all perspectives.

Most of the people on the Island, and in the single cells at least, don't enter into ideological debates. I would not openly stand and start criticising, running down the ANC. I know you are with the ANC, and we accept one another's position on the basis that you are not going to change me, and I am not going to change you. But other issues we will debate, and if part of our logical standpoints don't convert we will argue and discuss, and we will not allow intolerance ... We could talk to anybody as equals.[117]

CONTRIBUTION TO NATIONAL RESISTANCE AND RENEWAL

Robben Island represented an important site of continued resistance, organisation and defiance in South Africa during the period 1963–1976. This was a time (so it is generally felt) when there was relatively little opposition and a pervasive fear, even terror, that undermined organised opposition to National Party tyranny. There was of course some resistance inside the country, and many of its agents and products were to land up on the Island because of their opposition. These included James April, who in 1971 was arrested after infiltrating South Africa,[118] and nine members of the South African Students' Organisation, who were tried and convicted for their Black Consciousness convictions. But, in general, there is no doubt that political fear was pervasive and a sense of oppression gripped black South Africa. Saki Macozoma, for example, has commented that although the Eastern Cape in general, and Port Elizabeth in particular, had a reputation for being at the heart of anti-apartheid resistance, this was not his experience.

This may surprise many of you here as it goes against popular myth [but] ... the Port Elizabeth I grew up in the late sixties and early seventies was very apathetic politically. Port Elizabeth's townships had suffered so much from the repression of the early sixties that people would not even speak about the struggles of that period, [although] in fact people from this area constituted a majority on the Island.[119]

The first act of resistance the Islanders engaged in was to challenge the horrendous conditions of their existence. They took the enormous risk of publicly challenging the prison authorities, through a variety of actions, the most extreme of which were hunger strikes. They challenged the right of warders to be called *baas*, the right of the state to mete out arbitrary 'justice', and to treat them in a subhuman manner through providing inadequate food, medical care and clothing, and infrequent contact with their families.

In themselves, these protests and challenges to the system were far-reaching. They challenged power relations from the prisoners' position of extreme vulnerability, and achieved tangible and measurable improvements to their lives. Moreover, these achievements – the establishment of a minimum baseline of behaviour which it was dangerous for the authorities to transgress – allowed the prisoners to concentrate on using their imprisonment as productively as possible.

The second area where prisoners created a sense of victory was in the development of people both as persons and as political beings. While most prisoners seem to emphasise in retrospect their overt political training through political education, the prison experience in general contributed to the growth and sophistication of people and movements. For example, the sophisticated and complex society and culture that the prisoners developed taught them about administration, dealing with those they disagreed with, mutual support, and overt political and organisational development. When Jacob Zuma was asked in an interview whether it was perhaps axiomatic that leaders should emerge out of Robben Island, because it was leaders that had gone to the Island prison, he was quick to disagree, and in so doing provided what might be described as a curriculum vitae of his own years in prison:

> If I take my own example, when I went to Robben Island I was an ordinary young cadre ... I hadn't been a commander before, I hadn't been anything. I began to work in the smallest unit in the ANC [on the Island], as a member of the group and I was changed from one group to the other. I then at one point became identified to collect news for the cell, because we had a system where collectively we collect news and come and disseminate the news ... You would keep [the news] in your head because we were not allowed to write down anything ... At one time I was appointed a group leader, which was different than me serving as a group member ... Once you are a group leader you actually attend cell leadership meetings of all the groups. In other words you are now at the cell leadership collective grouping. At another point I was ... the public relations person in the cell ... At times we'd be asked to prepare a lecture ... By the time I left Robben Island I was the chairman of the political committee that was responsible for disseminating political lectures throughout the prison.[120]

As well as developing individuals, a third function of political resistance was to develop organisations. On the one hand, prison provided long periods of time for people to consider past strategies and tactics, and re-evaluate their organisation's thinking and practices. 'Because of the time [in prison] I had to reflect on the mistakes made in the early sixties, that is why I couldn't be arrested for a second time ... because I so understood them, I could predict their thinking wherever I'd be.'[121] Newer members and supporters were able to learn their organisation's and country's history, often a time-consuming luxury for those outside prison in the heat of political struggle or under repressive conditions. On the other hand, internal differences, whether based on ideology or personality, had to be overcome so as to prevent the state from abusing divisions within or between organisations. Perhaps this was less important for the ANC, which had managed to remain a fairly strong organisation despite pulls in different directions over the years. But the PAC had greater divisions and certainly seems to have fared better on Robben Island than in exile. On Robben Island it united, or at least its members found common cause. Many of its current leaders are Robben Island veterans and graduates. Robben Islanders were also vital in the work of rejuvenating the organisation in exile. Tom Lodge notes:

> During the 1970s the PAC had virtually fallen apart due to conflict among its leaders. In 1980 John Pokela, one of the PAC's founders, was released after being imprisoned for twenty years on Robben Island ... [I]n 1981 he was elected president of the exiled PAC ... During the early 1980s, Pokela managed to bring back into the fold some of the dissident factions that had been alienated by the erratic behaviour of previous leaders ... Pokela died in June 1985, and his mantle was assumed by another long-term Robben Islander, Johnson Mlambo. In 1989 ... Mlambo retained the executive functions of chairperson, and another recently released veteran, ... Zephania Mothopeng, became PAC president. After Mlambo became PAC president in 1985, the APLA [Azanian People's Liberation Army] began to launch guerrilla operations ... [122]

Closely related to the role the Islanders played in maintaining and developing organisations was their part in keeping the otherwise banned organisations alive inside the country, albeit mostly behind prison walls. For nearly thirty years, the only place in South Africa where the ANC and PAC could remain intact was on Robben Island. On the Island the liberation movements were organised as the ANC and as the PAC, an achievement which should not be underestimated. They discussed ideology and policy, educated their membership, cultivated leadership, and recruited new members.[123] While exiles would, unbeknown to themselves, have to wait till the 1990s to return to the country, most prisoners did contemplate a time when their sentences would end and they could reinsert themselves politically into South African society. In saying this, one should not understate or underestimate the weight of repression that faced former Islanders, and the incredible odds that worked against their continued political activism. But in fact many former Islanders did continue their

The entrance gate to Robben Island Prison (Mayibuye Centre)

work inside the country on release, although usually under enormous secrecy.

In this work inside the country, as well as in the struggles behind prison walls, the Robben Islanders laid the foundations for the next generation. The changes and improvements won by the prisoner struggles of the sixties and early seventies allowed the post-1976 generation of prisoners to emphasise politics from the start rather than begin their terms of sentence fighting for survival. Indeed, so much had the conditions improved, that the newcomers were often contemptuous of the older men, who they felt were submissive to authority.

Within the country, former Islanders were severely restricted by bannings, banishment orders, surveillance, and threats. They could seldom therefore act as visible beacons of the continuation of resistance politics, especially in the pre-1976 period. But they nevertheless found ways of being reference points for the youth, who took over much of the struggle in the 1970s. Jacob Zuma, with the help of Harry Gwala and others, reinvigorated the Natal ANC underground. Similarly, Martin Ramokgadi ran the Greater Johannesburg ANC underground in the mid-1970s, along with people like Joe Gqabi, who did much to recruit the disenchanted youth of the 1970s into uMkhonto weSizwe and the ANC. Nor was this confined to the major centres of the country. Peter Nchabaleng organised first of all the ANC underground and then the United Democratic Front in the northern Transvaal, and there are countless accounts of people who continued various forms of legal or underground political work in the Eastern Cape. The PAC, too, relied on former Islanders to maintain or rejuvenate their organisation and the spirit and practice of resistance. Simon Ramogale, a PAC member imprisoned on the Island in the 1960s, describes helping young Black Consciousness members in the early 1970s. Walter Tshikila, who had previously been on the Island for six years as a PAC member, was found guilty in 1977 in Grahamstown of being a PAC member, inciting people to leave the country for military training, and giving lectures on the PAC, and was sentenced to a further 13 years' imprisonment.[124]

Perhaps the most powerful set of evidence about the role of former prisoners was the number of Robben Islanders who served a second sentence in that prison, having continued their underground work upon their initial release. Indeed, not only was that the case with the PAC Bethal Trial of 1978–9, but the four former Robben Islanders involved – Zephania Mothopeng, Mark Shinners, Hamilton Keke, and John Ganya – were also charged with furthering the PAC while on the Island in the 1960s and early 1970s! Regarding Mothopeng, Lodge writes:

> Mothopeng was arrested again in August 1976 and endured, at the age of sixty-six, sixteen months of solitary confinement. A lengthy trial [the Bethal Trial] subsequently revealed his almost single-handed efforts to

resurrect the PAC as a political force in South Africa. Setting up a co-ordinating committee in Johannesburg, Mothopeng was able to bring within its ambit a string of youth and other associations that had been formed in the wake of the black consciousness movement. He made contact with the PAC in Swaziland and set up a recruitment pro-gramme. In 1978 he was sentenced to fifteen years under the Terrorism Act.[125]

Two major ANC trials also reflected the work of the Robben Islanders. One was known as the Joe Gqabi (or Pretoria Twelve) Trial of 1977–8, and while trialists Gqabi and Nchabaleng were both acquitted (and later killed), Martin Ramokgadi, a fellow Island veteran, was sent back for a second term. The other major trial took place in Pietermaritzburg in 1977: Harry Gwala and Msomi Matthews Meyiwa were again convicted and returned to Robben Island. There were other, smaller trials of Robben Islanders who had been caught continuing the struggle, and frequently it was their former fellow Island prisoners who were forced to give evidence, though many refused.

The Islanders' resistance also fulfilled another function, of facilitating cross-generational communication between different age-sets of activists who were thrown into prison. At times relationships could be tense, especially in the post-1976 period, but generally the prisoners worked to understand each other and build their organisations from the perspective of different genera-tions. This meant, *inter alia*, that former prisoners leaving the Island to resume activism would carry with them the knowledge and insights of multiple peri-ods of struggle, as well as the ideology and histories of the outlawed organi-sations.

CONCLUSION

This chapter has attempted to show that not only did the use of Robben Island as a political prison continue the Island's long history as a site of repression, but it also continued its role as a site of resistance. Moreover, I have argued that resistance was found in many forms, often with far-reaching conse-quences, that affected not only the life chances of the men in the prison, but also the life chances of the anti-apartheid struggle outside the prison. From demanding to be treated as human beings, to academic and political educa-tion, to developing mandates for prisoners returning to the struggle outside, Islander resistance shaped the history of the prison, as well as influencing national history. Survival and growth of the prisoners and their organisations on the Island thus defeated the government's aim of destroying opposition to apartheid. Dingake's comment on his release from Robben Island is an appro-priate conclusion:

I had done well in gaol, if one can do well there. I was leaving Robben Island in one piece, unbroken in spirit and flesh. Not only could I boast a PG (Prison Graduate), I could boast three academic degrees obtained through correspondence with the University of South Africa. During my 15 years, I had served our prison community through a variety of committees.

I also served in all the underground structures of the ANC, from the committee responsible for drawing the organisation's study programme to the highest committee entrusted with day-to-day administration and organisational discipline in the section.

I had lived a full life in a 'basement' devoid of natural life.[126]

Most Robben Islanders insist that they and their organisations were able to find some way to benefit from imprisonment or at least minimise the negative effects of incarceration.[127] This did not mean there were no lasting ill-effects of imprisonment, for individuals or the polity. Furthermore, Robben Islanders would face new challenges as well as a continuation of existing conditions in the post-1976 era, which brought with it a more complex and contested political terrain.

How Best to Resist?
Robben Island after 1976

Fran Buntman

> I was particularly shocked when I realised that here is a ... [young man]
> coming from Port Elizabeth and the young man was born after I had
> been on Robben Island for more than a year. And here is this young man
> coming to serve his sentence ... I realised that the intervening period has
> been long enough to have someone born, grow up and to come and
> serve his own sentence on Robben Island ... It gave me ... a very, very
> great shock.
> —Johnson Mlambo, PAC member, who spent most of his twenty-year
> sentence on Robben Island

Despite the prison's isolation, the revitalisation of anti-apartheid politics in the
wake of the Soweto uprising was felt on Robben Island, not least because
waves of new, mainly young prisoners were sent to the Island prison after June
1976.* As a consequence of their arrival the years between 1977 and 1980
were marked by considerable conflict among political prisoners. While there
were ideological and strategic disagreements that developed within and
between organisations, the differences based on generational perspectives were
also an important reason for conflict. Ultimately, however, as in the pre-1977
period,[1] these generational conflicts were successfully mediated, to the point
where a large degree of convergence was achieved and agreement was reached
about how to conduct the struggle in prison and upon release.

Arguably, at the heart of the dissension among prisoners over the appropriate ways to conduct themselves in prison lay a debate about resistance: what
actions constituted resistance, what criteria should be used to assess the effec-
tiveness of resistance, and what were the most effective means of resistance?
Two different strategies to deal with imprisonment can be identified: resistance
as a point of political principle (or categorical resistance), and resistance as a
means towards the end of *realpolitik*[2] (or strategic resistance). Categorical
resistance is defined in direct relation to the enemy; it is concerned with negat-
ing the enemy's attempts to affect or influence political prisoner behaviour.
Strategic resistance, on the other hand, is defined more as a response to the

system and structure being challenged. While strategic resistance became the predominant strategy of resistance on Robben Island in the period under discussion, categorical resistance continued to play a vital role in informing debates about, and options for, individual and collective resistance.

POLITICAL CONTEXT

On 16 June 1976 about 15,000 schoolchildren in Soweto left their schools to march down the streets of the township and protest against a recent government edict that they be taught certain subjects in Afrikaans.[3] They met the might of the apartheid state in the form of over-zealous policemen who began shooting at them. Their protest and the state's response 'broke the fear'[4] that had gripped the country since the political repression of the 1960s. In the wake of 16 June, the country was engulfed for months by waves of sympathetic protest action around South Africa and by continued police brutality. 'At least 150 lives were lost during the first week of the Soweto uprising, most of them black schoolchildren and most of them shot by police. By October the following year a total of 700 [people] had died in disturbances arising out of … apartheid grievances. Over ninety per cent of the dead were less than twenty-three years old.'[5] With the wisdom of hindsight, one can see that the 1976 uprising was a turning point in the long journey to the end of apartheid. One of the paths to political liberation ran via Robben Island prison.

The activism of 16 June had not occurred in a vacuum. Most opposition to apartheid had been crushed in the early 1960s by 'the suppression of the nationalist movements and the imprisonment, banning or exile of an entire generation of politicians and trade unionists'.[6] From the late 1960s, however, the outlines of future resistance were being sketched, with the emergence of Black Consciousness (BC) organisations on black university campuses and in a wave of strikes in 1973 in the industrial port city of Durban. At the same time, two buttresses of apartheid were undermined: the South African economy began to show signs of crisis after 1972, and in 1975 Mozambique gained its independence from Portugal. The coup in Portugal in April 1974, which 'brought within reach a transition of power in Mozambique',[7] proved to be especially important, at least in the short term, for much of the leadership of the BC-aligned South African Students' Organisation (SASO). SASO and its ally, the Black People's Convention, organised a rally to honour Frelimo (the Front for the Liberation of Mozambique). This was banned by the government, and nine SASO and BPC leaders – Saths Cooper, Zithulele Cindi, Mosiuoa 'Terror' Lekota, Aubrey Mokoape, Strini Moodley, Muntu Myeza, Pandelani Nefolovhodwe, Nkwenkwe Nkomo and Kaborane Sedibe – were subsequently charged, convicted and sent to Robben Island.

These men, and the Black Consciousness Movement (BCM) which they represented, had already begun to have a significant influence on black South African politics, especially among younger, more educated and urban black people. Certainly, the rhetoric and some of the substance of psychological and self-liberation that formed part of the core message of Black Consciousness were influential in the Soweto and subsequent uprisings.[8] The various youth and school organisations of the time, such as the South African Students' Movement (SASM), the Soweto Students' Representative Council (SSRC) and the National Youth Organisation (NAYO), as well as the mass of students who participated in the rebellions,[9] tended to identify with Black Consciousness ideas and sometimes with Black Consciousness organisations.[10] When the young men who had participated in the uprising arrived on Robben Island, they usually came identifying themselves with the Black Consciousness Movement.

OVERVIEW OF 1977–1990

Prison conditions

Conditions in the prison had largely improved by 1977, and they were to improve further in the next decade, albeit unevenly. A new head of the prison, Captain John Harding, was appointed in November 1977, bringing with him what was, for the most part, a more relaxed attitude to his charges.[11] Hard labour in the quarries was brought to an end in 1977. In 1978, the authorities began to pipe pre-recorded and censored radio news to the inmates,[12] and in 1980 one of the most hard-fought prisoner struggles was won when 'A'-class prisoners were allowed to read newspapers, though these were often censored – once again, evidence of the 'zig-zag' nature of prison reform. Increased access to news and media was gained when television was introduced in December 1986. About ten years after prisoners were allowed to sleep on beds rather than on the concrete floors, sheets were first given out in 1986.[13]

The uneven nature of improvements is indicated by two examples from this period. Tertiary-level studies were banned in 1977, and that ban was only rescinded in 1981.[14] In the same year Harding was succeeded by a Major Badenhorst, who 'attempted to apply the prison regulations rigidly, unlike his predecessor'.[15] His rigidity led in 1981 to a hunger strike, which was successful in changing his attitude and achieving certain other demands, such as improved food, greater time for visits (from 30 to 45 minutes), the right of prisoners to have their children visit them, and an increase in the quota of letters that could be written and received.[16] There were in fact numerous hunger strikes during the 1980s, some of which were widely supported by the majority of prisoners, while others had the support of smaller groups. For example, James Mange of the ANC has mentioned embarking on hunger strikes a number of times, often with the support of PAC and Black Consciousness-affiliated Islanders. Denmark Tungwane recalled a hunger strike in 1987 that received support from the vast majority of prisoners.[17]

The political prisoner community

When the 1976 uprising occurred, Robben Island was in political terms a fairly stable community divided between two liberation movements, the ANC and the PAC, with the former in the majority. There were also a few members of the BCM and the African People's Democratic Union of South Africa (APDUSA). It was, for the most part, an ageing population. When the attitudes of soccer players in the prison were investigated in the mid-1970s, the results indicated that one of the problems that soccer on the Island faced was 'a decline of fitness and the increasing chronicity of injuries'.[18] No doubt there was also a certain degree of resignation and depression among prisoners as their long sentences took their toll. The apparent political lull outside prison did little to encourage them. Certainly, this was the impression of the younger prisoners who began arriving from the mid-1970s, and it is also confirmed in the records of sports bodies on the Island. In the same investigation quoted above, other problems identified were 'A general saturation level ... [due to the fact that the] present clubs have played one another ... so frequently that it can be predicted to a high level of accuracy which clubs will win and which tactics will be used or attempted ... [Furthermore, the] effects of imprisonment are becoming noticeable ... [In addition, a] more mature outlook towards sport has been attained. We do not now feel the need to prove ourselves narcissistically in our sport any more ...'[19]

Although the prisoners on Robben Island were not to know about the June uprising until August,[20] the arrival of the 'children of '76' made an impact that shook the prison to its core. These new prisoners were, for the most part, different from the existing population in at least two respects: they were generally much younger, and they mostly identified with or were members of Black Consciousness groupings. Both these differences were to cause conflict, and much of the period from 1977 to 1980 was characterised by intense disagreements, at times leading to physical fights, over questions of ideology, recruitment, leadership, and appropriate strategies to deal with the authorities. While elements of dissension continued after 1980, the conflict largely ended in a high level of convergence about the rules, formal and informal, governing the prisoner society. By the early 1980s, too, the ANC had re-established its dominance on the Island. This appears not to have been undermined by the state's removal of Nelson Mandela, Walter Sisulu, Raymond Mhlaba, Ahmed Kathrada and Andrew Mlangeni from the Island to Pollsmoor Prison on 31 March 1982, or the 'early' releases of Harry Gwala and Govan Mbeki in 1987. Indeed, the ANC's underground structures on the Island appear to have become much more sophisticated by the late 1980s.[21]

Releases and the prison after 2 February 1990

February 1990 marked a turning point in South African history. In that month, President F. W. de Klerk unbanned the ANC, PAC and other organisations, and released Nelson Mandela and certain other political prisoners. These steps initiated the negotiation process that would take South Africa beyond apartheid, into a nascent democracy, over the next four and a half years. It was, of course, good news for the prisoners on Robben Island, and the announcement had a liberalising effect on the prison. But for most of the prisoners there was nothing immediate about their release. Indeed, political prisoner releases were the subject of protracted negotiations for more than two years after the February announcement. For Tom Winslow, a human rights activist who worked in support of Robben Islanders in prison and upon their release, the period after February 1990 created enormous stress for prisoners, whose fates were uncertain.

> That whole [release] process, I think, was designed deliberately to desta-
> bilise the individuals involved, to use political prisoners as pawns in the
> negotiating process. It was used by the government as a lever against
> what the ANC was doing. It was a very, very cruel thing to do ...
> [P]eople were released without any notice. They tended to be released
> when there were major overseas initiatives ... We begged and pleaded
> with the authorities, the prisoners begged and pleaded with the author-
> ities, their families begged and pleaded with the authorities – please give
> them advance warning. They refused to do it. They refused to give a
> timetable, they refused to give them the exact time or place. They need-
> ed a draw card. On an individual, emotional level it caused tremendous
> stress and strain on people. Some people say it was probably the most
> stressful time in the Island's history. Just that sheer uncertainty of know-
> ing the hour and the day when you would come out and not letting fam-
> ilies know was incredibly painful for people.[22]

In practical terms, the prisoners hastened their own release with a series of protests and hunger strikes. In February, soon after De Klerk's speech, 143 prisoners on Robben Island went on a hunger strike to demand 'the immediate and unconditional release of all political prisoners'.[23] The next month protesters outside prisons marched for the release of political prisoners. These actions had little immediate effect. In May, the government and the ANC signed the Groote Schuur Minute, thus beginning the process of facilitating political prisoner releases. In June 1990, while Nelson Mandela was on a world tour, a number of Islanders were released, but the majority still remained imprisoned. In August, 15 more political prisoners were released in terms of the Pretoria Minute, another negotiated agreement, according to

Ex-prisoners attending a news conference after their release in October 1989.
From left to right: Raymond Mhlaba, Oscar Mpetha, Andrew Mlangeni, Walter
Sisulu, Ahmed Kathrada, Elias Motsoaledi, Wilton Mkwayi (Mayibuye Centre)

which all political prisoners were to be released by 30 April 1991.

The Pretoria Minute required that prisoners sign an indemnity agreement
before they were released. This caused considerable disagreement among the
prisoners on Robben Island,[24] as many felt they should not have to ask the
government for pardon. An ANC legal team attempted to persuade all the men
to sign the indemnity, but was unsuccessful, in part because it tried to get prisoners to do this before the ANC on Robben Island had had a chance to discuss the matter fully. Other prisoners, in support of the ANC leaders negoti-
ating with the government, did sign the indemnity forms, and expected to be
released by 30 April. It took a visit from Nelson Mandela in late April to persuade the remainder to sign. Although there were some releases effected by 30
April, not all political prisoners were released at that stage, including some of
those who had signed the indemnity. The majority of prisoners therefore
decided to embark on another hunger strike to pressurise the government to
release them. After a lengthy hunger strike most prisoners were set free.
Political prisoners finally left Robben Island in May 1991, although some of
them were transferred to other prisons before being released.[25]

THE CRITICAL YEARS OF CONFLICT: 1977–1980

In recent years, there has been an increasing tendency to portray Robben Island as a site of resistance, where prisoners were able to overcome the state's attempt to marginalise and destroy them as individuals and political beings, and to transcend the conditions that would make the prison a place of perpetual struggle for survival. This view has been challenged by critics, including former political prisoners, as romantic.[26] 'These little movies and other things people have put out [are] actually a romanticised version [of Robben Island]. ... What I am objecting to is this idyllic picture of [Robben Island as a] great university, [where there was a] sharing of experiences.'[27] It is certainly true that there has been some romanticising of the prison experience, but it is equally true that former Islanders themselves are often insistent about the positive things they were able to achieve in prison for themselves, their organisations and the struggle. (That people remember the positive experiences within prison does not mean they do not simultaneously recall the pain, loss, anger and abuse associated with their imprisonment.)

One corrective to the narratives of Robben Island that emphasise mutual respect of political organisations, avoidance of conflict in cases of differing ideological perspectives, and rejection of physical violence as a means of resolving disputes, must be a consideration of the period between 1977 and approximately 1980. At this time there was a no-holds-barred competition to recruit the (mostly) young men who had been sent to the prison in the wake of the 1976 uprising.

Saths Cooper, who was on Robben Island between December 1976 and the early 1980s, offers this bleak diagnosis: 'When the sordidness of prison behaviour is examined there is little difference between common law and political prisoners generally. Where the former are often organised into deadly rival gangs, the latter are organised into often warring political groupings.'[28] When asked to comment on this perspective, Murphy Morobe – a leader of the Soweto uprising who secretly identified with the ANC even when involved in SASM and the SSRC before being sent to Robben Island – accepted and at the same time refuted Cooper's argument.

> Given what was happening at that point in time [in the late 1970s when conflict inside the prison was at its height] it would have been difficult to find a difference. What was different between what the criminals were doing as members of the 26s [a criminal gang] ... and [what] the politicals are doing? The actions were the same, but the reasons, the motives behind it, were different. ... [Arguably], our ideas are much more morally acceptable reasons to actually get into a fight.[29]

Murphy Morobe (Mayibuye
Centre)

In Morobe's view, Cooper was not wrong in his assessment – 'there's no situation which is total harmony' – but he did not fairly reflect the overall picture on the Island, where the 'preponderant majority' were fighting against 'gangsterish type of behaviour'. 'If you look at it purely in terms of the ... various conflagrations that took place there, and you get overwhelmed by these, you then will not see the difference between Robben Island and what was happening [in criminal prisons]. But if you look at it in its totality ... you will see it very differently.'[30]

Kgalema Motlanthe, also an ANC member on the Island, has completely rejected the argument that the political organisations on the Island were little different from criminal gangs, 'because political organisations were never established to fight each other. They were primarily established to ... turn adversity or disadvantage into an advantage.' He strongly believes that political organisations had a transformative function both in developing prisoners on the Island through political education and in furthering the struggle upon their release.[31]

Internal conflict

It is, however, indisputable that there was significant conflict among prisoners. Disagreement between generations was an important element in the debates, but it was not the only basis of conflict. There was great conflict between organisations, which involved physical violence as well.

Organisational conflict came about primarily because the ANC and PAC wished to recruit the new arrivals who had been imprisoned in the wake of the 1976 uprising. Most of these youth were affiliated, to a greater or lesser degree, to Black Consciousness organisations. Even if they were not, they would probably have been aware of the rhetoric and ideas generated by Black Consciousness ideologues and groupings. On one level, then, they came to Robben Island identifying with, or affiliated to, the Black Consciousness Movement. At another level, however, this political identification was often not very strong. Many of the people who participated in the uprising were not at the time very politically conscious. Petros Mashigo, for example, recalled that he joined the march of 16 June because of his difficulty in learning Afrikaans.[32] Others who joined the rebellion were caught up in the crowds or in anger at a specific event. Islanders often refer to a 'tsotsi' (delinquent or gang member) element that had joined the uprising (or had been unlucky to be at the wrong place at the wrong time), later to be imprisoned on Robben Island.[33] Such tenuous links with political organisations and ideologies tended to be undermined even further on the Island as other political groupings in the prison with long histories and significant political experience began to compete for new members.

Recruitment on Robben Island was not a new phenomenon. As long as there were people uncommitted or wavering in their allegiance, political organisations would seek to enlist them. But with the political community largely stable in the early 1970s, there was little need to recruit. Mature leaders recognised that recruitment might indeed have a destabilising effect on the political community, and would only want to risk that for good reason. But the waves of new, Black Consciousness prisoners did provide 'good reason'. For one thing, the Soweto uprising was the most significant political event in resistance politics for over a decade. An organisation that ignored the new arrivals did so at the risk of its continued existence. Secondly, the older men who had spent so many long years in prison did not want to see Black Consciousness established as a third rival to the ANC and PAC. Then again, when affiliations were unclear, recruitment was seen as necessary to ensure that every inmate came under a political discipline. Any prisoner not subject to organisational discipline was susceptible to co-option by 'the system', both in the prison and on release.[34] Finally, the inmates on Robben Island had always regarded it as their duty to produce capable activists who would eventually on release go back into their communities. The youth of '76 were crucial to the prospects of the movements and the liberation struggle. These were the future activists, leaders and soldiers, and their recruitment was a necessity. Recruitment was, of course, a starting point for the vital process of training activists, teaching them organisational histories, ideologies and strategies, and preparing them for their political obligations and mandates upon release. The new arrivals from the Soweto uprising made older prisoners aware 'that you had a political force that could fall either way'.[35]

According to accounts of many former Islanders, PAC members assumed that a natural alliance existed between themselves and the new BC supporters because of the similarity of their political philosophies. In some accounts, this meant that the PAC's approach to recruitment was more low key, stemming from a belief that the natural affinities would inevitably bring the Black Consciousness groupings into the PAC fold.[36] Others argue that the PAC and BCM entered into a formal alliance.[37]

The ANC, on the other hand, appeared to want to recruit or, at least, actively engage the new prisoners from the outset. Prisoners record, in the words of Black Consciousness leader Nkosi Molala, that the ANC made 'no bones about its position vis-à-vis the Black Consciousness Movement' – its desire to recruit the new inmates.[38] ANC members, in contrast, have claimed that 'as an organisation, we had decided, especially in our [leadership] section, not to go out of our way to recruit'.[39] The ANC had, however, long made it a practice to write to new arrivals, welcoming them, and usually engaging in political interchange. Mosibudi Mangena recalls:

> Like many other prisoners, I had a pen pal in another section. This was one of the ways in which we kept in touch with prisoners in different sections who were not supposed to communicate with one another. The clandestine 'postal system' would deliver the letters we wrote to each other every now and then. More often than not, the notes we exchanged involved comments and debates on political and ideological issues. Because many of us in the BCM were generally younger, most older people in the older compartments of the liberation movement imagined we ought to be targets of their political education exercises. Thus, when one or the other of them had an opportunity to correspond with one or another of us, he would almost invariably launch himself into ideological questions.[40]

More direct or personal engagement or recruitment was often difficult, for most of the '76 arrivals were placed in a new section of the prison, Section E. It was also called the 'klipgooier' section (*klipgooier* means stone-thrower in Afrikaans), as many of its inmates were young militants who had been charged with throwing stones at police or similar acts of public violence. Their placement effectively meant they were cut off from the other prisoners and constituted an almost exclusively Black Consciousness section. This changed when ANC adherents charged with Harry Gwala were placed in Section E, and new tensions and attempts at recruitment began.[41]

Within the Black Consciousness groupings themselves there was much self-

'Terror' Lekota at a UDF rally (Mayibuye Centre)

questioning and soul-searching. The most significant case was that of 'Terror' Lekota, one of the SASO Nine. As a result of Lekota's decision to leave the Black Consciousness Movement in late 1977 and identify with the ANC, he was attacked by some of his former comrades with a garden fork, after he had tried to justify the democratic legitimacy of recruitment.[42] A second dramatic incident of violent assault occurred when 'some ANC guys were beaten up' because of ANC recruitment efforts, 'and the ANC guys laid charges'.[43] While these incidents of physical violence have acquired legendary or infamous status, they were not unique. The prison had in fact become extremely tense because of organisational and generational differences, in addition to the endemic tensions of prison life.

High levels of conflict and especially physical confrontation were always dangerous to the political prisoner community, for prisoner unity was one of the community's most significant weapons against the state. But the dissension about recruitment fundamentally undermined this. Cooper argues that recruitment ended when ANC leaders approached the BCM leaders calling for a speedy resolution to the crisis in view of the fact that the state was becoming involved.[44] While this is not the only account of the period,[45] it is widely accepted that by 1980 new agreements had been established between the organisations, setting out mutually acceptable protocols regarding recruitment and the prevention of further conflict. But by then, the ANC was already the largest organisation on the Island, in part as a result of the arrival of captured uMkhonto weSizwe guerrillas, and in part because of the success of its recruitment campaigns. As an organisation that included members of the older generation, the ANC had also managed to persuade the younger men of the merit of its strategies for coping with prison life.

The relation between generational and organisational conflict

Generational and organisational conflict are specific phenomena. Although former Islanders tend to explain conflict in terms of ideology and movements, age grouping and generational consciousness are also important in explaining events and processes on Robben Island, especially after 1976. Moreover, there is a significant intersection between organisational and generational factors. For one thing, the BCM was largely the expression of a younger generation. Black Consciousness was developed by university students at a time when the older liberation movements appeared dormant, if not dead. It articulated the perspectives of a new, younger generation, as well as a political philosophy of liberation. Then again, on Robben Island the BCM was often not taken seriously as a political organisation by the older men in the established movements precisely because it was composed of youth. This is to some extent captured by Mangena's description of the ANC's letter writing to the new Black Consciousness inmates, cited above. Cindi similarly comments that

> they would treat us as youth. We would always correct them and say: Look, we may be young in age, but our organisation is on a par with your organisation. It's not a youth organisation. It's a political organisation. So it must be accorded the same status. There's no youth political organisation, as it were. It's just one political organisation. But there would be resistance. And naturally, people always wanted us to be submerged under them.[46]

Moreover, there was a significant overlap between the political identity of the youth and the BCM as well as between the older men and the ANC and PAC. The youth, as a grouping with a generational consciousness, and the BCM, as a grouping with an ideological consciousness, shared a political identity which demanded militant defiance or categorical resistance as a matter of

course. Indeed, they identified such defiance as the core of their political identity, and believed it required them to challenge the regime's authority publicly
at all times. For their part, the generational consciousness of the older men
was intertwined with their experiences as long-term political prisoners who
had developed a curiously and ironically intimate understanding of the behaviour of their enemy in prison. The older men's perspective tended to cut across
ideological and factional lines. It embodied a consensus that prisoner resistance demanded a careful strategic approach. In this logic of strategic resistance, resistance might be less visible but not necessarily less effective.

UNDERSTANDING THE GENERATIONAL CONFLICT

As has become clear, the tensions and conflicts on Robben Island between
1977 and 1980/1 arose, in significant part, out of a struggle for ideological
and organisational dominance, which the ANC won.[47] There was also a struggle over the appropriate understanding of and methods of resistance that political prisoners should adopt in an apartheid gaol.[48] As such, these competing
logics tended to be the divergent understandings of two generations of political activists.

By the mid-1970s, the attitude to resistance of the older men, who had mostly been in prison since the 1960s, had been shaped by three main factors.
Firstly, having experienced extreme brutality at the hands of the state, they
measured their current conditions and attitudes against their past experiences.
In that sense, they recognised the enormous improvements they had won in
prison conditions, and may have measured progress more according to what
had been than according to what ought to be. Secondly, there was probably at
least some sense of resignation to the status quo. While no prisoner celebrates
the imprisonment of a comrade, the relative paucity of new prisoners who
came into the prison in the late 1960s and early 1970s no doubt had a depress-
ing effect, as it tended to confirm the widespread view of the struggle as at a
standstill. This was probably not helped by the ageing of the men who were
beginning their second decade of imprisonment from 1972 or 1973. Thirdly,
these men had come to embrace a very pragmatic understanding of resistance.
They had come to believe that if one was to withstand and make productive
use of imprisonment, one could not expend one's energies on constant fights
with the authorities. One had to strive continually for basic rights and privileges; beyond that, one had to continue the anti-apartheid struggle in prison
by developing organisations and the members that composed them.

This attitude of pragmatic resistance is exemplified in the following comment by Nelson Mandela:

> We soon became aware that in terms of our daily lives ... an ordinary
> warder, not a sergeant, could be more important to us than the
> Commissioner of Prisons or even the Minister of Justice. If you went to
> the Commissioner of Prisons or the Minister and said, 'Sir, it's very cold,
> I want four blankets', he would look at the regulations and say, 'You
> can only have three blankets ... more would be a violation of the regu-
> lations ... ' If you went to a warder in your section and said, 'Look, I
> want an extra blanket', and if you treated him with respect, he'd just go
> to the storeroom, give you an extra blanket, and that's the end of it.[49]

There were times, in this view, to make a public or principled stand or
launch a protest on an issue or demand, but that was not all the time. If one
wanted to achieve results, one at times took a pragmatic route, which could
include being polite to the enemy. Indeed, Mandela acknowledges the efficacy
of this approach: he recounts a lesson he learned when prisoner grievances
were ignored because he had publicly challenged the authority of a prison official. 'The best way to effect change on Robben Island was to attempt to influence officials privately rather than publicly. I was sometimes condemned for
appearing to be too accommodating to prison officials, but I was willing to
accept the criticism in exchange for the improvement.'[50] While Mandela is the
best-known exemplar of this perspective, and was perhaps the most extreme,
he was certainly not alone. When Harry Gwala – usually considered one of the
ANC's most hardline and uncompromising representatives – was asked in an
interview whether the youth were right in their criticism of the older leadership as too conciliatory, he replied that the new young prisoners 'were very
much inexperienced ... Those people in prison were very militant by all means.
Otherwise they would never be inside [prison] for militant actions. But ... [we]
always distinguished between when to embark on mass action and when to
talk. Whereas at times young people's actions bordered on anarchy.'[51]

In contrast, the young men and (often) boys of the 1976 generation tended
to define themselves proudly as militants, who would resist everywhere and
always. This militancy and deliberate defiance can be explained in a number
of ways. In the first place, they too had experienced the severities of apartheid.
They were coming of age in the overcrowded homes, schools and townships
that apartheid had created, at a time when the already poor standard of living
showed signs of further decline, with rising inflation and declining employment.[52] On top of this, they had experienced the brutal repression of their
1976 rebellion: teargassing, beatings, shootings, detention without trial, torture in gaol, and unjust trials. They tended to feel that little could be lost and
much might be won by a militant expression of anger and pain.

Then again, the youth of the seventies were often appalled at the silence and
acquiescence of their parents, teachers, and the older generation as a whole,

who had been subdued into silent submission. In an anguished editorial, Aggrey Klaaste, editor of the black newspaper *Weekend World*, berated the parents of the Soweto youth: 'We are cowards.'[53] For these youth, Black Consciousness ideology appeared to provide an antidote to the older generation's meekness: 'The militant proselytising of Biko and his colleagues imbued in their younger counterparts in SASM a sense of rebellion and self-assertion – the beginnings of a generational consciousness.'[54] Steve Biko and his colleagues who shared his vision were concerned to resocialise the youth generation, by persuading them to take responsibility for their actions whatever the situation they found themselves in, and not to wait for others to take the initiative. If the white apartheid regime wanted the compliance and resignation of mutes, they would be the opposite: militant, vocal, and angry. 'At least among urban youth,' Anthony Marx notes, 'the days of bowing and scraping were long gone, with the positive self-identity consistent with BC expressed as an angry desire to tear down rather than build up.'[55] These were the boys and men who were to arrive on Robben Island and clash violently with the authorities and, in turn, come into conflict with an older generation of prisoners, who often had very different notions of appropriate strategies and tactics.

As well as the broad trends that defined the youth who came of age in the 1970s, there were particular factors or experiences which shaped the outlook of specific groups. One important example in this regard is that of the SASO Nine. In their trial, which began in August 1975 and ended in December 1976, the defendants were determined to take advantage of the public nature of the hearings, turning the court into a stage and lectern wherever possible so as to instruct the public about the meaning and implications of Black Consciousness, and to stand up to the authorities at every turn.

> Leading by example, the *Cooper* defendants set out to make the most of the political theater of the courtroom. They maintained their combative stance throughout the trial, managing also to convert the courtroom into a forum for mature political instruction. In May 1976 when the defense subpoenaed Biko as a witness and he testified for five days with all his customary persuasiveness, the court and the public through the press were audience to an open seminar on the history, aims and principles of black consciousness ... uncompromising in its moral assertiveness.[56]

In the SASO Nine trial, and in many other incidents in the growing confrontation between the state and the militant youth from the mid-1970s, the new younger generation of activists distinguished themselves both by standing up to the authorities and by impressing a wide popular audience. These younger men were therefore often deeply disappointed with the behaviour of the older men whom they confronted in prison. Zithulele Cindi, one of the SASO Nine, commented bitterly:

> We were the first of the younger generation on the Island. [We were then] followed by an avalanche of the post-June '76 people ... But it was partly a disappointing experience. People never lived up to our expectations. Remember we were charged partly for eulogising them, calling them our leaders ... saying our leaders were on Robben Island. But you meet them and they don't match expectations ... We came with our vibrant militancy and our outright defiance ... We got there and we found these people who we look up to as our leaders ... sheepishly [cringing] ... [When] we went through the corridor ... they literally turned their backs on us and faced the wall. Now that's a practice that is being enforced in these prisons ... There's a prison command that you face the wall. So they would always turn and face the wall. But this was not what we had expected – the black man we had always eulogised now turning his back on us ... So we then had to embark on a defiance now of the warders. We would say 'Hey', black style [clenched fist up], and they'd say 'Keep quiet'. And we'd say, 'There's nothing wrong in greeting ... this is our form of greeting.' ... So they accepted that. We scored a victory. Then we moved it a step further ... [The point of it was to] restore their dignity.[57]

In turn, the older men tended to feel that the new activists and prisoners did not understand the enormous improvements in conditions they had achieved, and the tremendous costs associated with those changes. Nor did they believe that defiance for defiance's sake was always the wisest strategy. Johnson Mlambo of the PAC recalls:

> by and large all the people that came in after '76 felt that the old organisations [the PAC and ANC] were more or less dead and that they are everything. Even when we advised them how to handle the prison authorities etc., they felt that, well, some of our advice was uncalled for. And some of the things we predicted actually happened ... Here is the group of people now coming in, and they ... mix with other people of the Black Consciousness Movement but there is no one ... enlightening them because of their, you know, over-assertiveness ... They were a younger generation who perhaps felt that 'why is this like this, why is this like that?', and who did not want to give credit to what had gone on before. What we were, where we were, [was] because of so many struggles ... They were to some extent also a little reckless as far as the militancy [was concerned] ... [But that is] always to be expected from

young people ...[58]

The generational conflict was in many ways epitomised in the disagreements over classification. A standard feature of South African prisons was the classification of prisoners into four categories – 'A' being the highest and 'D' the lowest[59] – rewarding good behaviour with certain privileges and punishing bad behaviour with the retraction of those privileges. Thus 'A'-group prisoners were, for example, allowed to buy food and, after 1980, newspapers. This was denied those in lower classifications. One's classification also determined one's right to study, the number of letters one could send and receive, and the number and length of visits (and, later, whether these would be contact visits or not). Political prisoners had always challenged classification, arguing that political prisoners should not be classified. 'We are all prisoners. Why should there be differentiation? If there's to be a privilege we [should] all get it.'[60] They also opposed the fact that political prisoners would initially be classified at the lowest 'D' rung, whereas criminals would initially receive a 'B' rating.[61] Yet although the older Robben Islanders opposed classification, they had accepted it as a necessary evil. Ahmed Kathrada comments:

> On the question of classification we never took a decision that we are going to refuse classification. Our demand was always that all political prisoners should be treated as 'A' groups. There should be no discrimination among political prisoners, because the rationale for promotion was your so-called behaviour, and we said it's an insulting thing to tell us how to behave ... So we never used to ... ask ... to be classified ... but we said we won't refuse if we appear before the [classification] board. PAC was the same, you see, PAC never refused classification ... Neville Alexander ... [of the Unity Movement] resisted for a while, but he eventually became 'A' group.[62]

In contrast, the Black Consciousness leaders rejected classification (although Mangena seems to have believed it was necessary or wise to accept it).[63] In part they rejected it for the same reason that the older generation of political prisoners had done so: that it was 'prison apartheid' which assumed the state had the right to judge political prisoners and manipulate their behaviour by using the carrot and stick of classification to reward and punish prisoners. In addition, the Black Consciousness adherents, at least from the time of arrival of the SASO Nine, saw classification as creating a hierarchy among prisoners that would lend itself to divide and rule tactics by the state, as well as other undesirable effects. In particular, once the ANC (and, to a lesser extent, the PAC) began recruiting or approaching the new wave of prisoners, BCM members argued that classification became a means of bribery. In effect, Black

Consciousness members who opposed both classification and recruitment by
the other organisations accused the older men of seducing vulnerable young
activists into their organisations with privileges like food. For the younger generation, this was a complete violation of the behaviour appropriate to political prisoners. The Black Consciousness leader Pandelani Nefolovhodwe elaborates:

> All cadres belonging to our organisation went in being classified 'D' and
> went out being 'D'. We saw in the classification process of the South
> African prison authorities, that disorder and that bribery and that
> which will destroy the spirit of comrades. So we formulated a policy, as
> the Black Consciousness Movement ... that we are not going to be clas-
> sified. That as I get in, I'll go out as I am. (I think some of our cadres
> were then classified later, when there were very few [BC members],
> when we had all gone out; I think there were about 20 or less than that,
> then there was no longer any question of us [the different organisations]
> clashing.) [Earlier, however,] ... we were many and you could have
> imagined that one of us become 'A', enjoy certain privileges, and the rest
> of the people are not 'A'. It causes a lot of friction. [Those who had
> accepted 'A' classification before the SASO Nine arrived were allowed
> to keep it.] [The authorities] sometimes used to offer [classification]:
> 'We think you are behaving very well and we would want you to be a
> B.' We say, 'No, keep it. I'm all right where I am. I eat your food free, I
> don't need to buy biscuits.'[64]

Nefolovhodwe argued that even if organisational abuses were excluded,
accepting what in prison were luxuries could lead to a form of dependence,
which might then be used against one. This pragmatic asceticism was not
unique to the Black Consciousness; another member of the militant younger
generation was the ANC's James Mange, who constantly fought the seductive
lures of the state and his organisation.

> [When] I got [to Robben Island] I had been graded 'C' whereas every-
> body started [with being graded 'D'], and instead of going up I went
> down. [*Laughs*] I went the other way down. I stayed a 'D' grade I think
> from '81 to 1990. You know the privileges that goes with that and so
> on. And each time there would be pressure from friends and family and
> so on, because I couldn't get contact visits and they tried talking me
> around to changing. In the first place I shouldn't have been here [in
> prison] – [the] circumstances that brought me here are war ... As far as
> I'm concerned I'm still on enemy territory. And in order to preserve my
> sanity, my strengths, I'll have to learn to do without. Prison can become

very frustrating if you learn not to do without. That stick that always lands above your head, you can write five letters, you can have seven visits or whatever, contact visits, that sort of straitjackets you ... I had dreadlocks this long, you know. [*Indicates*] And prison regulations doesn't have room for that. But that was one of my weapons. Because that said to me victory all the time ... I can't exchange my will-power for the small nothings that you are offering.[65]

There was certainly sound political sense in the argument that classification was not only offensive, but a clever divide-and-rule strategy which the state could manipulate to the detriment of anti-apartheid struggles. Furthermore, while the privileges of higher classification might make for a life in prison that was a little less harsh and even more 'liberal', liberalisation of the prison could also create problems for organisational coherence. Petros Mashigo, an ANC member, has noted that often support for hunger strikes (intended to improve conditions or challenge the state in some way) would be divided along the lines of classification: those with higher classifications and therefore more privileges would oppose hunger strikes, and those with lower classifications and a harsher existence would support the strike strategy.[66] This lends significant support to Mange's contention that 'in a resistance movement it is only rebelling that keeps you brave',[67] and that acceptance of privileges in prison can blunt the resistant and defiant edge of prisoners. Not only can the absence of an all-powerful enemy lead to apathy or (greater) divisions in the ranks, but political organisations may also have less to offer members when there are the competitive attractions of movies, television and a relatively undisciplined life. Saki Macozoma reminds one that 'there is another pole to prison life, where people spend all day talking about movies they have seen and women they have known – and manufacture the stories in any case. The counter-attractions increased with the liberalisation of the prison, when there were more movies, sport, and so on.'[68]

There were, however, a number of problems with the principled argument against classification. Firstly, while it was undoubtedly difficult to renounce privileges that might mitigate the hardships of prison life, it was also true that those who had very long sentences would be hurt most by this strategy. The SASO Nine were given five- and six-year sentences, and most of the '76 militants were given sentences of similar lengths.[69] In contrast, many of the older generation had received much longer sentences. Arguably, for men dealing with long-term imprisonment, the relative gains made by strategic asceticism could be outweighed by the greater losses of renunciation.[70] For example, the more prisoners were able to draw on support from families through letters or visits, the more they were likely to cope with their sentences.[71]

Then again, practical problems began to emerge with the refusal to accept improved levels of classification. For example, Ahmed Kathrada of the ANC was critical of some people in the Black Consciousness Movement who denounced classification but accepted its benefits:

> A number of Black Consciousness chaps came ... with the idea ... they shouldn't accept classification. So what these Black Consciousness chaps did is they used to work with this PAC chap who was in the tuck shop, and he used to wangle his books, so they used to order food. [And when the authorities allowed newspapers but said] newspapers are only for 'A' groups, so they used to read all our newspapers ... So it was all a sham, this thing of boycotting classification.[72]

Finding ways around classification was not necessarily denied by those who opposed it. Saths Cooper did not accept classification, he said, but 'I got classified unknown to me, and then discovered I was "B" group, so I said why should I deny myself writing all these letters ... and I wrote the letters.' That did not lead to tension, because

> the thing that was most problematic was the 'A' group status, because that allowed you foodstuffs, and you see it was also an elitist thing because most prisoners came from very humble backgrounds, no money whatsoever, so it caused all those types of tensions[73] ... There was a time when I benefited from getting bought foodstuff without being classified [*chuckle*] because the guy who was in charge of the shop would just write it ... to account for the amount rather than the items, so he would give me the stuff.[74]

What for Cooper was a clever manipulation of the system was for Kathrada a lack of honesty in the way one carried out the strategies of struggle. The point is not to judge the perspective of either man, or others like them, but rather to demonstrate that the strategy of avoiding classification could be as vulnerable to problems of principle and practice as using classification directly. Certainly, in the rumour mill that is prison,[75] with the tensions existing between generations, organisations and factions, these competing approaches to dealing with the state on this issue did not resolve the conflict. Kgalema Motlanthe has argued that the contradiction between Black Consciousness leaders denouncing classification and then reaping the benefits of classification was one reason why some BC supporters left that organisation.[76]

Finally, rejecting classification ignored the achievement and fundamental insight of the older generation: that prisoner struggles to create improvements not only provided material benefits that helped people survive their incarceration with the least possible harm to their own and their organisation's well-being, but were used by the prisoners to create new gaps and contradictions within which to continue the struggle. In other words, improving conditions was not only an end in itself; improved conditions and increased privileges and rights were used to further the struggle. One obvious example of this concerns academic studies. The constant struggle for academic studies achieved several important goals. On an individual level, it helped keep people mentally alert, and increased the worth of their daily lives. In addition, it could provide people with the means to make a living upon release. Seen in terms of the collective political ends of the various organisations, academic study allowed people the intellectual sophistication to master complex ideological arguments, and also provided a steady stream of books that were vital to political education in the prison. (Because their use was of course outlawed, prisoners would transcribe whole books so that the handwritten copies could provide a library after the student had returned them!)[77]

The utility of privileges for political ends was not only seen in study rights. Prisoners also used contact visits to smuggle in contraband – in one case, money to bribe a warder to buy a short-wave radio, essential for communication.[78] On another occasion a photograph was used to smuggle codes from the ANC on Robben Island to the ANC in exile, to facilitate communication.

> That secret message and hundreds like it were smuggled between prisoners and their officials in exile over the 30 years that the ANC was banned. They formed a fabric of interwoven instructions and information that would help determine the shape of South Africa's democracy...
> ... [Mac Maharaj explained that aside from the importance of being informed about events beyond the prison for psychological well-being],
> 'we could debrief prisoners about problems they had encountered infiltrating the country or trying to carry on the struggle in South Africa. That information would be passed on to the leadership in Lusaka.' ...
> [Prisoners' letters] had to deal strictly with family business. Consequently, the codes were built around words like children and parents ...[79]

In these examples, the use of privileges provides examples of resistance to incarceration and to the political conditions that sustained that imprisonment. In this context, then, resistance can be seen as a constructive political act that aimed at challenging the status quo not only by opposition, but by creative and imaginative use of material conditions.

In discussing appropriate means found by prisoners to resist apartheid within the prison, one has to consider the warders. Once again, the older generation, usually irrespective of their organisational affiliation, claimed there were benefits in 'taming' the warders. Mandela's view that 'The most important person in any prisoner's life is ... the warder in one's section' is based on the understanding that a non-conflictual and even cordial relationship with warders could have an enormous impact on a prisoner's daily existence.[80] Mlambo recounts his experience that the humanity of prisoners helped to change the perspective of the warders, who 'had been conditioned to treat you as animals, but, by and large, with the march of time, some of them start to see the human being in you.'[81] Alexander, too, recalls this lesson learnt on the Island:

> Perhaps the greatest irony of all was that eventually we became the teachers, literally, of some of these warders ... The authorities quickly realized that they couldn't keep any set of warders for too long because the danger of fraternisation was obviously very great ... I want to underline the role of people like Nelson Mandela and Walter Sisulu in particular [in teaching us how to deal with the authorities] ... While we were terribly impetuous and would have run ourselves suicidally against the prison walls ... [t]hey realized that if we adopted a particularly humane, dignified, friendly attitude (short, of course, of collaborating in our own indignity) that eventually we would break through.[82]

The older generation sought to persuade the younger men that the best interests of anti-apartheid resistance within and without the prison demanded a strategic approach. Mandela has argued that by working with or at least neutralising warders, these state functionaries at times changed their prejudiced views, even to the point of recognising the wisdom of the ANC's position. Furthermore, as Mandela points out, 'Having sympathetic warders facilitated one of our most vital tasks on Robben Island: communication. We regarded it as our duty to stay in touch with our men in F and G, which is where the general prisoners were kept. As politicians, we were just as intent on fortifying our organization in prison as we had been outside.'[83] If one of the highest forms of resistance is to continue (and even to further) one's political struggle within[84] or as a result of prison, this kind of resistance was crucial.

Gradually, the younger generation came to accept the perspective of the older men. For some, this was achieved through joining the older liberation movements, most notably the ANC, though the PAC also won new recruits on the Island. Identifying with or joining an organisation was not, however, the only or even the most important means of embracing a more far-reaching vision of resistance. Saths Cooper made the following comment on 'Terror' Lekota's suspension from the Black Consciousness Movement. What Lekota was saying, Cooper argues, was:

> 'Shouldn't we look at what the ANC guys are saying in terms of our

principled position, we objecting to many of these practices? Maybe they have explanations for some of these things and maybe ... because they come from a different time they're accepting classification. We're rejecting it – shouldn't we actually find out?' And because of that heavy idealist militant youth orientation, everyone said, 'No, we can't do it.'[85]

After release from prison, Cooper held leadership positions in the Azanian People's Organisation, before adopting a position of independent non-affiliation. Likewise, Mike Xego, who came into Robben Island as a Black Consciousness adherent, but joined the ANC on Robben Island, recalls:

Our perception of the old comrades [was] that they were too compromising with the warders. We would punch the warders. If warders touched us, we would quickly punch back. There were daily skirmishes ... Gradually Madiba [Mandela] and the others were told to tame us. It was not the regime but the ANC that cracked us. One by one, the ANC underground on Robben Island worked on us – on individuals – talking with us and smuggling notes to us.[86]

This is not to suggest that the learning process was all one way. In the first place, the generation of '76 helped to push further back the boundaries which the state had imposed on political prisoner life. It is probably no coincidence that the cessation of hard labour in the quarries, and the opening up of more useful occupations such as carpentry and sewing, began at a time when the state came under greater pressure to give in to these demands, both from the militant prisoners and from heightened external monitoring. Secondly, at least in the ANC, the youth (including the increasing numbers of captured MK guerrillas) appear to have developed a more sophisticated underground structure for their organisation in prison. Thirdly, the younger generation played a critical role in revitalising prison life: they were a reminder to the older, long-term and life prisoners that the struggle had continued, and imprisonment was not in vain. They also were an invaluable source of news and contemporary culture to those on an island that had been deliberately, if not entirely successfully, cut off from the world for over a decade. With the arrival of the '76 youth, sport again flourished, not least because there were now some professional soccer players.[87] Lastly, the youth exposed the older men to new thinking, and forced them to rethink their attitudes on many crucial points. For instance, the older generation came to accept their view that 'black people' referred to all the oppressed, African, Indian and coloured[88] – an enduring legacy of the Black Consciousness philosophy – and to understand the sense of alienation and anger that young black South Africans experienced. The significance of this alienation of black South African youth is poignantly captured in Nelson Mandela's account of the lesson he learned from Strini Moodley after the single-cell prisoners had watched a documentary about the Hell's Angels, which 'depicted the Hell's Angels as reckless, violent, and anti-social, and the police as decent, upstanding, and trustworthy'. In the ensuing discussion, almost all the prisoners criticised the bikers for their lawlessness, until Moodley pointed out the similarities between the rebellion against authority of the Soweto youth of 1976 and the Hell's Angels.

> [Strini] reproached us for being elderly middle-class intellectuals who identified with the movie's right-wing authorities instead of with the bikers ... the larger question that concerned me was whether we had, as Strini suggested, become stuck in a mind-set that was no longer revolutionary. We had been in prison for more than fifteen years; I had been in prison for nearly eighteen. The world that we left was long gone ... Prison is a still point in a turning world, and it is very easy to stay in the same place in prison while the world moves on.[89]

The mutual benefit of the generational mix can be illustrated by two comments made by Kgalema Motlanthe. On the one hand, he comments that in some respects his 'most enriching lesson that I picked up throughout my [ten year] stay on the Island in prison' was learning to accept, and help others accept, that although an enthusiastic young activist might find a way to make time for five political discussions or classes a day, there are 'elderly people who would want to take part in political education classes ... twice [or] a maximum of three times a week, and not more than that.' The older man's inability to absorb the same material did not make him any less competent. This was an important lesson. On the other hand, Motlanthe notes, 'I think that one of the things that sustained the older comrades ... was the fact that there was always an intake of new people and they could see their efforts, those of political education, transforming people, and those people actually leaving prison to go out and actually contribute in the struggle.'[90]

The importance of generational differences and convergence on Robben Island continued beyond the early 1980s, as the following three examples illustrate. In about 1985, Motlanthe was removed from Robben Island for a few months and sent to prisons near Cape Town. Here he encountered youth who identified with the ANC (they had come from United Democratic Front organisations) but were affected by the 'wild element of violen[ce]' engulfing the country at the time. When they were all brought back to the Island, 'we then joined other groups that came from exile and some comrades from the University of the Western Cape, and then we generally stabilised the group in the mainstream structures of the Island'.[91]

In 1988, ANC member Lassie Chiwayo, at the age of 22, was sent to

Robben Island after harrowing experiences at the hands of the state, including physical torture and an attempt to blackmail him after his father's death, itself a result of his detention. Furthermore, 'there was apparently an attempt by prison officials to break us [in Witbank and Bethal prisons]; they did not think that being in prison was enough of a punishment'. As a result he and his fellow prisoners adopted 'very serious antagonistic attitudes against whites ... All that we knew was that any person that is white, especially prison warders, deserved [to be] assault[ed].' This was to be fundamentally challenged on Robben Island. 'But with the sort of leaders we found on Robben Island we were, to a very large extent, transformed. I would say we were completely transformed, but completely different, new attitudes.'[92] Chiwayo also mentioned that he was shocked by the 'very healthy relations' between the different organisations on the Island, in sharp contrast to the attitude outside prison where organisations viewed each other as enemies that had to be suppressed.

The third example suggests the continuing legacy of negotiations with the authorities in the name of the smooth running of the prison, but to the advantage of the prisoners. By 1988, most of the older-generation leaders in 'B' sections had been replaced by the arrivals of the late 1970s and early 1980s, many of whom were uMkhonto weSizwe cadres. In turn, 'A' section had come to be used for new arrivals. Because communication between sections was always a sought-after goal, the 'B'-section Recreation Committee attempted to persuade the authorities that the sections be allowed to mix for recreational and sporting purposes. Arguments were based on practical grounds: because new prisoners had a difficult time adjusting, this would cause problems for warders, who would need to deal with the resulting tensions; older prisoners could also play an orientation role. The following are the minutes as they appear in the 'Book of Occurrences, Recreation Committee'.

B-SECTION RECREATION COMMITTEE
MEETING WITH W/O VAN DER MESCHT
AUGUST 30 1988
PRESENT[:] AUTHORITIES: W/O van der Mescht
DELEGATES: W. Mkwayi, M. Sexwale, J. Legoabe
Proceedings
(1) B-RC [Recreation Committee] request that their section should be allowed to mix with A-Sec[tion] and form one team for sporting purposes and video/films viewing.
MOTIVATIONS
(a) Both Sections (A:B) are already playing *AGAINST* one another.
(b) Due to 'Manpower' shortages particularly in B, games such as Soccer, Rugby and other outdoor games cannot be played. Mixing A & B will alleviate this shortage.

(c) A consists of new arrivals to this Island. Problems of adjustment in warder–prisoner relationships which normally occur due to tensions are likely to be avoided as B-sec. old inmates can have a positive influence on A-sec.

(d) Viewing videos/films together will assist in cost reduction measures by the GRC [General Recreation Committee] as TV screens and projectors are to run lesser under a mixing scheme.

(e) The GRC is also faced with the problem of having to purchase new sporting equipment, offices and footwear ... for A-section. This duplication can be avoided when A & B are allowed to play together.[93]

Negotiations such as this attempted to promote contact and communication among prisoners and ensure the influence of older prisoners on the newer inmates. They were also excellent training in dealing with the enemy, the apartheid state, and as such would presage the negotiations with the National Party government, which began less than two years later, in 1990. It is important to recognise negotiations between prisoners and the authorities, recorded here for example in the General Recreation Committee minutes, as instances of strategic resistance. The appropriate balance between strategic and categorical resistance was forged through both conflict and convergence, much of it generational, on Robben Island.

IMPLICATIONS FOR RESISTANCE

The two generations who met and interacted on Robben Island had conflicts of understanding about the nature of anti-apartheid struggle and the response it demanded within the prison walls. Although the arrival of the '76 generation did not mark the first time there were debates over how to fight apartheid in the prison, their arrival brought a new depth to the debates. These were complicated by inter-organisational differences, particularly as the BCM emerged as a significant force in liberation politics. Resolving the inter-generational conflict (and, to a lesser extent, their organisational conflict) involved identifying strategies appropriate to the nature and forms of resistance. Essentially, the two groups had two different understandings of resistance, categorical and strategic resistance.[94] In the first (categorical resistance) there is an understanding that resistance is required as a matter of political principle. In the second (strategic resistance), resistance operates on a strategic basis; this does not necessarily require that political prisoners resist always, everywhere, and overtly.

In the face of a state that wanted pliant and servile black people who knew their place, and in the face of parents who seemed to be too accepting of that role, the black urban youth of South Africa rose up to say, clearly and defiantly, 'No!' To quote Shaun Johnson again, that 'sense of rebellion and self-assertion [which formed] the beginnings of a generational consciousness' created a political identity that largely defined itself in opposition to anything suggesting the authority of the apartheid state. Going to apartheid prisons, Robben Island included, was a journey into the very heart of the regime. Here it would have to be confronted in a far more intimate, controlling, and total way than anything apartheid represented on the 'outside'. In prison the white regime was personified by the warders and the militarised prison hierarchy. These had, in the logic of categorical resistance, to be confronted at every turn. The warders' provocation provided a further basis for the anger and militancy of the youth – 'our vibrant militancy and our outright defiance'.[95] The prisoners were determined to match every action of their enemy, and their enemy's very existence, with militant resistance. Resistance was their raison d'être; resistance *was* their political identity as young, angry, black and proud political prisoners.

The conviction that underlay categorical resistance was not exclusive to the youth or Black Consciousness adherents. Thami Mkhwanazi, who was convicted of recruiting youths for military training, while not publicly questioning his organisation, the ANC, presents himself as a militant who resisted wherever possible. He writes that he and PAC lifer Jeff Masemola 'were bound by the principle of telling the prison authorities where to get off.'[96] Similarly, he describes Toivo ya Toivo, the SWAPO leader, as 'militant and hostile to members of the Prisons Service. He refused to appear before the institutional board for classification, thereby denying himself any chance of upgrading so he could buy food or subscribe to newspapers.'[97] James Mange rejected both the PAC and the BCM as viable movements or philosophies, and despite his fraught relationship with the ANC on the Island, was for a long time a high-profile member of that organisation. For Mange, and indeed other revolutionaries and militants, confrontations with the authorities were necessary as a matter of principle. For them, the sense of purpose needed to live as prisoners of war on enemy terrain demanded that there be no compromises or personal or organisational indulgences.

Ironically, the state was not the only focus of opposition for the defiant prisoners. (Indeed, state opposition would largely reinforce categorical resistance, because that approach was defined in terms of, and against, the state and its representatives.) Another source of challenge to the younger men was their fellow political prisoners, those mostly from a different generation. The dissonance between the groups was originally put down to generational (and organisational) differences. A generational difference implies that individuals and groups occupy separate historical spaces with associated sets of perceptions and experiences. Different generations have different collective experiences and world views that shape their identities. For instance, the youth who rebelled in 1976 were born into an environment virtually devoid of any political resistance, to parents who apparently acquiesced in their own subordination. The youth's response to that was to do and be the opposite: to be militant, defiant and overt in their resistance. In contrast, the older generation had seen their protests of the 1950s and early 1960s crushed, and had gone on to experience the limits to automatic protests in prison in the 1960s and early 1970s. In this context, resistance had to be very strategic; it had to guarantee conditions of survival, and use the prison to achieve far-reaching political change of the kind discussed. On arrival on Robben Island the younger men did not immediately see that the older generation *did* engage in resistance, but the resistance involved a different understanding and status. For the youth, resistance constituted their moral and practical core as political prisoners. For the older generation, resistance was a strategy, not necessarily a principle; a means, not necessarily an end.

Strategic resistance required prisoners to expend time and energy developing themselves and their organisations in a way that would affect the political terrain both within and beyond the prison. This certainly did not imply ignoring the state – apart from anything else, that was impossible, as the very conditions of political organisation and education on the Island violated rules and were by definition acts of resistance against the prison regulations. What it did demand (at least, this was the interpretation of its practitioners) was that prisoners attempt to reach in effect a truce with the authorities and thereby create the space for organisational development within and beyond the prison. Such an approach required knowledgeable and disciplined members who would, upon release, rejuvenate, support or redirect external anti-apartheid struggles. This was what a good graduate of Robben Island was meant to do, and South Africa's political history has been shaped by many of these 'alumni'.

According to this understanding, strategic resistance is less a moment than a continuum, less a point than a process. In this continuum, resistance forms the baseline of prisoner life, and resignification, reconstrual and emancipation the objects of that life.[98] Resignification here applies both to the prison and to the broader society; it suggests that resistance – a negative baseline refusal – is a means to the end of resignification, a positive act of remaking and reconstruing the dominant world.

Strategic resistance does not deny the place or importance of categorical resistance. Older prisoners (at least in the ANC) were, for example, 'encouraged by [the] ... radicalism' of captured uMkhonto weSizwe soldiers who were sent to Robben Island in the early 1970s.[99] The youth of '76 had a similar rejuvenating effect on the prison. Furthermore, categorical resistance is often a necessity, and its absence may prove dangerous, as when prisoners come to rely on official privileges. It is significant that, for example, prisoners with higher classifications were less likely to support hunger strikes than those with lower classifications.

Often, however, the different imperatives of categorical resistance and strategic resistance proved incompatible on Robben Island. For instance, one tactic of the state in a hunger strike would be to raid cells and seize contraband political material. In this case, the need for immediate improvements or the satisfaction of an urgent demand as expressed in the hunger strike might have put the broader goals of political education or communication in danger. This contradiction between the two forms of resistance was probably unavoidable. It may at times have been necessary to stress an immediate and militant public protest even if longer-term goals or resistance was undermined. Similarly, the reverse is true. Recognising these inevitable and difficult choices, neither 'right' nor 'wrong', and trying to balance them, in many respects captures the generational convergence achieved by political prisoners on Robben Island. It also suggests the specificity of the conditions shaping understandings of resistance, in this case the conditions and history of Robben Island.

CONCLUSION

Before his murder, Steve Biko saw the 1976 uprising and the subsequent state repression as 'a very useful weapon in merging the young and old. Before then there was a difference in the outlooks of the old generation and the younger generation.'[100] His observation involved astute analysis and excellent foresight, both for much of South Africa's recent political history and for the narrower history of Robben Island. From conflict and then convergence between generations and organisations on Robben Island, the political prisoners, young and old, derived one of their great achievements: most of them did not 'stay in the same place in prison as the world moved on'. This was crucial in allowing them to influence the course of the anti-apartheid struggle on Robben Island, and also upon release. Their achievement was partly the product of the debates about, and the actual employment of, different forms of resistance – categorical and strategic resistance. For they constantly assessed the extent of their relative power and powerlessness, and attempted to find the most appropriate means of improving their conditions, to ensure the maintenance and growth of their organisations and the individuals that composed them.

These lessons were taken back into the mass struggles of the 1980s, and the struggles and negotiations of the post-1990 period.[101] While a detailed account of the role of Robben Islanders after release and their tactics of resistance outside prison is beyond the scope of this chapter, their post-prison roles are significant and observable. In the 1980s, for example, ex-Robben Islanders became amongst the most important leaders in both the United Democratic Front and its affiliates, and in AZAPO and the National Forum. They worked as trade union leaders in both the Congress of South African Trade Unions and the National Council of Trade Unions and their affiliates. Former Islanders were also active in leadership positions in religious groupings, non-governmental and human rights organisations, and in the banned liberation movements in exile. All of these sectors played key roles in challenging apartheid. Robben Islanders continue to be active in all these sectors today, as well as in government, not only in the person of President Nelson Mandela, but also as cabinet ministers, members of parliament, premiers and ministers of provincial governments, members of provincial legislatures, and chairpersons of government commissions. There are many reasons why incarceration on Robben Island proved to be an advantage in these positions. Not least of these was the ability for very different tendencies and generations of political activists to learn about each other and from each other while imprisoned on Robben Island.

Released prisoner arriving at Cape Town docks from Robben Island (Mayibuye Centre)

References

Chapter 1
INTRODUCTION

Thanks to Nigel Penn for providing some of the material in this chapter.

1. The most complete study of the history of Robben Island available to date is Simon de Villiers, *Robben Island: Out of Reach, Out of Mind* (Cape Town, 1971). This is a rather uneven, anecdotal book, characterised by some extraordinary judgements. More modern studies include Nigel Penn, Harriet Deacon and Neville Alexander's *Robben Island: The Politics of Rock and Sand* (Cape Town, 1992); Harriet Deacon's Ph.D. thesis, 'A history of the medical institutions on Robben Island, 1846–1910' (University of Cambridge, 1994); Fran Buntman's BA (Honours) thesis, 'From 'Hell-hole' to a 'Blessing in disguise': a study of politics on Robben Island, 1963-1987' (University of the Witwatersrand, 1988) and her forthcoming doctoral thesis on the ways in which Robben Island, designed as an institution of repression, was transformed into a site of resistance by the political prisoners imprisoned there after 1962. There are a number of autobiographical accounts of experiences on the Island including J. Fish, *Robben Island* (London, 1924), M. Dlamini, *Hell-hole Robben Island* (Nottingham, 1984), I. Naidoo, *Island in Chains: Ten Years on Robben Island* (Harmondsworth, 1982), N. Alexander, *Robben Island Dossier, 1964–1974* (Cape Town, 1994).

2. That is, with the exception of John Murray's grant of land in 1806, which was relinquished in 1823, and a grant of land for the Church of the Good Shepherd in 1895 which still remains the property of the Anglican 'Church of the Province of South Africa'. See Pat Riley, 'Conservation survey of Robben Island' (unpublished survey, National Monuments Council, 1993).

3. For more information on this, see J.N. Theron and R. Hill, 'Ekskursie na Robben Eiland, 6 Oktober 1990', Report for the Geological Society of South Africa, Western Province Branch, 1990; D. Miller, 'A geological description of Robben Island', *South African Lapidary Magazine*, 23, 2 (1991), pp. 5–8.

4. The information in this paragraph has been taken from B. S. Werz and J. C. G. Deacon, 'Operation Sea Eagle: final report on a survey of shipwrecks around Robben Island' (unpublished report, National Monuments Council, 1992).

5. For more information on this, see J.W. Lloyd and M.T. Linger, 'Report on the vegetation of Robben Island', in *'n Natuurbewaringsondersoek van Robben Eiland* (Department of Nature Conservation, Cape Provincial Administration, January 1986).

6. Pat Riley, 'Conservation survey of Robben Island'.

7. Accepting the Jawaharlal Nehru Award for International Understanding in New Delhi, 1980, on behalf of Nelson Mandela who was then imprisoned on Robben Island. O. Tambo, *Preparing for Power* (Oxford, 1987), p. 199.

8. G. Lubbe, 'Robben Island: the early years of Muslim resistance', *Kronos*, 12 (1987), p. 49. See also J.H. Jacobs, 'Narrating the Island: Robben Island in South African literature', *Current Writing*, 4 (1992), p. 74.

9. J.H. Jacobs, 'Narrating the Island', p. 74.

10. P. Stallybrass and A. White, *The Politics and Poetics of Transgression* (London, 1986), pp. 2-3.

11. P. Stallybrass and A. White, *The Politics and Poetics of Transgression*, pp. 130–32.

12. M. van Wyk Smith, *Shades of Adamastor: An Anthology of Poetry* (Grahamstown, 1988), pp. 1-13.

13. Quoted in M. van Wyk Smith, *Shades of Adamastor*, p. 9.

14. N. Penn, 'From penguins to prisoners: Robben Island, 1488-1805' in N. Penn, H. Deacon and N. Alexander, *Robben Island*, p. 6.

15. A. W. P. Pinkerton, 'Introductory lecture on climate' (Edinburgh Medical School, Edinburgh, 1857), p. 10.

16. A. W. P. Pinkerton, 'Introductory lecture on climate', p. 11.

Chapter 2
ROBBEN ISLAND 1488-1805

1. There are two volumes in the Cape Archives (CA) which contain the names of prisoners on Robben Island in the eighteenth century. The first of these is CA CJ 3188, Bandieten Rollen, 1728–1795 and the second is CA CJ 3189, Lists of Convicts sent to Robben Island, 1758–1802. Actually CA CJ 3189 has lists up until 1806.

2. Eric Axelson, *The Portuguese in South East Africa, 1488–1600* (Cape Town, 1973) does not mention any visit.

3. P. Kolben, *The Present State of the Cape of Good Hope* (London, 1731), p. 15.

4. S. de Villiers, *Robben Island* (Cape Town, 1971), p. 4.

5. Quoted by R. Raven-Hart, *Before Van Riebeeck: Callers at South Africa from 1488 to 1652* (Cape Town, 1967), p. 6.

6. Raven-Hart, *Before Van Riebeeck*, pp. 9–11.

7. In 1620 the French mariner Augustin de Beaulieu commented that on the Island 'great numbers of sea-bears are found, which bleat like sheep, but are very unlike them in taste, and for my part I could not eat them, nor the penguins, because they too much tasted of fish oil … although most of our crew found them good and preferred them to bacon …' In Raven-Hart, *Before Van Riebeeck*, p. 103.

8. David Middleton of the *Consent*. In Raven-Hart, *Before Van Riebeeck*, p. 33.

9. An anonymous sailor of Sir Henry Middleton's voyage of 1604. In Raven-Hart, *Before Van Riebeeck*, p. 30.

10. An anonymous account of Sir James Lancaster's voyage of 1601. In Raven-Hart, *Before Van Riebeeck*, pp. 24–5.

11. Sir Henry Middleton's voyage. In Raven-Hart, *Before Van Riebeeck*, p. 30. See also David Middleton in Raven-Hart, *Before Van Riebeeck*, p. 33.

12. John Jourdain of the *Ascension*. In Raven-Hart, *Before Van Riebeeck*, p. 43.

13. According to David Pietersz de Vries in 1627. In Raven-Hart, *Before Van Riebeeck*, p. 125.

14. According to the recorder of Sir James Lancaster's voyage of 1601. In Raven-Hart, *Before Van Riebeeck*, p. 24.

15. Account of Cornelis Matelief. In Raven-Hart, *Before Van Riebeeck*, pp. 39–40.

16. Account of Jon Olafsson of the *Christianshaven*, 1623. In Raven-Hart, *Before Van Riebeeck*, p. 111.

17. The English word derives from the Dutch word *traan*, meaning tear, applied to the oil because of the form of its drops.

18. See account of Nicholas Downton of the *Peppercorn* in 1610. In Raven-Hart, p. 47.

19. See account of John Saris in 1611. In Raven-Hart, *Before Van Riebeeck*, p. 47.

20. In Raven-Hart, *Before Van Riebeeck*, p. 24.

21. In Raven-Hart, *Before Van Riebeeck*, p. 28.

22. In Raven-Hart, *Before Van Riebeeck*, p. 26–8.

23. Quoted in Raven-Hart, *Before Van Riebeeck*, p. 35.

24. For Aldworth's report see Raven-Hart, *Before Van Riebeeck*, p. 61.

25. See Raven-Hart, *Before Van Riebeeck*, note on p. 78.

26. See account of Walter Peyton of the *Expedition*, 1615; in Raven-Hart, *Before Van Riebeeck*, pp. 71–7.

27. See account of Edward Dodsworth, 1615; in Raven-Hart, *Before Van Riebeeck*, pp. 67–9. It is possible that the Portuguese had left some convicts or *degredados* on the Island in 1525 but this is hard to verify.

28. For Pring's account see Raven-Hart, *Before Van Riebeeck*, p. 69.

29. Walter Peyton's report, 1617, in Raven-Hart, *Before Van Riebeeck*, p. 75.

30. Edward Terry's account, 1616, in Raven-Hart, *Before Van Riebeeck*, p. 84.

31. See Raven-Hart, *Before Van Riebeeck*, p. 84.

32. Humphrey Fitzherbert's account, 1620, in Raven-Hart, *Before Van Riebeeck*, pp. 106–7.

33. For details about Coree, see Richard Elphick, *Khoikhoi and the Founding of White South Africa* (Johannesburg, 1985), pp. 78–82. Also Raven-Hart, *Before Van Riebeeck*, pp. 54, 64–6, 72–90, 98, 114, 120–1, 148.

34. Elphick, *Khoikhoi*, p. 80.

35. For details of Autshumato see Elphick, *Khoikhoi*, pp. 84–94, 101–13.

36. See Raven-Hart, *Before Van Riebeeck*, pp. 129, 138, 143–4, 148–9, 153, for evidence for the residence on and removal of Khoikhoi from the Island between 1632 and 1640.

37. Peter Mundy, 1634, in Raven-Hart, *Before Van Riebeeck*, p. 143.

38. See the account of Hendrik Brouwer, 1636, in Raven-Hart, *Before Van Riebeeck*, p. 144. Eight less fortunate fellow conspirators were summarily drowned. In 1642 more Dutch mutineers were marooned on the Island but they were later taken off by an English ship. See F. Caron, 1642, in Raven-Hart, *Before Van Riebeeck*, p. 155.

39. See account of Johan von Mandelslo, 1639, in Raven-Hart, *Before Van Riebeeck*, p. 153.

40. Account of Artus Gijsels, 1638, in Raven-Hart, *Before Van Riebeeck*, p. 148.

41. For an account of this incident see the documents in Raven-Hart, *Before Van Riebeeck*, pp. 166–78.

42. De Villiers, *Robben Island*, p. 10, believes that without Robben Island it would have taken another one hundred years for a colony to be established at the Cape.

43. H. B. Thom (ed.), *Journal of Jan Van Riebeeck*, vol. 1, 1651–1655 (Cape Town, 1952), pp. 221–3.

44. This was the opinion of the Swedish botanist Thunberg. See V. S. Forbes (ed.), *Carl Peter Thunberg: Travels at the Cape of Good Hope, 1772–1775* (Cape Town, 1986), p. 123.

45. This was the name given to the Peninsular Khoikhoi.

46. Thom, *Van Riebeeck's Diary*, vol. 1, p. 103.

47. H. B. Thom (ed.), *Van Riebeeck's Diary*, vol. 2, 1656–1658 (Cape Town, 1954), pp. 306–12.

48. H. B. Thom (ed.), *Van Riebeeck's Diary*, vol. 3, 1659–1662 (Cape Town, 1958), p. 161. See also Elphick, *Khoikhoi*, pp. 103–16.

49. Thom, *Van Riebeeck's Diary*, vol. 2, p. 121.

50. Thom, *Van Riebeeck's Diary*, vol. 2, p. 133.

51. See 'Extract of a letter from Dassen Island, 12 Oct 1654', in D. Moodie, *The Record; or A Series of Official Papers Relative to the Condition and Treatment of the Native Tribes of South Africa* (Cape Town, 1838; reprint, Cape Town, 1960), Part 1, p. 54.

52. Moodie, *The Record*, p. 253; Thom, *Van Riebeeck's Diary*, vol. 2, p. 85 n1, p. 101.

53. See Thom, *Van Riebeeck's Diary*, vol. 2, p. 139.

54. Thom, *Van Riebeeck's Diary*, vol. 2, p. 148.

55. Thom, *Van Riebeeck's Diary*, vol. 2, p. 243.

56. Thom, *Van Riebeeck's Diary*, vol. 2, pp. 263–5.

57. Thom, *Van Riebeeck's Diary*, vol. 2, p. 277.

58. Thom, *Van Riebeeck's Diary*, vol. 2, p 383; vol. 3, pp. 65–6, 72, 122.

59. Thom, *Van Riebeeck's Diary*, vol. 3, p. 305.

60. Thom, *Van Riebeeck's Diary*, vol. 3, p. 417.

61. Thom, *Van Riebeeck's Diary*, vol. 3, p. 309.

62. D. B. Bosman, 'Uit die biografie van 'n Hottentottin: 'n eksperiment in beskawing', *Huisgenoot*, 3 July 1942, p. 7.

63. For a sensitive account of Krotoa's history see V. C. Malherbe, *Krotoa, Called Eva: A Woman Between* (Centre for African Studies, University of Cape Town, Communications No. 19, 1990).

64. Quoted by Malherbe, *Krotoa*, p. 51.

65. Moodie, *The Record*, pp. 273, 275.

66. See Abstract of Criminal Convictions before the Court of Justice, Cape of Good Hope, 1662–1672. In Moodie, *The Record*, pp. 311–15.

67. Extracts from Wagenaar's Memorandum; in Moodie, *The Record*, p. 295.

68. Extract of the Despatch from Acting Commander Van Brugel; in Moodie, *The Record*, p. 319.

69. In Moodie, *The Record*, p. 323 and n2.

70. CA CJ 3188, Bandieten Rollen, 1738–1795.

71. A. J. Böeseken (ed.), *Resolusies van die Politieke Raad*, vol. 3, 1681–1707, 26 Nov. 1682, p. 55.

72. Apart from CA CJ 3188, details concerning prisoners from the East may be found in CA CJ 3186–3187 (Note Books, Convicts, 1722–1757, 1786) and CA CJ 2562–2568 (Papers received relative to persons banished from Batavia, etc., 1722–1789). See also R. Shell, 'The establishment and spread of Islam at the Cape from the beginning of Company rule to 1838' (BA Hons. thesis, UCT, 1974).

73. CA CJ 3188, 1728; G. C. de Wet (ed.), *Resolusies van die Politieke Raad*, vol. 6, 1720–23, 22 Dec. 1722, p. 2211; vol. 8, 1729–34, 7 April 1733, p. 283.

74. De Wet, *Resolusies*, vol. 6, 24 Nov. 1722, p. 216; CA CJ 3188, 1747.

75. Gordon became the commanding officer of the Cape garrison. He travelled extensively in the Cape interior in the 1770s and 1780s.

76. See CA CJ 359, Criminele Proses Stukken, 1751, p. 357.

77. See Chapter 4.

78. See CA CJ 339, Criminele Proses Stukken, 1735, p. 220.

79. See CA CJ 786, Criminele Proses Stukken, 1740, pp. 327–32.

80. In 1751 for instance a European convict, Michiel van Embreelen, and an *Indiaanen,* Arend van de Velde, were in charge of the Island's boat. See CA CJ 359, p. 371.

81. A. J. Böeseken (ed.), *Resolusies*, vol. 3, 29 Sept. 1692, p. 260.

82. De Wet (ed.), *Resolusies*, vol. 5, 3 March 1716, pp. 36–7; 22 Feb. 1718, p. 257.

83. De Wet (ed.), *Resolusies*, vol. 5, 22 Feb. 1718, p. 257.

84. CA CJ 3188, 1731.

85. Coenraad van der Walle managed this in 1737 and Thomas Detutrepon in 1740; CA CJ 3188, 1737, 1740; CA CJ 3188, 1742, 1743, 1746.

86. De Villiers, *Robben Island*, pp. xiii–xiv.

87. A. J. Böeseken (ed.), *Resolusies van die Politieke Raad*, vol. 4, 1707–1715.

88. De Wet (ed.), *Resolusies*, vol. 6, 1 July 1721, pp. 117–18.

89. De Wet (ed.), *Resolusies*, vol. 6, 22 July 1723, p. 328.

90. See CA CJ 339, pp. 236–8 for mention of crayfish.

91. See CA CJ 359, pp. 369–71. Daing Manganam was released in 1771. CA CJ 3189, 1771.

92. Details of this case may be found in CA CJ 339, pp. 218–38 and in CA CJ 17, Criminele Regts Rollen, 1735, pp. 57–61.

93. CA CJ 339, pp. 236–8.

94. 'Slaeniet, ek heb het gedoen, send my maar op.'

95. CA CJ 3188, 1728.

96. CA CJ 339, pp. 233, 218–32.

97. CA CJ 339, pp. 230–3.

98. *Daggetjes* were presumably little pieces of metal tied in the thongs of a cat-o'-nine-tails.

99. CA CJ 339, pp. 230–2, 218–25.

100. CA CJ 339, p. 226.

101. The summary of the case stated: 'nademaals den Eerste (i.e. Jacobsz) reeds op Batavia met die misdaet is beschuldigt geweest, en daer over voor vijfentwintig jaaren op het England gebarren hebbende.' CA CJ 339, p. 225.

102. CA CJ 17, pp. 57–61.

103. See CA CJ 786, pp. 327–32.

104. 'Daar komt dat bulderbeert al weeder aan om mij te radebraaken zoor als hij laats gedaan heeft, het is beeter een korte dood als een lange pijn.' The expression *radbraken* is figurative rather than literal.

105. CA CJ 786, pp. 330–2.

106. CA C 1517, Letters Despatched, 20 July 1740.

107. The details of this incident are to be found in CA CJ 359, pp. 319–71.

108. The Bouganese had a fearsome reputation amongst the Dutch for their violent vengefulness. See R. Ross, *Cape of Torments: Slavery and Resistance in South Africa* (London, 1983), pp. 19–20.

109. CA CJ 33, Criminele Regts Rollen, pp. 92–7.

110. CA CJ 3188, 1744.

111. CA CJ 3188, 1745. It is probable that Hadje Mattarm is the same person as Abdul Mattara whose *karamat* is on Robben Island.

112. CA CJ 3188, 1761. Cape Muslims express doubt about whether Said Aloeurie did become a Caffer (see M. A. Bradlow, 'Imperialism, state formation and the establishment of a Muslim community at the Cape of Good Hope, 1770–1840: a study in urban resistance', MA, UCT, 1988, pp. 129–30) but the archival record is ambiguous.

113. Ross, *Cape of Torments*, pp. 19, 33–5.

114. CA CJ 3188, 1744, 1761.

115. Achmat Davids, *The History of the Tana Baru* (Cape Town, 1985), pp. 48–52.

116. De Villiers, *Robben Island*, pp. 30–4.

117. CA CJ 3188, 1789, 1793. By 1793 these men had been put in chains alongside other notables such as Minse, the Prince of Ternaten, and Euginius Monoppo,

King of Bolongen Chongoda. Earlier VIPs on the Island included Daing Masfoeroe, a head of Macassar, sentenced in 1752. Minse was not the same Prince of Ternaten who had been on the Island between 1722 and 1747.

118. Ross, *Cape of Torments*, pp. 20–1; Davids, *History of Tana Baru*, pp. 35–9.

119. Davids, *History of Tana Baru*, p. 41; Shell, 'Establishment of Islam', pp. 31–5; Bradlow, 'Muslim community', pp. 143–5. Tuan Guru was also known as Imam Abdullah Kadi Abdus Salaam. In my researches I have found neither name listed in the Bandieten Rollen, although it is possible that Tuan Guru was the same man as Jina Apdula of Ternate.

120. Information based on CA CJ 3189.

121. CA VC 199(a), Report of Inspection of Robben Island, 18 April 1803.

122. CA CJ 3188, 3189.

Chapter 3
THE BRITISH PRISON ON ROBBEN ISLAND 1800–1896

Thanks to Dr V. C. Malherbe and Dr Nigel Penn for their help.

1. M. Boucher and N. Penn, *Britain at the Cape, 1795 to 1803* (Houghton, 1992).

2. M. Boucher and N. Penn, *Britain at the Cape*, pp.11, 14, mention Britain's military-strategic role and the administrative and economic changes it brought about at the Cape as the two major themes of Cape history in the nineteenth century.

3. Carmichael-Smyth papers, London, Public Record Office, 'Observations and reflections on the colony of the Cape of Good Hope', PRO 30/35/14, 11 Feb. 1827.

4. N. Mostert, *Frontiers: The Epic of South Africa's Creation and the Tragedy of the Xhosa People* (London, 1992), pp.xvii–xviii.

5. For example, C. Bayly, *Imperial Meridian: The British Empire and the World, 1780–1830* (London, 1989) and M. Boucher and N. Penn, *Britain at the Cape*.

6. C. Bayly, *Imperial Meridian*, pp.8-9.

7. H. van Wyk, 'Die geskiedenis van die gevangeniswese in die Kaapkolonie, 1806–1910' (unpublished Ph.D. thesis, University of South Africa, 1963), p.131.

8. S. Pete, 'The penal system of colonial Natal' (unpublished LL.M. thesis, University of Cape Town, 1985), p.22 and H.J. Deacon, 'A history of the Breakwater Prison, 1859-1905' (unpublished BA Hons. thesis, University of Cape Town, 1989), p.34.

9. D. van Zyl Smit, 'Public policy and the punishment of crime in a divided society: a historical perspective on the South African penal system', *Crime and Social Justice*, 21-22 (1984), p.147.

10. W.A. Newman, *Biographical Memoir of John Montagu* (London, 1855), p.16.

11. De Salis to Governor and Raaden, 7 August 1805, Cape Archives, Cape Town (CA) VC 199(b).

12. Lists of convicts sent to Robben Island, 1758-1802 [1806], CA CJ 3189, p.140/420.

13. Schultze to Governor, 20 December 1811, Memorials, CA CO 3885.

14. Memorials, January 1802, CA BO 120, doc.3; Robben Island was also used for quarantine purposes in 1816 (see Government Proclamation, 8 March 1816).

15. Memorial of Thomas Suter, 6 May 1820, CA CO 3918.

16. Memorials 1888-89, CA CO 4266, doc.B12.

17. Fitzpatrick to Baird, 15 Feb. 1806, CA CO 3859.

18. Memorials, 20 Oct. 1806, CA CO 3860, doc.581.

19. Commission of Inquiry into the State of the Cape of Good Hope, 1823, CA CO 202.

20. Murray to Earl of Caledon, 3 Jan. 1809, Memorials, CA CO 3871.

21. Commission of Inquiry into the State of the Cape of Good Hope, 1823, CA CO 202.

22. Plasket to Humphreys, 19 August 1826, CA CO 4893; Pedder to Bell, 21 Jan 1829, CA CO 366.

23. Holman, *Voyage around the World* (London, 1834), vol.2, p.144.

24. Schultze to Governor, 20 Dec. 1811, Memorials, CA CO 3885.

25. Inquiry into Commandant's conduct, Supt. of Police to Lieut-Gov., 6 Nov. 1826, Permanent sitting comm. (1826-27), CA 1/CT 16/19.

26. Plasket to Humphreys, 20 April 1826, CO 4893; Plasket to Humphreys, 31 August 1826, CA CO 4893.

27. Bell to Pedder, 6 May 1828, CA CO 4893.

28. Bell to Pedder, 7 Feb. 1833, CA CO 5111; Memorial, 13 Jan. 1826, CA CO 3930, doc.19.

29. Memorials 1840, CA CO 4004, doc.4; Memorial, 13 January 1826, CA CO 3930, doc.19.

30. See 'Return of convicts, detained prisoners and lunatics on Robben Island', January 1827, CA CO 334.

31. V.C. Malherbe, 'Khoikhoi and the question of convict transportation from the Cape Colony, 1820-1842', *South African Historical Journal*, 17 (1985), pp.21, 23, 25. Although allowed by Bathurst in 1815, transportation of Cape offenders to New South Wales was only put into practice in about 1819.

32. Memorial, 27 Sept. 1845, Medical Corr. 1829-50, CA CO 4372.

33. H. van Wyk, 'Die geskiedenis van die gevangeniswese in die Kaapkolonie', p.199.

34. 'Return of convicts, detained prisoners and lunatics on Robben Island', January 1827, CA CO 334.

35. Convicted criminals for 1814, CA CJ 3192A.

36. *Dictionary of South African Biography*, vol.4, ed. C. J. Beyers (Pretoria, 1981), p.642.

37. Sentences, CA CJ 803, 13 May 1809.

38. Return, Jan.1831, CA CO 401. Ten per cent was, however, probably considerably larger than the percentage of female convicts in the colony's mainland prisons.

39. V.C. Malherbe, 'Khoikhoi and the question of convict transportation', p.28.

40. Cape of Good Hope Blue Book for 1828, CA CO 5970, pp.208-9.

41. A 'prize negro' was a person who was 'rescued' from a slaving vessel by the British after the abolition of slavery in 1807. At the Cape, these people were apprenticed, mainly to colonists, for several years before they were given their freedom. A 'free black' was a freed slave

or a descendant of one. The term 'Kaffre' or 'Kafir', literally 'heathen', had broadened and altered its meaning by the nineteenth century at the Cape to indicate a Bantu-speaking African, especially a Xhosa (in the previous century the 'caffers' of Cape Town were low-ranking policemen). 'Kafir' was used in this descriptive sense by government officials and colonists. Nowadays the word has very negative connotations, however. 'Return of convicts, detained prisoners and lunatics on Robben Island', January 1827, CA CO 334.

42. 'Monthly return of convicts on Robben Island', Jan. 1844, Letters from Robben Island, CA CO 533.

43. Cape of Good Hope Blue Book for 1828, CA CO 5970, pp.209, 211.

44. Convicted criminals for 1815, CA CJ 3192A.

45. Convicted criminals for 1815, CA CJ 3192A.

46. H. van Wyk, 'Die geskiedenis van die gevangeniswese in die Kaapkolonie', p.149.

47. 'Return of convicts, detained prisoners and lunatics on Robben Island', June 1827, CA CO 334.

48. Cape of Good Hope Blue Book for 1828, CA CO 5970, p.212.

49. Letters, CA CO 533, 5 Jan 1844.

50. 'Monthly return of convicts on Robben Island', Jan. 1844, Letters from Robben Island, CA CO 533.

51. S. de Villiers, *Robben Island* (Cape Town, 1971), p.44.

52. Petrie to Bird, 17 Feb. 1820 and 22 March 1820, CA CO 122.

53. Petrie to Bird, 22 March 1820 and 9 August 1820, CA CO 122 and Bird to Petrie, 16 August 1820, Letters from the Governor, CA CO 4843.

54. Criminal sentences, 16 Dec. 1820, CA CJ 814, p.314.

55. Petrie to Bird, 9 August 1820, CA CO 122.

56. Criminal sentences, 16 Dec. 1820, CA CJ 814, pp.300-2.

57. Criminal sentences, 16 Dec. 1820, CA CJ 814, pp.314-15.

58. Criminal sentences, 16 Dec. 1820, CA CJ 814, p.290.

59. V.C. Malherbe, 'David Stuurman: "Last chief of the Hottentots,"' *African Studies*, 39, 1 (1980), p.60.

60. Criminal sentences, 16 Dec. 1820, CA CJ 814, pp.318-20. Four of these prisoners – Jacob, Jakawa, Piet and Battie – were later commended by the Commandant as 'the best behaved prisoners on the Island' (Commandant to Plasket, 18 June 1827, CA CO 334).

61. V.C. Malherbe, 'David Stuurman', p.58. See CJ 3661, Diverse Proses Stukken, p.77.

62. V.C. Malherbe, 'David Stuurman', p.59.

63. V.C. Malherbe, 'David Stuurman', pp.47, 50.

64. V.C. Malherbe, 'David Stuurman', pp.52, 54.

65. V.C. Malherbe, 'David Stuurman', p.55.

66. V.C. Malherbe, 'David Stuurman', p.59.

67. N. Mostert, *Frontiers*, p.428 and chapter 13.

68. Letters, CA CO 4841, 11 Oct. 1819.

69. B. Maclennan, *A Proper Degree of Terror: John Graham and the Cape's Eastern Frontier* (Johannesburg, 1986), p.221.

70. Criminal cases, Appeal Court, 1820, CA CJ 778, p.44.

71. S. de Villiers, *Robben Island*, pp.37ff.; Capt. T. Boteler, *Narrative of a Voyage of Discovery* (London, 1835), describes the request by the commander of the *Leven*, Capt. F.W. Owen, for interpreters from Robben Island in 1822.

72. Criminal cases in Appeal Court, 1821, CA CJ 778.

73. J. Mason, 'Slaveholder resistance to the amelioration of slavery at the Cape', paper presented at the Western Cape Roots and Realities Conference, University of Cape Town, 1986, pp.21-2.

74. Memorial, 1 June 1825, CA CO 3928, doc.309.

75. Government proclamation, 12 Jan. 1821, CA CO 5958.

76. Two slaves and a free black woman were, however, convicted in 1822, possibly after an escape from Robben Island (Klad boek, 17 Jan. 1822, CA CJ 3192A).

77. H. van Wyk, 'Die geskiedenis van die gevangeniswese in die Kaapkolonie', p.147.

78. Cape of Good Hope Blue Book for 1828, CA CO 5970, p.211.

79. Bell to Pedder, 25 Oct. 1828, CA CO 5111; Moore-Craig to Wolfe, 29 Nov. 1841, CA CO 5112; Wolfe to Montagu, 31 March 1844, CA CO 533.

80. Plasket to Humphreys, 27 Oct. 1826, CA CO 4893.

81. S. de Villiers, *Robben Island*, p.44.

82. H. van Wyk, 'Die geskiedenis van die gevangeniswese in die Kaapkolonie', p.114.

83. Plasket to Superintendent of Police, 8 Nov. 1826, CA CO 4891.

84. Plasket to Superintendent of Police, 8 Nov. 1826, CA CO 4891.

85. Plasket to Superintendent of Police, 8 Nov. 1826, CA CO 4891.

86. Plasket to Pedder, 7 May 1827, CA CO 4893.

87. Plasket to Superintendent of Police, 8 Nov. 1826, CA CO 4891.

88. Pedder to Plasket, 15 Jan. 1827, CA CO 334; Plasket to Pedder, 20 June 1827, CA CO 4893.

89. 'Return of convicts, detained prisoners and lunatics on Robben Island', January 1827, CA CO 334.

90. Holman, *Voyage*, p.140.

91. Acting Secretary to Govt. to Pedder, 5 Sept. 1829, CA CO 5111.

92. Pedder to Plasket, 11 July 1827, CA CO 334.

93. Bell to Pedder, 23 Sept. 1828, CA CO 5111.

94. Pedder to Plasket, 11 July 1827, CA CO 334; Bell to Pedder, 9 Jan 1828, CA CO 4893.

95. Convicts to Somerset, 1825, Memorials, CA CO 3928; Plasket to Pedder, 10 July 1827 and 28 July 1827, CA CO 4893.

96. Pedder to Plasket, 5 Sept. 1827, CA CO 334.

97. Bell to Pedder, 14 April 1830, CA CO 5111.

98. Bell to Pedder, 7 Feb. 1833, CA CO 5111.

99. S. de Villiers, *Robben Island*, p.44.

100. *Dictionary of South African Biography*, vol.2, p.75. On Wolfe, see R.T. Wolfe, *The Wolfes of Forenaghts, Blackhall, Baronrath, Co. Kildare, Tipperary, Cape of Good Hope etc.*, 2nd ed. (Guildford, 1893), p.80.

101. Great Britain Army Medical Department and War Office, 'Statistical reports on the sickness, mortality and invaliding among the troops in Western Africa, St. Helena, the Cape of Good Hope and Mauritius', section 2B2, p.5b.

102. Brink to Wolfe, 5 June 1834, CA CO 5111.

103. Cape of Good Hope Blue Book for 1828, CA CO 5970, p.212; Brink to Wolfe, 23 July 1834, CA CO 3968.

104. Brink to Wolfe, 14 Nov. 1834, CA CO 5111.

105. Brink to Wolfe, 4 Nov. 1834, CA CO 5111; Bell to Wolfe, 4 July 1836, CO 5112; Brink to Wolfe, 15 Oct. 1833, CA CO 5111; Bell to Wolfe, 14 Sept. 1836, CA CO 5112.

106. Bell to Wolfe, 28 Nov. 1836 and 6 March 1838, CA CO 5112.

107. Rules and Regulations for the Prison on Robben Island, CA CO 533, 31 March 1844.

108. Replies to the Queries of the Robben Island Committee from Albany, 26 August 1842, Letters from Albany, CA 1/AY 8/27; Memorials, CA CO 4025, doc.309, June 1845.

109. Replies to the Queries of the Robben Island Committee from Albany, 26 August 1842, Letters from Albany, CA 1/AY 8/27. This was Montagu's view as well.

110. Memorials, 1845, CA CO 4025, doc.309.

111. Memorials, 1840, CA CO 4004, doc.87.

112. Memorials, 1842, CA CO 4013, doc.249.

113. Letters from Robben Island, 5 May 1855, CA CO 659.

114. Letters from Robben Island, 11 May 1855, CA CO 659.

115. Letters from Robben Island, 11 May 1855, CA CO 659; J. Peires, *The Dead Will Arise* (Johannesburg, 1989), p.301.

116. Letters from Robben Island, 7 Jan. 1862, CA CO 797.

117. J. Peires, *The Dead Will Arise*, p.302.

118. Letters from Robben Island, 2 August 1862, CA CO 797; J. Peires, *The Dead Will Arise*, p.302.

119. T.J. Stapleton, 'The memory of Maqoma: an assessment of Jingqi oral tradition in Ciskei and Transkei', *History in Africa*, 20 (1993), p.321.

120. T.J. Stapleton, 'Reluctant slaughter: rethinking Maqoma's role in the Xhosa Cattle Killing (1853-57)', *International Journal of African Historical Studies*, 26, 2 (1993), p.346. Stapleton has also published a biography of Maqoma called *Maqoma: Xhosa Resistance to Colonial Advance* (Johannesburg, 1994).

121. T.J. Stapleton, 'The memory of Maqoma', p.321.

122. 'Report of the Commission of Inquiry into the General Infirmary and Lunatic Asylum on Robben Island', CA G31-1862, p.69.

123. Letters from Robben Island, 1 Nov. 1858, CA CO 724.

124. 'A visit to Robben Island', *Cape Monthly Magazine*, 6 (September 1859), p.191.

125. Letters from Robben Island, 24 Sept. 1861, CA CO 779.

126. J. Peires, *The Dead Will Arise*, p.301.

127. Letters from Robben Island, 12 April 1858, CA CO 724.

128. N. Mostert, *Frontiers*, pp.1228-29.

129. Public Works Department, Letters, 4 Feb 1863, CA PWD 1/835.

130. Annual Report on Robben Island for 1863, CA G3-1864, p.29.

131. Robben Island Chaplains' Diaries, University of the Witwatersrand Manuscripts Collection (UWMC), 19 April 1869.

132. Letters from Robben Island, 10 Sept. 1873, CA CO 972.

133. On exhumation of what were claimed to be Maqoma's bones, a bullet hole was found in the shoulder blade which revived the murder claims. T.J. Stapleton, 'The memory of Maqoma', pp.324-25, 328-29.

134. *Dictionary of South African Biography*, vol.2, pp.383-84. A (rather old-fashioned) biography of the man is N. Herd's *The Bent Pine: The Trial of Chief Langalibalele* (Johannesburg, 1976).

135. J.A. Spear, 'Cape reactions to the Langalibalele affair: a study of Eastern and Western Province attitudes' (unpublished BA Hons. thesis, UCT, 1977), p.65.

136. Letters from Robben Island, 29 Jan. 1875, CA RI 2.

137. J.A. Spear, 'Cape reactions to the Langalibalele affair', pp.38, 48.

138. Report by the chief wives of Langalibalele, 7 January 1876, South African Library Manuscripts, MSB 299 Folder 1(1), item 7.

139. Letters, 26 July 1880, CA CO 1125.

140. Annual Report on Robben Island for 1880, CA G22-1881, p.4. The close connection between the Breakwater Prison and Robben Island was a result of the creation of a branch convict station of the Breakwater Prison on the Island in 1866 to provide criminal prisoners as workers for the Robben Island hospital. On the Breakwater Prison, see Harriet Deacon, 'A history of the Breakwater Prison, 1859-1905' (unpublished BA Hons. thesis, University of Cape Town, 1989).

141. Letters received by the Home Office from the Colonial Office, South Africa, 1881, Public Records Office, London, GH 1/411.

142. Annual Report on Robben Island for 1880, CA G22-1881, p.4; Letters received by the Home Office from the Colonial Office, South Africa, 1881, GH 1/411 in Public Records Office, London.

143. T. Strauss, *War along the Orange* (University of Cape Town African Studies Centre, Communications No.1, 1979), p.116.

Chapter 4
THE MEDICAL INSTITUTIONS ON ROBBEN
ISLAND 1846–1931

Thanks to Professor John Iliffe, my PhD supervisor.

1. Great Britain, 'Papers respecting a plan for improving the discipline of convicts at the Cape of Good Hope received during the years 1843 and 1844, *Accounts and Papers* 1847, vol. 48, 359–458: 'Report on Robben

Island', 6 Jan. 1844, p.449.

2. Maitland to Secretary of State, 23 Dec. 1844, London, PRO, Original Correspondence, CO 48/245.

3. B. Kruger, *The Pear Tree Blossoms: A History of the Moravian Mission Stations in South Africa 1737–1869* (Genadendal, 1966), p.211.

4. Admissions Register for Old Somerset Hospital, CA, Old Somerset Hospital Papers, HOS 58.

5. Memorial of Hicks et al., 3 Sept. 1846, CA, Memorials received by Colonial Office, CO 4029, doc.296.

6. T.E. Kirk, 'Self-government and self-defence in South Africa' (D. Phil. thesis, University of Oxford, 1972), pp.280-84.

7. F. Madden and D. Fieldhouse (eds.), *Imperial Reconstruction 1763–1840: The Evolution of Alternative Systems of Colonial Government* (New York, 1987), p.xxxiv.

8. 'Requisition for medicines', 12 May 1847, CA, Medical Committee, MC 20.

9. 'Return of chronic sick, lunatics and lepers in the General Infirmary', Select Committee of 1855, CPP, A9-1855, p.17.

10. Wolfe to Montagu, 14 Sept. 1846, CA, Letters received by Colonial Office on medical matters 1831-46, CO 4372.

11. 'Return of chronic sick, lunatics and lepers in the General Infirmary', Select Committee of 1855, CPP, A9-1855, p.17.

12. Admissions registers of the Old Somerset Hospital (CA, Old Somerset Hospital Papers, HOS 58) and of the Robben Island lunatic asylum (CA, Robben Island Papers, RI 181).

13. 'Return of chronic sick, lunatics and lepers in the General Infirmary', Select Committee of 1855, CPP, A9-1855, p.17.

14. Dr. Landsberg to Colonial Secretary, 10 Dec. 1886, CA, Letters received by Colonial Office, CO 1364.

15. Memorial of Tinehan, 18 Nov. 1851, CA, Memorials received by Colonial Office, CO 4062, doc.T18.

16. Annual report for 1855 (Old Somerset Hospital), CPP, G12-1856, p.2. This order probably lapsed in 1852 when the Admissions Register stops recording patients as 'coloured late apprentices'.

17. Annual report for 1855 (Old Somerset Hospital), CPP, G12-1856, p.2.

18. 'Management of Somerset Hospital', 1840, CA, Cape Town Municipality Papers, Minutes of Wardmasters, 3/CT 1/2/1/1.

19. Dr Bickersteth's memo on amended regulations for the Old Somerset Hospital and Pauper Asylum, [1845(?)], CA, Letters received by Colonial Office on medical matters 1831-46, CO 4372.

20. Memorial of De Vries, 21 April 1853, CA, Memorials received by Colonial Office, CO 4072, doc.84. Outpatients outnumbered inpatients by about three to one in 1855 (Annual report for 1855 (Old Somerset Hospital), CPP, G12-1856, pp.2, 4).

21. M. Vogel cited in H. Marland, 'Lay and medical conceptions of medical charity during the nineteenth century: the case of the Huddersfield General Dispensary and Infirmary', in J. Barry and C. Jones (eds.), *Medicine and Charity before the Welfare State* (London, 1991), p.149.

22. Landsberg, Minutes of evidence, Select Committee of 1865 (Old Somerset Hospital), CPP, A27-1865, pp.16-17.

23. Report, Commission of 1861-2, CPP, G31-1862, p.ix.

24. Ebden, Minutes of evidence, Commission of 1861-2, CPP, G31-1862, pp.252-53.

25. Peirce, Minutes of evidence, Commission of 1861-2, CPP, G31-1862, p.109.

26. Annual report for 1871, CPP, G18-1872, p.8.

27. Dr Ebden, Minutes of evidence, Select Committee of 1865 (Somerset Hospital), CPP, A27-1865, p.39.

28. East London, Annual reports for 1882 (Civil Commissioners, Resident Magistrates and District Surgeons), CPP, G91-1883.

29. Memorial of Widow Hennessy, 13 Nov. 1863, CA, Memorials received by Colonial Office, CO 4130, doc.H43.

30. Memorial of Davies, 12 March 1859, CA, Memorials received by Colonial Office, CO 4108, doc.D20.

31. Cape of Good Hope Blue Book for 1846, pp.176-77.

32. Birtwhistle to Montagu, 16 Dec. 1848, CA, Robben Island Papers, Letterbook, RI 1; Medical Committee to Colonial Secretary, 19 May 1855 in Select Committee of 1855, CPP, A9-1855, p.4.

33. Young, Minutes of Evidence, Inquiry of 1852, Papers relating to the Select Committee of 1854, CPP, A37-1855, p.20.

34. For example, James Nutt (see Memorial of Nutt, 6 Feb. 1884, CA, Memorials received by Colonial Office, CO 4243, doc.N4; Parson to Webb, 25 Feb. 1884, CA, Letters received by the Breakwater Prison 1881-1885, PBW 2; Nutt, Minutes of evidence, Commission of 1894-5, CPP, G10-1894, p.327); Alexander Rose (see Memo from Jane Rose to Lieut-Governor, Inquiry of 1853, Papers relating to the Select Committee of 1854, CPP, A37-1855, p.98).

35. Dr Birtwhistle to Piers, 14 Sept. 1855, CA, Robben Island Papers, Letterbook, RI 1.

36. Nutt, Minutes of evidence, Commission of 1861-2, CPP, G31-1862, p.168.

37. 'Leper papers', Papers relating to the Commission of 1854, CPP, A37-1855, p.94.

38. Birtwhistle to Secretary to Government, 16 Feb. 1853, CA, Robben Island Papers, Letterbook, RI 1; Verreaux, Minutes of evidence, Commission of 1861-2, CPP, G31-1862, p.158.

39. Watson, Minutes of evidence, Inquiry of 1852, Papers relating to the Select Committee of 1854, CPP, A37-1855, p.19.

40. Parsons, Minutes of evidence, Select Committee of 1883, CPP, A23-1883, p.5.

41. *Cape Monitor*, 29 April 1862.

42. In 1845 the total cost of the (civil) medical establishment at the Cape was £7124 including initial repair costs for Robben Island (P. Laidler and M. Gelfand,

South Africa: Its Medical History (Cape Town, 1971), p.222); in 1850, it was about £6600 ('Estimated expenses for colonial medical establishment' c.1849, London, Wellcome Institute Archives, Sir John Hall papers, Box 48, RAMC 397, DRM 3/3).

43. Memorial of D. Thompson, 6 April 1852, Inquiry of 1852, Papers relating to the Select Committee of 1854, CPP, A37-1855, p.1.

44. Birtwhistle to Commissioners, 6 Sept. 1854, Papers relating to the Select Committee of 1854, CPP, A37-1855, p.122.

45. Memorial of D. Thompson, 6 April 1852, Inquiry of 1852, Papers relating to the Select Committee of 1854, CPP, A37-1855, pp.1-2.

46. Kirk, 'Self-government and self-defence in South Africa', p.460.

47. D. Foster, pers. comm., 1991.

48. Impey, Minutes of evidence, Commission of 1894-5, CPP, G10-1894, p.104.

49. Abercrombie, Minutes of evidence, Commission of 1861-2, CPP, G31-1862, p.237.

50. Wodehouse to Newcastle, 7 Aug. 1863, Correspondence 1863-1865, CPP, A9-1865, p.10; Conolly considered 1:17 the lowest acceptable staff–patient ratio in pauper asylums (the ideal was 1:12), rising to 1:13 in troublesome wards (I.L. Patch, 'The Surrey County lunatic asylum', *British Journal of Psychiatry*, 159 (1991), p.74).

51. Edmunds to Colonial Secretary, 10 Aug. 1864, CA, Letters received by Colonial Office, CO 827.

52. Annual report for 1862, CPP, G7-1863, p.4.

53. Annual report for 1862, CPP, G7-1863, p.1.

54. *South African Advertiser and Mail*, 6 Jan. 1864.

55. Dr Ross, Minutes of evidence, Select Committee of 1865 (Somerset Hospital), CPP, A27-1865, p.25.

56. Dr Ross, Minutes of evidence, Select Committee of 1865 (Somerset Hospital), CPP, A27-1865, p.24.

57. Although the original plans had been delayed to make use of Conolly's suggestions for the model asylum, these were deemed too expensive, and a modified plan was used.

58. Edmunds, Minutes of evidence, Select Committee of 1871, CPP, A3-1871, p.3.

59. Select Committee of 1855, CPP, A9-1855, p.17.

60. Admissions database. Because the census data for 1875 is not aggregated by class or disaggregated by occupation it is difficult to compare the proportion of 'better class' Robben Island patients with the general proportion in the Cape District, or the Colony as a whole.

61. Z. Gussow, *Leprosy, Racism and Public Health* (London, 1989), p.203.

62. Laing et al. to Colonial Secretary, 19 May 1855, Select Committee of 1855, CPP, A9-1855, p.4.

63. 'Minute re disturbances at Robben Island', Loch to Lord Marquis, 4 Sept. 1893, London, PRO, Original Correspondence, CO 48/522.

64. Petition of leper Franz Jacobs to the Queen, Aug. 1892 in Loch to Lord Marquis, 4 Sept. 1893, London, PRO, Original Correspondence, CO 48/522.

65. Memorial of F. Diedrichs, 3 Jan. 1895, CA, Health Branch, Robben Island 1895, CO 7192.

Translated from the Dutch by the author.

66. 'Minute re disturbances at Robben Island', Loch to Lord Marquis, 4 Sept. 1893, London, PRO, Original Correspondence, CO 48/522.

67. Waterston, Minutes of evidence, Commission of 1894-5, CPP, G10-1894, p.259.

68. Annual report for 1893, CPP, G24-1894, p.88.

69. Commissioner to UCS, 3 March 1889, CA, Robben Island Papers, Letters despatched, RI 59; 'Minute re disturbances at Robben Island', Loch to Lord Marquis, 4 Sept. 1893, London, PRO, Original Correspondence, CO 48/522.

70. Dixon, Minutes of evidence, Select Committee of 1889, CPP, G3-1889, p.17.

71. P.D. von Blomberg, *Allerlei aus Süd-Afrika* (Gutersloh, 1899), pp.56-57.

72. De Smidt, 'Minute re disturbances at Robben Island', Loch to Lord Marquis, 4 Sept. 1893, London, PRO, Original Correspondence, CO 48/522.

73. De Smidt, 'Minute re disturbances at Robben Island', Loch to Lord Marquis, 4 Sept. 1893, London, PRO, Original Correspondence, CO 48/522.

74. Commissioner to UCS, 27 March 1899, CA, Robben Island Papers, Letters despatched, RI 59.

75. Chute, 'Abstracts of Replies', Commission of 1894-5, CPP, G4-1895, p.89.

76. Impey, the ex-Superintendent of Robben Island, was accused of doing this in 1908 (MOH to UCS, 16 July 1908, CA, MOH Papers, Leprosy Commission, 1904-1908, MOH 353, Folio C121a).

77. Impey to UCS, 22 Sept. 1893, CA, Health Branch, Leprosy Commission 1893-1903, CO 7663, fol.1258.

78. S.P. Impey, 'The non-contagiousness of anaesthetic leprosy', *SAMJ*, 6, 1 (May 1898), p.7.

79. 'Leprosy notification', *SAMJ*, 6 (July 1898), p.64.

80. 'Lepers in name only', *South African Review*, 12 October 1908.

81. Minutes of evidence, Select Committee of 1909, CPP, A12-1909, p.15.

82. Piers to UCS, 22 Feb. 1898, CA, Health Branch, Robben Island 1898, CO 7210.

83. Copy of statistics given in the House of Assembly, Aug. 1899, CA, Health Branch, Robben Island lepers 1896-1902, CO 7509, fol.635.

84. Verreaux, Minutes of evidence, Commission of 1861-2, CPP, G31-1862, p.158.

85. *The Lantern*, 11 Oct. 1884, p.1.

86. 'Lepers at the Cape', *Blackwoods Edinburgh Magazine* (Sept. 1889), p.294. This comment may just have been sensationalist.

87. Government notice 520, 1892.

88. Rules drawn up before 1894 were not provided for in law. The 1894 Amendment Act was intended to provide for such regulations, which were finally passed in 1902.

89. Annual report for 1895, CPP, G27-1896, p.86.

90. Commissioner to UCS, 12 Sept. 1910, CA, Robben Island Papers, Letters despatched, RI 75.

91. Commissioner to UCS, 15 Oct. 1901, CA, Robben Island Papers, Letters despatched, RI 61.

92. Commissioner to UCS, 27 Sept. 1901, CA, Robben Island Papers, Letters despatched, RI 61.

93. Commissioner to UCS, 22 May 1907, CA, Robben Island Papers, Letters despatched, RI 69.

94. Loch to Lord Marquis, 4 Sept. 1893, London, PRO, Original Correspondence, CO 48/522.

95. Commissioner to UCS, 1 June 1904, CA, Health Branch, Lepers 1904-1908, CO 8053.

96. Commissioner to UCS, 27 Aug. 1904, CA, Health Branch, Lepers 1904, CO 7862.

97. Engleheart to Commissioner, 3 Sept. 1904, CA, Health Branch, Lepers 1904, CO 7862.

98. Commissioner to UCS, 10 Aug. 1904, CA, Health Branch, Lepers 1904, CO 7862.

99. Annual report for 1904, CPP, G57-1905, p.100.

100. Commissioner to UCS, 8 Sept. 1910, CA, Robben Island Papers, Letters despatched, RI 73.

101. Commissioner to UCS, 11 Nov. 1910, CA, Robben Island Papers, Letters despatched, RI 73.

102. Editorial, *South African Health Society Magazine* (Oct. 1927), pp.1-2.

103. Annual report for 1913, UPP, UG24-1913, p.6.

104. Annual report for 1920, UPP, UG8-1922, p.383.

105. Annual report for 1922, UPP, UG9-1922, p.297.

106. Annual report for 1929-1930 (Public Health), UPP, UG40-1930, p.62.

107. J.M. Hunter and M.C. Thomas, 'Hypothesis of leprosy, tuberculosis and urbanization in Africa', *Social Science and Medicine*, 19, 1 (1984), p.27.

108. 'The principles of the prophylaxis of leprosy', *First General Report of the Leprosy Commission, League of Nations Health Organization* (Geneva, 1931), p.5.

Chapter 5
ROBBEN ISLAND AND THE MILITARY
1931–1960

1. CA, PAS File MM 558, correspondence 27 April 1926–8 Aug. 1930.

2. Map 'Building No. 8132/2', Public Works Department, Cape Town. With acknowledgment to Lieutenant-General G. Dunbar Moodie.

3. *Die Huisgenoot*, 30 Jan. 1931 (photograph and caption).

4. L. G. Green, *Islands Time Forgot* (London, 1962), pp. 14–21.

5. Debates, House of Assembly, 20 Feb. 1931, p. 639.

6. *Cape Times*, 7 Nov. 1934.

7. Debates, House of Assembly, 14 Feb. 1933, pp. 653–4.

8. Debates, House of Assembly, 2 May 1934, pp. 3035–42.

9. Debates, House of Assembly, 17 March 1936, p. 1395.

10. L. C. F. Turner, H. R. Gordon-Cumming and J. E. Betzler, *War in the Southern Ocean 1939–1945* (Cape Town, 1961), p. 7.

11. CA, CAD 2/1/1/58, C 14/96, Dichmont to C. Graham Botha, 20 Sept. 1937.

12. Debates, House of Assembly, 23 March 1939, pp. 2279–80; A. K. du Toit, *South Africa's Fighting Ships, Past and Present* (Rivonia, 1992), pp. 19–22.

13. Lawrence Green's description evoking memories of a once formidable German island-fortress.

14. N. Orpen and H. J. Martin, *Salute to Sappers* (Johannesburg, 1981), Pt 1, pp. 17–8.

15. *Weekend Argus*, 8/9 May 1993 (Article by G. D. Moodie).

16. *Vlootnuus/Navy News*, June 1987 (Article by Commander W. M. Bisset).

17. *Official Year Book of the Union of South Africa*, No. 23–1946 (Pretoria, 1947), p. 18.

18. J. W. Yates-Benyon, *The Weak and the Wicked* (Cape Town, 1959), p. 52.

19. For mention of these AA armaments see G. de Vries, *Wingfield. A Pictorial History* [Cape Town, 1991], p. 191. Searchlights were deployed, but there is uncertainty about the translation of the blueprint for the guns into actuality.

20. N. Orpen, *The Cape Town Highlanders 1885–1985* (Cape Town, 1986), p. 6.

21. L. Crook, *Young's Field. A History of the Anti-Aircraft School* (Kimberley, 1991), pp. 15, 17.

22. Orpen and Martin, *Salute the Sappers* (Johannesburg, 1982), Pt II, p. 383.

23. H. J. Martin and N. D. Orpen, *South Africa at War* (Cape Town, 1979), pp. 122–3.

24. UG 8–1939: Annual Report for 1937, Department of Defence, p. 17.

25. Lieutenant-General G. Dunbar Moodie (Interview).

26. See M. H. Hill, *Look-in after 40 Years: The Story of the Artillery Specialists WAAS, 1941–1945* (Johannesburg, *c.* 1985).

27. *The Nongqai*, Jan. 1943, p. 12.

28. P. Brain, *South African Radar in World War II* (Cape Town, 1993), pp. 46, 83.

29. Martin and Orpen, *South Africa at War*, p. 265.

30. For comprehensive coverage of this unit see M. H. P. Laver and others, *Sailor-Women, Sea-Women SWANS: A History of the South African Women's Auxiliary Naval Service 1943–1949* (Simon's Town, 1986). Also *Cape Times*, 27 Dec. 1968 (Recollections of Lieutenant-Commander G. J. Perkins, RNR).

31. Martin and Orpen, *South Africa at War*, p. 238.

32. Martin and Orpen, *South Africa at War* (Map inside back cover 'South Africa and its Coastal Waters 1939–1945').

33. Martin and Orpen, *South Africa at War*, p. 193.

34. 'Salute the women of Robben Island' by Lieutenant-General G. Dunbar Moodie in *Weekend Argus*, 8/9 May 1993.

35. *Cape Argus* cutting [late 1946] referred to 'hundreds of excellent buildings awaiting tenants'.

36. Debates, House of Assembly, 16 April 1947, col. 2797.

37. CA, Provincial Education Department, PAE vol. 1663, C 32/830/G, 1946–1952.

38. *Government Gazette*, 10 Aug. 1951, Notice 2061, p. 14.

39. Orpen, *The Cape Town Highlanders 1885–1985*, p. 26.

40. *Commando*, March 1957, p. 45.

Chapter 6
RESISTANCE ON ROBBEN ISLAND 1963–1976

*This and the following chapter represent work in progress for a PhD dissertation on Robben Island politics and its implications for South African politics and theories of resistance. I would be most grateful to receive comments and criticisms from readers, especially former Robben Islanders and other political prisoners. These can be sent to me at 7 Haven Road, Greenside, 2193, Johannesburg, South Africa.

I would like to thank the following people for their help. First and foremost, I thank everyone who has allowed me to interview them. Second, thank you to everyone who read and commented on drafts of this chapter, including the participants of the Institute for Advanced Social Research seminar at the University of the Witwatersrand where a draft of this chapter was presented; Rachidi Molapo of the Mayibuye Centre, University of the Western Cape; the members of my dissertation discussion group at the University of Texas at Austin; and Barbara Buntman, Penny McKenzie and Manuel Orozco who provided moral support and logistical help as well as reading the chapter. I am most grateful to the Mayibuye Centre for their financial support for the transcription of my interviews. Finally, my very grateful thanks to Gail Gerhart and Tom Karis for not only reading and commenting on my work, but being so very generous in sharing their own resources with me.

1. Robben Island here refers to the maximum security political prison, although the prison accounted for only a portion of the Island's use of space. As will become clear below, this prison also housed common-law or non-political prisoners until about 1970. The literature and interviews with former Islanders give different dates as to when the common-law prisoners left or were housed in a separate prison on the Island. After the non-political prisoners were removed from the political prison, criminal prisoners came to be housed in a separate, medium-security prison on the Island. This prison will not be considered in this chapter.
2. Tom Lodge, *Black Politics in South Africa* (London, 1985), p. 231.
3. Lodge, *Black Politics*, p. 241.
4. Fikile Bam interview, 22 September 1994; Neville Alexander interview, 18 April and 26 October 1994. In the case of the Yu Chi Chan Club and the National Liberation Front (NLF), four men were each sentenced to ten years' imprisonment for merely discussing and reading about armed struggle. The NLF arose from a group of members of the Non-European Unity Movement (NEUM). But NEUM rejected consideration of the armed struggle and expelled Neville Alexander, one of the chief protagonists. He notes that they were known on Robben Island 'not as Unity Movement but as National Liberation Front' (Alexander interview). Many of the Robben Islanders do, however, refer to this group as the 'Unity Movement'. According to Fikile Bam (interview), the NLF–Unity Movement grouping did not organise as a political body on the Island.
5. Natoo Babenia, 'Cast in Stone on a Hell Hole' (manuscript, Mayibuye Centre, University of the Western Cape), p. 182. Prisoner estimates of the number of inmates vary, both in total number and in terms of the breakdown of organisational affiliation. For example, Indres Naidoo (interview, by Victoria Butler, in Karis–Gerhart collection) remembered that when he arrived there in December 1963, 'the Island had over 1000 political prisoners. Of the 1000 only about 35 were ANC. The rest were PAC. By 1965 their number had been reduced to less than 500. Ours had increased to over 1000.'
6. I. Naidoo, *Island in Chains: Ten Years on Robben Island as Told by Indres Naidoo to Albie Sachs* (Harmondsworth, 1982), pp. 228–9.
7. N. Alexander, *Robben Island Dossier 1964–1974* (Cape Town, 1994), p. 40; see also Naidoo, *Island in Chains*, p. 72.
8. Hansard, 1974, col. 6296.
9. Little information exists about the conditions before 1963.
10. Joe Shithlibane (interview, 20 November 1994), then a common-law prisoner, recalls being imprisoned there from 1960.
11. D. M. Zwelonke, *Robben Island* (London, 1987), p. 14.
12. Ahmed Kathrada, interview, June and 31 October 1994. Mandela's first incarceration on Robben Island was as a convicted prisoner. He had received a five-year sentence for inciting African workers and leaving the country illegally.
13. M. Dingake, *My Fight Against Apartheid* (London, 1987), p. 217.
14. Alexander, *Robben Island Dossier*, pp. 11–12.
15. The literature is filled with discussion about the warders, an important topic, unfortunately beyond the scope of this chapter.
16. Dlamini, *Robben Island*, pp. 165, 170.
17. Other criminal prisoners remained, or were brought to the Island prison, however. Dlamini (*Robben Island*, p. 164) notes: 'When they [the hardened criminals and gang members] realised that ... the date of their departure [from Robben Island] was getting nearer, the gang warfare began again. While they were at each other's throats, a draft of short term criminal convicts arrived. It was obvious they had come to replace them.'
18. Accurate periodisation is often difficult. For example, Indres Naidoo (*Island in Chains*) does not mention Badenhorst, and instead he implies a slow, gradual improvement up until the end of his sentence in 1973.
19. Alexander, *Robben Island Dossier*, pp. 13–14.
20. Alexander, *Robben Island Dossier*, p. 13. Understanding state perspectives is largely a matter of speculation as, at least at the time of writing, access to state archives and related sources has been denied. More broadly, the question of the relationship between the prison authorities and the state more broadly is also largely a matter of speculation, and is beyond the scope of this chapter. There is no doubt, however, that incarceration on Robben Island was 'supervised' by the security branches of the state, as well as the Prisons Service.
21. Alexander, *Robben Island Dossier*, p. 14.

22. Because he was white, Denis Goldberg was not allowed to be with the rest of the Rivonia group, and was instead sent to Pretoria Central Prison.

23. The role the state had in defining and creating leadership is itself a matter for debate and evaluation. It is ultimately a speculative question, beyond the scope of this chapter.

24. The incarceration of the Namibians is not considered here. But see, for example, Helao Shityuwete, *Never Follow the Wolf: The Autobiography of a Namibian Freedom Fighter* (London, 1990).

25. Curnick Ndlovu, interview, 18 June 1994. See also N. Mandela, *Long Walk to Freedom* (Johannesburg, 1994), pp. 366–8.

26. Generational tensions were much more a product of the post-1976 period, as discussed in the next chapter.

27. Bam interview.

28. Alexander interview.

29. Regarding the racially discriminatory provision of clothing, Alexander (*Robben Island Dossier*, p. 38) summarises the situation as follows: 'Until approximately 1970 there was rigid discrimination in regard to the clothing worn by prisoners according to their official racial classification. Coloureds and Indians were given long pants, shoes and socks, besides a shirt, a jacket, and a jersey (in winter), whereas African prisoners were until that year given neither shoes nor socks, and were forced to wear short pants throughout the year ... African prisoners were given sandals even in winter, but a very large percentage had to go barefoot most of the year ... Whereas Coloureds and Indians were given black hats, which served a useful purpose ... Africans were given a most inadequate cap. Finally, however, almost all discrimination was swept away in the course of 1970. All prisoners now wear the same clothes except that until recently the differentiation between caps (Africans) and hats (others) was still maintained.' Apart from the racially discriminatory nature of clothing, clothing was inadequate by any definition and was often dirty. Lombard Mbatha (interview, December 1987–February 1988) and Martin Ramokgadi (interview, February 1988) both describe how they were given clothes that were far too small; the clothes soon fitted when they were engaged in hard labour and eating far less than they needed. (Interviews held between December 1987 and February 1988 cannot be dated more accurately because of the security constraints of the time.)

30. Alexander, *Robben Island Dossier*, pp. 36–7.

31. Kathrada interview.

32. Dingake (*My Fight Against Apartheid*, p. 211) is the exception to this. He argued that after the preparation of food improved, food was no longer a point of protest except as regards racially discriminatory diets.

33. But see, for example, Mandela, *Long Walk to Freedom*, p. 369. Mandela argues that hunger strikes were a problematic form of resistance or protest because they demanded the outside world knew about them, they were passive, and they punished the prisoners, not the authorities. He notes that he always supported decisions to go on hunger strikes once they had been agreed upon.

34. Alexander, *Robben Island Dossier*, p. 69.

35. Alexander, *Robben Island Dossier*, p. 69.

Alexander notes further that 'In the early sixties there used to be at least forty to fifty prisoners serving meal-stops every Sunday, and in really bad periods there were many more.'

36. D. Brutus, *A Simple Lust* (Oxford, 1973), p. 55.

37. Dikgang Moseneke, interview, December 1987–February 1988.

38. Alexander, *Robben Island Dossier*, p. 30.

39. Babenia, 'Cast in Stone on a Hell Hole', pp. 179–80.

40. Naidoo, *Island in Chains*, p. 83; Ramokgadi interview; Johnson Mlambo, interview, June and July 1994.

41. Zwelonke, *Robben Island*, p. 14.

42. Recent publicity has highlighted the damage done to Nelson Mandela's eyes because of the years of working in the quarry.

43. Harry Gwala, interview, 20 June 1994.

44. Jacob Zuma, interview, 20 June 1994.

45. Moseneke interview.

46. This is an example where state records might prove useful. That is, intra-state communication might convey what the state felt its pressures for change to be.

47. Nkosi Patrick Molala, interview, December 1987–February 1988.

48. Personal communication to author, 10 March 1988.

49. Alexander, *Robben Island Dossier*, p. vii.

50. Conversation with author, 9 March 1994.

51. Gwala interview.

52. Mlambo interview.

53. H. Lewin, *Bandiet* (London, 1981), pp. 88–97; United Nations Unit on Apartheid, *Maltreatment and Torture of Prisoners in South Africa* (New York, 1973), p. 42. None of the oral or written testimonies of ex-Robben Islanders mention the influence of the Strachan and *Rand Daily Mail* exposures in changing conditions on the Island. This may, however, be explained by the denial of newspapers to the prisoners, and the fact that the changes were gradual, so individual inmates may not have perceived any connection.

54. N. Alexander, 'The view from Robben Island', in R. Lee (ed.), *Values Alive: A Tribute to Helen Suzman* (Johannesburg, 1990), p. 64.

55. Gwala interview.

56. Helen Suzman, interview, December 1987–February 1988.

57. Naidoo's account also demonstrates the importance of taking advantage of gaps that have presented themselves, and thus the hunger strike is only possible once 'The chains [are] loosened'.

58. Dlamini, *Robben Island*, p. 181.

59. The separation of rights and privileges is closely linked to the classification system. The prison authorities would classify prisoners according to their behaviour, and consequently reward or punish them by giving or withdrawing privileges like the opportunity to study or, in later years, to buy food and newspapers. The classification system was always criticised by the political prisoners; in the post-1976 period it became an important focus of debate in the community.

60. Sonny Venkatrathnam, interview, 17 and 21 June

1994.

61. Brown cement bags had been the major source of paper for literacy classes, probably as well as for other means, throughout the 1960s. This is mentioned frequently in both interviews and books on the period.

62. Venkatrathnam interview.

63. Alexander, *Robben Island Dossier*, pp. 57, 67, 112 n31.

64. The post-1976 period is beyond the scope of this chapter, but there are a couple of examples that illustrate this point of 'zig-zag' conditions. Firstly, despite the fact that conditions had generally improved by this period, there were instances of inhumanity and brutality. For example, Walter Sisulu recalled that on 29 May 1977 an evening raid resulted in his being stripped naked in the cold when he was ill, and other prisoners were beaten up (see J. Schadeberg, *Voices from Robben Island* (Johannesburg, 1994), p. 27). Secondly, the late seventies and early eighties saw some apparently contradictory policies. On the one hand, there were improvements, like the ending of hard labour, the beginning of legal news, and the prisoners receiving beds for the first time. On the other hand, this was also a time when study rights beyond matric level were withdrawn; outside prison, in the 1978–9 Bethal Trial, PAC leaders were prosecuted for organising the PAC on Robben Island.

65. Naidoo, *Island in Chains*, p. 248.

66. Babenia, 'Cast in Stone', p. 234.

67. Moseneke interview.

68. Dingake, *My Fight Against Apartheid*, pp. 183–4.

69. Mbatha and Moseneke interviews; Babenia, 'Cast in Stone', p. 238.

70. Moseneke interview.

71. See, for example, 'Robben Island: our university' in Tom Lodge and Bill Nasson (eds.), *All, Here and Now: Black Politics in South Africa in the 1980s* (Cape Town, 1991), p. 301. Saths Cooper, who arrived on Robben Island in late 1976, argues that illiteracy on Robben Island was a serious problem, and it was 'only in the mid-seventies that serious literacy [education] began to happen.' He also contests the 'great idyllic picture of what a great intellectual' environment existed in the prison (Cooper, interview, 25 November 1994).

72. Gwala interview.

73. Suzman interview.

74. Dingake, *My Fight Against Apartheid*, p. 203.

75. Dingake, *My Fight Against Apartheid*, p. 175.

76. Bam interview.

77. H. Suzman in Hansard, 1974, col. 6295.

78. Also see Cheryl Roberts, *Sport in Chains* (Cape Town, 1994).

79. Schadeberg, *Voices from Robben Island*, p. 38.

80. The Robben Island Archives 1966–1991, at the Mayibuye Centre for History and Culture in South Africa, University of the Western Cape. Hereafter the documents from the collection are noted by 'Mayibuye' and their box and file number, for example Mayibuye 1.3.

81. Mayibuye 1.1.

82. Mayibuye 1.2.

83. Mayibuye 17.1.

84. Lodge and Nasson (eds.), *All, Here and Now*, p.

300; Brutus, *A Simple Lust*, p. 60.

85. Mayibuye, 44.1.

86. Babenia, 'Cast in Stone', p. 180.

87. I argue for the overt contribution of Robben Island to the anti-apartheid struggle for the 1963–1976 period. Arguably, however, that contribution was even stronger and more explicit for the people who left or went to Robben Island after 1976.

88. Kathrada interview.

89. Babenia, 'Cast in Stone', p. 182.

90. Babenia, 'Cast in Stone', p. 183.

91. Vocabulary is difficult here, because 'cell' can of course mean more than one thing. I have therefore tried to distinguish between physical prison cell and a human organisational cell of (about) four people per group.

92. Gwala interview.

93. Kathrada interview. It has often been quite difficult to get specific details of organisational structure in interviews. There are a number of possible reasons for this, including the following: former Islanders still consider these secret; certain prisoners did not know the exact structures of the liberation movements inside prison; structures were not especially precise, and it would be wrong to assume they were; structures changed over time and interviewees generalise for the experience throughout their term of incarceration, rather than identifying exact organisational definitions; and organisational structures differed in different sections, even within the general section.

94. Babenia, 'Cast in Stone', p. 183.

95. Ndlovu interview.

96. Alexander interview.

97. See for example, *Weekly Mail and Guardian*, 29 July–4 August 1994. Copies of the security police files on Mac Maharaj referred to here are now lodged with the Mayibuye Centre for History and Culture in South Africa, University of the Western Cape.

98. Mlambo interview.

99. Mlambo interview.

100. Babenia, 'Cast in Stone', p. 196.

101. Mlambo interview.

102. Babenia, 'Cast in Stone', pp. 223–4.

103. A. Odendaal, 'Robben Island: bridgehead for democracy' (paper presented to Mayibuye Winter School, University of the Western Cape, 1994), p. 8.

104. *Weekly Mail*, 14 August 1987.

105. Zuma interview. Certain people who were part of the ANC grouping on the Island may not have been ANC members before their incarceration. These would have included members of the South African Congress of Trade Unions (SACTU).

106. This chapter is not concerned with the content of the ideology of the movements, or internal debates. Mlambo, however, did give Mothopeng's answer to this question in the interview: 'He would say, "That is a negative type of question you are asking. Ask what we are going to do for the African. That is the question you should be asking ..." Sobukwe actually put it that in the new Africa there would be no reason why a predominantly black electorate cannot even have a white person representing them in Parliament because colour will be of no consequence.'

107. Mlambo interview.

108. Many of Mbeki's prison analyses have been collected in his book *Learning from Robben Island: The Prison Writings of Govan Mbeki* (Cape Town, 1991).

109. Dingake, *My Fight Against Apartheid*, p. 214.

110. See, for example, Naidoo, *Island in Chains*, p. 132 and Dingake, *My Fight Against Apartheid*, pp. 193–5.

111. The two most important periods of inter-organisational conflict on the Island appear to have been in the 1960s, and from 1976 to approximately 1981. In the 1960s unity needed to be forged both between the ANC and PAC, and within the PAC (as discussed above), in order to effectively challenge the state. On the other hand there were actually unity talks between the ANC and PAC in prison in the sixties, which were ultimately unsuccessful (Kathrada interview).

112. Indeed, in so far as there were inter- or intra-organisational tensions, bringing these to the attention of the state could well have proved very dangerous. Mark Shinners (interview, 12 September 1994) is a PAC member who was on Robben Island from 1963 to 1973. He was later tried in the 1978 Bethal Trial, only to be reconvicted and sent back to Robben Island. He said that the security police used discussions of tensions within the PAC in Indres Naidoo's *Island in Chains* as a basis of their interrogation.

113. In her autobiography she gives the same account, except that she remembers Eddie Daniels as being the person who directed her to Mandela on behalf of all of them.

114. Lodge and Nasson (eds.), *All, Here and Now,* p. 309.

115. Venkatrathnam interview.

116. Venkatrathnam interview.

117. Venkatrathnam interview.

118. Lodge, *Black Politics in South Africa*, p. 302.

119. S. Macozoma, 'Notes of a native son', *Monitor* (1989), p. 56.

120. Zuma interview.

121. Zuma interview.

122. Lodge and Nasson (eds.), *All, Here and Now*, pp. 191, 193. These events were of course in the 1980s, not the pre-1976 period. The point, however, is that these men were a product of the prison from the 1960s, and reflect the difference from the previous exiled (as opposed to imprisoned) leadership.

123. The most vigorous recruitment campaigns on the Island and, from the ANC's perspective, the most successful were those of the post 1976 period, where many (primarily) Black Consciousness adherents were recruited to the ANC. But this was certainly neither the first nor last recruitment initiative, as all organisations maximise their strength through larger numbers of members.

124. Simon Ramogale, interview, 24 July 1994; SAIRR, *A Survey of Race Relations in South Africa 1977* (Johannesburg, 1978), p. 139.

125. Lodge and Nasson (eds.), *All, Here and Now,* p. 193.

126. Dingake, *My Fight Against Apartheid*, p. 227.

127. At least in this researcher's interviews and readings of the growing literature about life on the Island.

Chapter 7
HOW BEST TO RESIST?
ROBBEN ISLAND AFTER 1976

*This chapter represents work in progress. Comments and feedback are requested and welcomed. I thank Gail Gerhart, Barbara Buntman and my dissertation discussion group for reading an earlier draft of this chapter, and especially appreciate the advice and encouragement of Barbara Harlow. I am most grateful to Manuel Orozco for helping me conceptualise and work through key arguments of this chapter. An enduring thank you to those I interviewed, and to Gail Gerhart and Tom Karis for providing me with the key materials of this work.

1. This chapter builds upon certain information set out in the previous chapter.

2. *Realpolitik* is a German term that refers to power politics. It emphasises political (and policy) approaches where considerations of practical power have more weight than those of principle. This is not to suggest that those who practise strategic resistance are not also concerned with principle or morality.

3. The march was conceived of and organised by a high school students' organisation, the South African Students' Movement (SASM), and the Soweto Students' Representative Council (SSRC).

4. Ahmed Kathrada, interview, 19 June and 31 October 1994.

5. Heidi Holland, *The Struggle: A History of the African National Congress* (New York, 1990), p. 183.

6. Tom Lodge, *Black Politics in South Africa since 1945* (Johannesburg, 1985), p. 321.

7. Anthony W. Marx, *Lessons of Struggle: South African Internal Opposition 1960–1990* (New York, 1992), p. 56.

8. Lodge, *Black Politics*, pp. 330–4, reviews much of the academic debate as to the relative influence or role of Black Consciousness in the uprising. My own research, while not specifically concerned with this question, does suggest the significant influence of Black Consciousness.

9. Anthony Marx provides the following figures to give one some sense of the magnitude of the protest and the response: 'Before they were quelled by continuing repression, protests had been staged in townships throughout South Africa, and a quarter of a million students had boycotted classes, leaving one thousand dead and twenty-one thousand prosecuted for related offenses by September 1977' (*Lessons of Struggle*, p. 69). Furthermore, many people left the country in the wake of the rebellion: 'The uprising was succeeded by the exodus of thousands of young men and women to Lesotho, Swaziland and Botswana and many of these were to provide Umkonto [*sic*] with a new army of. . . saboteurs' (Lodge, *Black Politics*, p. 339).

10. Gail Gerhart argues that the school students were deeply impressed by the SASO students 'who had put political commitment above the promotion of their own careers' when actively confronting the authorities in protests and university boycotts in 1972. 'One consequence by the end of 1972 was an upsurge in political consciousness among high school students, leading to

the formation of a welter of political youth organizations across the country. The most notable of these, and the ones which were to provide the organizational impetus behind the township youth uprisings of 1976, were the South African Students' Movement, formed in Soweto high schools, and the National Youth Organisation, a federation of youth groups in Natal, the Transvaal, and the eastern and western Cape.' See G. Gerhart, *Black Power in South Africa* (Berkeley, 1978), p. 297.

11. Former prisoner interpretations of Harding's behaviour and approach do, however, differ substantially. More broadly, it has been possible to procure significantly more information on the state from the late 1970s onwards than for the earlier period, covered in the previous chapter. Nevertheless, an analysis of the state is beyond the scope of this chapter.

12. Nelson Mandela, *Long Walk to Freedom* (New York, 1994), p. 434. Mandela writes of the end of manual (quarry) labour in early 1977. This followed 'the second year of a go-slow strike at the quarry, demanding a complete end to all manual labour.' Mandela argues that Section B inmates were also released from hard labour because the authorities were anxious 'to deal with these young lions' (p. 424). Zithulele Cindi, who arrived in December 1976, notes that their 'first resistance was when we managed to break this question of working in the quarry', that is, end manual labour, and this seems to have been within the first nine months of their arrival (Cindi, interview by Gail Gerhart, 5 July 1989).

13. Thami Mkhwanazi, 'My Years on the Island', *Weekly Mail*, 4–10 September and 14–20 August 1987. The improvements were due to a number of factors, including, but not necessarily limited to, prisoner resistance and demands for improvements; pressure brought on the state by national and international actors including family members, lawyers, human rights organisations, anti-apartheid pressure groups, and the International Committee of the Red Cross; the rise of reformist and technocratic actors in the Prisons Service and state; and the use of the legal system.

14. Michael Dingake, *My Fight Against Apartheid* (London, 1987), pp. 181, 183. Former Robben Islander, Sibusiso Ndebele, recalls that 'the Nationalist Party said to us that people have been burning schools, we [political prisoners] cannot now start going to school [in prison]. So they just banned ... post-matric studies' (Ndebele, interview by Tom Karis, 15 December 1989).

15. Mkhwanazi, 'My Years on the Island', *Weekly Mail*, 14–20 August and 4–10 September 1987.

16. Mkhwanazi, *Weekly Mail*, 4–10 September 1987.

17. James Mange, interview, 2 August 1994; Denmark Tungwane, interview, 3 November 1994.

18. Mayibuye 17.1, memo of 14 April 1974.

19. Mayibuye 17.1, memo of 14 April 1974.

20. Mandela, *Long Walk to Freedom*, p. 420.

21. Petros Mashigo, interview, 25 August 1994.

22. Tom Winslow, interview, 4 November 1994.

23. SAIRR, *Survey 1989/90*, p. 168.

24. This interview on which this paragraph is based was with an ANC member, who asked to remain anonymous and who made it clear that his comments refer to processes within the ANC, rather than to Black Consciousness or PAC adherents on the Island. The relationship of other organisations to the release process has yet to be fully researched. The South African Institute of Race Relations reported that 'the secretary general of the Pan-Africanist Congress (PAC), Mr Benny Alexander, said that the PAC would not enter into any negotiations regarding their release' (SAIRR, *Survey 1992*, p. 65). 'In April 1991 AZAPO repeated its demands for the unconditional release of all political prisoners and the return of all exiles. The newly elected president of AZAPO, Mr Pandelani Nefolovhodwe, said that this demand was not negotiable and added that it rejected "the definition of political prisoners and exiles as stated in the *Pretoria Minute*"' (SAIRR, *Survey*, p. 22).

25. SAIRR, *Survey 1991/92*, p. xi.

26. Russell Ally, the chair of a seminar at the Institute for Advanced Social Research (the University of the Witwatersrand, 17 October 1994) to which an earlier version of the previous chapter was presented, included in his comments the following: '[I]t was also difficult at the end of the paper to maintain my credulity. Now, far be it for me to call into question the fact that many people did come off the Island better educated, more politicised, more committed to the struggle, and so forth, but are there no stories of disillusionment? Was nobody's spirit broken on the Island? I ask this question not to belittle the experiences of any of the political prisoners ... but rather to alert ourselves to the danger of romanticising our history.' This is, of course, an important and a well-taken point, and the short answer is yes, of course, there were people whose spirits were broken and who suffered profound psychological damage from their incarceration. Perhaps the more significant question, and one beyond the scope of this chapter, is how and why people emphasise or suppress certain parts of their memory. A cursory comment is that damage and growth from an experience are not mutually exclusive, and that the current South African political context, as well as certain cultural mores which inform the interview process, is often more conducive to emphasising the fact of overcoming rather than succumbing to the apartheid regime's intent to destroy its opponents. I think here of a former Islander I interviewed who only told me of the problem with alcohol that he developed upon release once we had established a personal and social relationship; that is, well beyond the interview context.

27. Saths Cooper, interview, 25 November 1994. Reflecting the brutal reality, the first books on modern Robben Island – by Naidoo, Dlamini and Zwelonke – emphasised the prison as 'hell-hole'. Videos include Lindy Wilson's *Robben Island: Our University* (1988) and the Schadebergs' *Voices from Robben Island* (1994). Thami Mkhwanazi's series in the *Weekly Mail* was probably the first exposure of Robben Island to begin to explore the Island's internal political structure and its political implications. There has been little scholarly treatment of the modern Robben Island phenomenon, but one recent corrective is by Tom Karis, who is including a chapter on Robben Island in his and Gail Gerhart's forthcoming fifth volume of *From Protest to Challenge*.

28. Saths Cooper, 'The psychological impact of polit-

ical imprisonment and the role of the psychologist', in L. J. Nicholas and S. Cooper (eds.), *Psychology and Apartheid* (Durban, 1990), p. 141. Cooper qualifies this somewhat in the paragraph in which these comments are made. He notes that 'Imprisonment can bring out the best or the worst in human beings; there hardly seems to be a middle ground! ... However, the sense of camaraderie and political commitment can never be overwhelmed by self-serving individualism which characterises common-law prisoners.'

29. Murphy Morobe, interview, 17 November and 1 December 1994. Morobe emphasised that he had not read the article, and was relying on my explanation.

30. Morobe interview.

31. Kgalema Motlanthe, interview, 7 and 9 December 1994.

32. Mashigo interview.

33. Mangena describes his conversation with Darkie, who might be described as a politicised *tsotsi*, but was probably representative to some degree of many less politicised men who ended up in prison. Darkie made his living as a thief, and rationalised his choice in political terms: 'I will repossess money and other things from these rich settlers [whites], which I will then share with my family and others in the black community.' When the uprising began, Darkie related that 'some of my friends concentrated on hijacking delivery goods such as flour, mielie-meal [corn meal], cooking oil, liquor and so on in the townships.' Although he did not originally become involved in either the protests and demonstrations or the hijackings, he felt compelled to protest when he saw soldiers randomly shooting at children. His protests earned him a bullet in his stomach, and a charge of public violence, which brought him to Robben Island. See Mosibudi Mangena, *On Your Own* (Johannesburg, 1989), pp. 101–5.

34. Saki Macozoma, interview, December 1987–February 1988.

35. Macozoma interview.

36. Macozoma interview; Nkosi Patrick Molala, interview, December 1987–February 1988.

37. Thomas Velaphi Masuku, December 1987–February 1988.

38. Molala interview.

39. Kathrada interview.

40. Mangena, *On Your Own*, p. 86.

41. Macozoma interview.

42. Patrick 'Terror' Lekota, interview, by Gail Gerhart and Tom Karis, 17 February 1990. Lekota had been suspended from the Black Consciousness Movement in late 1977 (Cooper interview). In turn, Joe Shithlibane said he and fellow ANC members beat up the men who assaulted Lekota and they were therefore charged by the authorities (Shithlibane interview). Mandela records that 'in the interests of harmony, we advised Terror not to lodge a complaint' (Mandela, *Long Walk to Freedom*, p. 423).

43. Cooper interview. While there were numerous incidents where physical fighting was involved, this appears to have been a particularly important one. If we assume they are the same incidents, Mandela notes that the ANC men were charged by the authorities, while

Cooper notes that the ANC men charged their Black Consciousness counterparts. Sizane speaks of a 'faction fight – BCM people fighting ANC people' that resulted from BCM and PAC accusations that the head of the prison, Colonel Harding, was supporting recruitment for the ANC rather than the other two organisations. He dates this fight, which appears to be the same one that Mandela and Cooper refer to, as occurring on 19 February 1979 (Phumelele Sizane, interview by Gail Gerhart and Tom Karis, 4 May 1990).

44. Cooper interview.

45. Greater detail and divergent accounts of this period will be covered in my forthcoming Ph.D. dissertation.

46. Cindi interview.

47. In 1980, there were about 500 political prisoners on Robben Island and 'The overwhelming majority of inmates were Freedom Charter supporters' (Mkhwanazi, *Weekly Mail*, 14–20 August 1987, p. 14).

48. These clearly had implications for resistance outside the prison, which is beyond the scope of this chapter.

49. Nelson Mandela in J. Schadeberg, *Voices from Robben Island* (Johannesburg, 1994), pp. 18–19.

50. Mandela, *Long Walk to Freedom*, pp. 364–5. In many ways, this comment is a metaphor for both Mandela's initiation of negotiations with the South African government and the advantage the state took of engaging prisoners in private conversation when they could not speak to the banned ANC itself, in terms of the public rules the government had established.

51. Harry Gwala, interview, 20 June 1994.

52. See, for example, Marx, *Lessons of Struggle*, pp. 61–3.

53. Lodge, *Black Politics in South Africa*, p. 334.

54. S. Johnson, 'The soldiers of Luthuli: youth in the politics of resistance' in S. Johnson (ed.), *South Africa: No Turning Back* (Bloomington, 1989), p. 100.

55. Marx, *Lessons of Struggle*, p. 61.

56. Gail Gerhart, 'The Black Consciousness Movement: Confronting the State, 1972–1976' in Tom Karis and Gail Gerhart (eds.), *From Protest to Challenge*, forthcoming. I am indebted to Gail Gerhart for sharing her insights and unpublished work about the SASO Nine trial and its public impact.

57. Cindi interview.

58. Johnson Mlambo, interview, 8 and 19 July 1994.

59. Dingake writes that 'In 1980 political prisoners on Robben Island who were in Group One were accorded the privilege of buying newspapers' (*My Fight Against Apartheid*, p. 192). This suggests that at some point in the late 1970s or early 1980s the classification system changed from an A-B-C-D basis to three numbered groups, where group one was the highest and group three was the lowest. This is not, however, reflected in the interviews, as Islanders continue to talk about their classifications as 'A', 'D', and so on.

60. Cindi interview.

61. Mandela, *Long Walk to Freedom*, pp. 347–8; N. Alexander, *Robben Island Dossier 1964–1974* (Cape Town, 1994), pp. 76–80; Macozoma interview.

62. Kathrada interview.

63. Mangena, *On Your Own*, p. 97.

64. Pandelani Nefolovhodwe, interview, 13 September 1994.

65. James Mange, interview, 2 August 1994.

66. Mashigo interview.

67. Mange interview.

68. Macozoma interview. Denis Goldberg, who served his sentence in Pretoria Central Prison, similarly comments that 'I will say that as the conditions began to improve, so the tensions would arise in our community. There was less a need to face a common enemy every minute of the day. The community also changed because we were of a particular generation initially (Goldberg, interview, 3 March 1995).

69. A former Robben Islander who was incarcerated for five years for recruiting soldiers for uMkhonto weSizwe said the older men laid such emphasis on the fact that five years was a short sentence, that he only realised well after his release what a long sentence five years in prison really is, especially for a young person, barely out of his teens (anonymous interview). Similarly, Sibusiso Ndebele, who also was on Robben Island, said that a seven-year sentence is not considered a long sentence for South Africa (Ndebele, interview by Tom Karis, 15 December 1989).

70. James Mange, a member of the ANC who often differed with the leadership, was probably the most insistent on rejecting classification as inimical to the demands of being a political prisoner. He ultimately accepted 'A' classification when it was offered with no strings attached (Mange interview).

71. Former prisoners do not necessarily make the argument that those with longer sentences would be hurt most by the loss of privileges. It does, however, seem clear that the loss of benefits would be greatest for them. Michael Dingake, who had a fifteen-year sentence and who only had three visits during that time, wrote that 'Letters are a prisoner's lifeline, not only letters, visits and other channels of communication, photos' (*My Fight Against Apartheid*, pp. 159–60). Nelson Mandela explains that he asked his wife Winnie Mandela to forgo her protest against carrying a pass, so that she would be allowed to visit him. He writes that 'I thought it more important that we see each other than to resist the petty machinations of the authorities, and Winnie consented to carry a pass. I missed her enormously and needed the reassurance of seeing her, and we also had vital family matters to discuss' (*Long Walk to Freedom*, p. 370). One can well imagine that Mandela, or others in a similar position, might have taken a different approach if they were faced with a 'short' sentence, rather than a life sentence.

72. Kathrada interview.

73. The question of money raises another hornet's nest in the history of recruitment. Some of the ANC's opponents have accused it of selectively supplying funds (through external funders) to some of its prison members but not others, as well as using the promise of financial support as a weapon in recruitment (Mange interview, Cindi interview). Furthermore, as I am trying to make clear in this broader point, the accusations of abuse of finances could and did go in more than one direction. Kgalema Motlanthe (interview) argues that 'In

[the] Black Consciousness Movement the SASO groups came with funds, and had access to funds because they had Shun Chetty, one lawyer, who was working for them almost full time.'

74. Cooper interview.

75. Motlanthe interview.

76. Motlanthe interview.

77. A few examples of these transcriptions can be found in the Mayibuye Centre archives at the University of the Western Cape.

78. Vronda Banda, interview, 5 September 1994.

79. *Sunday Independent*, 25 June 1995, p. 5.

80. Mandela, *Long Walk to Freedom*, p. 365.

81. Mlambo interview.

82. Neville Alexander, 'Robben Island: a site of struggle', in N. Penn, H. Deacon and N. Alexander, *Robben Island: The Politics of Rock and Sand* (Cape Town, 1992), pp. 77–8.

83. Mandela, *Long Walk to Freedom*, p. 366.

84. See previous chapter.

85. Cooper interview.

86. Mike Xego, interview, by Tom Karis, 8 October 1993.

87. Mlambo interview.

88. Cindi interview.

89. Mandela, *Long Walk to Freedom*, p. 437.

90. Motlanthe interview.

91. Motlanthe interview.

92. Lassie Chiwayo, interview, 4 November 1994.

93. Mayibuye 41.1.

94. Of course, neither generations nor understandings of resistance are in reality reducible to neat, two-dimensional boxes. My reading of this period of Robben Island's history does, however, suggest there is a value to highlighting the role of generations in informing understandings of resistance. As one looks beyond the larger categories of 'younger' and 'older' generations, particular distinctions can be discerned. For example, Gail Gerhart has pointed out that for the SASO Nine, taking initiative, accepting responsibility and not waiting to take their cue from others were so critical to their political identities and sense of self, that not following that perspective (which so often implied categorical resistance) would 'have seemed to some of them like a betrayal of their movement and of Biko himself (who was notorious for being cheeky to policemen and authorities generally)' (Correspondence with author, 23 August 1995).

95. Cindi interview. The generation of prisoners that arrived in the wake of the 1976 uprising appear to have had to deal with provocative warders and authorities. Prisoners were set upon by dogs in the quarry when warders believed the prisoners were avoiding work on 20 January 1977. The prisoners made a complaint of assault to the head of the prison, but most refused to make statements without consulting with their legal representatives. In order to do so, a court application was made, and the judgment directed 'the Commissioner of Prisons to permit applicants to consult with their attorney and, if necessary, counsel in connection with alleged assaults upon them and allow applicants' legal representatives to take full instructions from applicants as to any

actions that they may desire to institute arising out of the said alleged assaults' (*Cooper and Others* v *Minister of Prisons* 1977 (4) SA 166 (C) Cape Provincial Division at 168).

96. Mkhwanazi, *Weekly Mail*, 21–27 August 1987.

97. Mkhwanazi, *Weekly Mail*, 21–27 August 1987.

98. Barbara Harlow, *Barred: Women, Writing and Political Detention* (Hanover, 1992), p. 5; Jan Nederveen Pieterse (ed.), *Emancipation, Modern and Postmodern* (London, 1992).

99. Mandela, *Long Walk to Freedom*, p. 404.

100. Steve Biko, *I Write What I Like* (London, 1978), p. 146.

101. As was the case on Robben Island, learning among generations (and tendencies and organisations) was not without difficulties or tensions. Outside prison, political conditions did not allow for time-consuming discussions and careful political education campaigns, which often made the process of inter-generational communication and consensus building very difficult.

Index

Index